Studies in Scripture

VOLUME EIGHT **Alma 30 to Moroni**

Studies in Scripture

VOLUME EIGHT Alma 30 to Moroni

Edited by Kent P. Jackson

Deseret Book Company
Salt Lake City, Utah

Studies in Scripture Series
Volume 1: The Doctrine and Covenants (Randall Book Co., 1984)
Volume 2: The Pearl of Great Price (Randall Book Co., 1985)
Volume 3: The Old Testament—Genesis to 2 Samuel (Randall Book Co., 1985)
Volume 4: The Old Testament—1 Kings to Malachi (future volume, Deseret Book Co., 1989)
Volume 5: The Gospels (Deseret Book Co., 1986)
Volume 6: Acts to Revelation (Deseret Book Co., 1987)
Volume 7: 1 Nephi to Alma 29 (Deseret Book Co., 1987)
Volume 8: Alma 30 to Moroni (Deseret Book Co., 1988)

First printing August 1988

Library of Congress Cataloging-in-Publication Data

Alma 30 to Moroni / edited by Kent P. Jackson
        p.   cm. — (Studies in Scripture ; v. 8)
    Includes bibliographies and index.
    ISBN 0-87579-166-2 : $15.95 (est.)
    1. Book of Mormon—Criticism, interpretation, etc.   I. Jackson,
Kent P.   II. Title: Alma thirty to Moroni.   III. Series: Studies in
Scripture (Salt Lake City, Utah) ; v. 8.
BX8627.A45   1988
289.3'22—dc19   88-15978
                                                        CIP

CONTENTS

PREFACE

Nothing bears a stronger testimony to the mission of the Prophet Joseph Smith than the Book of Mormon. Its detailed historical narrative, intricate and consistent geographical presentation, and profound description of human nature demonstrate beyond doubt that no uninspired person could have produced such a book. More importantly, its unparalleled description of the doctrine of God and its uncompromising testimony to the mission of Jesus Christ shout from the housetops that the Book of Mormon is true—the work of the Lord—and that Joseph Smith, through whom God brought it forth, was the Lord's servant.

We Latter-day Saints gratefully acknowledge the Book of Mormon as the keystone of our religion, revealed by the Lord to provide a sure foundation of our faith. In the Church we accept not only the truthfulness of its doctrine, but also the historicity of the events it describes. Those who choose to do otherwise not only deny the Lord's witness concerning it (see D&C 17:6) but also forfeit the blessings that attend those who read it, love it, and abide by the doctrine and precepts to which it bears testimony.

Studies in Scripture, Vol. 8: Alma 30 to Moroni was written to accompany one's personal study of the Book of Mormon. The authors and the editor acknowledge that there is no substitute for carefully searching the scriptures themselves, and we encourage all to do so. The Studies in Scripture series is presented as a resource to help readers in that effort.

This volume emphasizes the teachings of the Book of Mormon. The authors have stressed the messages contained in the sermons and writings of its prophets. At the same time, they have discussed Book of Mormon history in order to clarify the narrative and emphasize the lessons that are taught through historical events. Since the primary purpose of the Book of Mormon itself is to teach and bear testimony of the gospel of Jesus Christ, our purpose in this volume has been to do likewise. Thus we have considered external evidences of the Book of Mormon, as well as contextual and comparative studies, to be of lesser value for this work.

Each of the contributors is responsible for his or her own conclusions. This book is a private endeavor and not a production of either Brigham Young University or The Church of Jesus Christ of Latter-day Saints. Although the writers and the editor have sought to be in harmony with the teachings of the scriptures and the leaders of the Church, the reader should not regard this work as a primary source for gospel understanding but should turn instead to the scriptures and the words of modern prophets for authoritative doctrinal statements.

I express my appreciation to the management and staff of Deseret Book Company, to my assistant Charles J. Baldwin, and to the contributors to this volume, whose knowledge and spiritual sensitivities are apparent throughout its pages. I am also most thankful for the expert assistance of my colleagues Robert E. Parsons, Rex C. Reeve, Jr., and Robert L. Millet, whose wisdom and advice have added much to this book.

KENT P. JACKSON

1

KORIHOR THE ANTI-CHRIST
(Alma 30)

LaMar Garrard

After the people of Anti-Nephi-Lehi left their homeland among the Lamanites, they were allowed to live among the Nephites in the land of Jershon, where they were called the people of Ammon. Later came a great battle between the Lamanites and the Nephites in which the Lamanites were defeated. After this great battle was a period of peace throughout the land. Then appeared a man named Korihor, who came into the land of Zarahemla and preached against the prophecies of the coming of Christ. He also went to the land of Jershon and preached among the people of Ammon. However, these people took him before their high priest, who commanded him to be carried out of the land. Korihor then went to the land of Gideon to preach and was eventually brought before Giddonah, the high priest there. When Giddonah saw the hardness of Korihor's heart, he had him brought before Alma, the chief judge and governor over the land. Alma 30 discusses what Korihor taught in Zarahemla, Jershon, and Gideon; his trial before Alma; and his downfall.

The writer of this account is Mormon, who called Korihor an anti-Christ. Alma 30 is part of an abridgment made by Mormon—under the direction and inspiration of the Lord—from a larger, more detailed account by earlier prophets. In vision Nephi saw that this record would eventually come forth in the latter days for the benefit of our modern generation. (1 Ne. 13:32-36.) Keeping this in mind,

---

LaMar E. Garrard is professor of Church history and doctrine at Brigham Young University.

why would the Lord direct Mormon to devote an entire chapter to the details of the teachings and final destiny of Korihor when so many other things were written on the original plates? As we compare the teachings of this man and the beliefs of those today who advocate the philosophy of naturalism, we see a striking similarity. I believe that the Lord foresaw the adverse effects of naturalism on our modern world and therefore purposely directed Mormon to include the teachings of Korihor in his record. Those who read and accept the Book of Mormon are thereby warned against accepting the philosophical assumptions of naturalism. What one believes about the universe is important because it affects one's behavior, for "as [a man] thinketh in his heart, so is he." (Prov. 23:7.)

The Rise of Naturalism

E. A. Burtt, in his book *The Metaphysical Foundations of Modern Physical Science*, traces cosmological thinking from medieval to modern times. He points out that the naturalistic viewpoint has made great inroads into the thinking of many of our modern generation. Even though we may not all be philosophers or scientists, still the philosophies of those around us affect our thinking even though we may not realize it. Burtt explains that sometimes we accept a philosophical position without being aware of its implications and hence it produces a subtle and pervasive control over our thinking.

> How curious, after all, is the way in which we moderns think about our world! And it is so novel, too. The cosmology underlying our mental processes is but three centuries old — a mere infant in the history of thought — and yet we cling to it with the same embarrassed zeal with which a young father fondles his new-born baby. Like him, we are ignorant enough of its precise nature; like him, we nevertheless take it piously to be ours and allow it a subtly pervasive and unhindered control over our thinking.[1]

Bertrand Russell was a renowned mathematician and philosopher who advocated the naturalistic viewpoint. He claimed that as science has arisen in the past 300 years and has become so pragmatically successful in our lives, it has become a dominant factor in determining the beliefs of educated people: "As a result of the new control over the environment which scientific knowledge has conferred, a new philosophy is growing up, involving a changed conception of man's place in the universe."[2] He went on to explain that it is our personal acceptance of the premises on which the scientific method was based that has changed our way of thinking about the world around us:

> Out of the work of the great men of the seventeenth century a new outlook on the world was developed, and it was this outlook, not specific arguments, which brought about the decay of the belief in portents, witchcraft, demoniacal possession, and so forth. I think there were three ingredients in the scientific outlook of the eighteenth century that were specially important.
>
> (1) Statements of fact should be based on observation, not on unsupported authority.
>
> (2) The inanimate world is a self-acting, self-perpetuating system, in which all changes conform to natural laws.
>
> (3) The earth is not the center of the universe, and probably Man is not its purpose (if any); moreover, "purpose" is a concept which is scientifically useless.[3]

We advocate the philosophy of naturalism (whether we realize it or not) when we no longer regard these statements as restricted outlooks to be taken only in scientific endeavors but shift to the following positions: knowledge cannot be gained by any other means than by the use of the natural senses, the universe is really an inanimate self-acting and self-perpetuating system, and there is no real purpose in the existence of the universe.[4] This chapter will compare these fundamental assumptions of naturalism with Korihor's teachings to show the similarity between the two. The implications of accepting these assumptions will then be examined.

Methods of Gaining Knowledge

Science has become successful in predicting, controlling, and explaining many natural events by making the restriction that in any scientific endeavor all conclusions must be based upon public, repeatable observations using the natural senses. This has proved advantageous for the progress of science, but if we allow this restriction to become part of our personal epistemology or method of gaining knowledge of the world around us, it automatically eliminates any knowledge coming to us from God through the living prophets, the scriptures, or personal revelation.

Korihor took the naturalistic viewpoint. He advocated that what the prophets say and have said (their recorded words, or scriptures) are foolish traditions (Russell's unsupported authority), since we cannot know of anything that does not come through the natural senses (things we cannot see): "O ye that are bound down under a foolish and a vain hope, why do ye yoke yourselves with such foolish things? Why do ye look for a Christ? For *no man can know of anything which is to come.* Behold, these things which ye call prophecies, which ye say are handed down by holy prophets, behold, *they are foolish traditions of your fathers.* How do ye know of their surety? Behold, *ye cannot know of things which ye do not see.*" (Alma 30:13-15; emphasis added.)

Because of Korihor's position that we cannot know anything of the world around us except through empirical observation, he claimed we cannot know that there is a God, "a being who never has been seen or known, who never was nor ever will be." (Alma 30:28.) When Alma confronted him directly and asked him if he believed in a God, he answered no (Alma 30:38) and went on to explain that he would believe in God only if he were given a sign, some empirical evidence: "If thou wilt show me a sign, that I may be convinced that there is a God, yea, show unto me that he hath power, and then will I be convinced of the truth of thy words." (Alma 30:43.) Later he took more of an agnostic rather than an atheistic position, but he still maintained his position that knowledge of such things comes only by empirical observation: "I do not deny the existence of a God, but I do not believe that there is a God . . . and except ye show me a sign, I will not believe." (Alma 30:48.)

Alma, on the other hand, held that we can obtain knowledge from God by revelation as well as through the natural senses. By not hardening our hearts, we can receive revelation to our spirits that confirms to us that the words of the prophets and the scriptures are

4

true.[5] Alma rebuked Korihor, saying that he was resisting the prompt-ings of the Holy Spirit; otherwise he would accept the words of the prophets and the scriptures and believe in God:

> And now what evidence have ye that there is no God, or that Christ cometh not? I say unto you that ye have none, save it be your word only. But, behold, I have all things as a tes-timony that these things are true; and ye also have all things as a testimony unto you that they are true; and will ye deny them? Believest thou that these things are true?
>
> Behold, I know that thou believest, but thou art possessed with a lying spirit, and *ye have put off the Spirit of God* that it may have no place in you. . . .
>
> Will ye say, Show unto me a sign, when ye have *the testimony of all these thy brethren,* and also *all the holy prophets?* The *scriptures* are laid before thee, yea, and all things denote there is a God. . . . And yet do ye go about, leading away the hearts of this people, testifying unto them there is no God? And yet will ye deny against all these wit-nesses? And he said: Yea, I will deny, except ye shall show me a sign.
>
> And now it came to pass that Alma said unto him: Behold, I am grieved because of the hardness of your heart, yea, that *ye will still resist the spirit of the truth,* that thy soul may be destroyed. (Alma 30:40-42, 44-46; emphasis added.)

The Nature of the Universe

Russell's second point was that science has become pragmatically successful by assuming that the world around us is a self-acting, self-perpetuating system in which all changes conform to natural laws. Russell explains that before the rise of modern physics, it was thought that all motion resulted from the action of living beings with souls:

> Before Galileo it had been thought that a lifeless body will not move of itself, and if it is in motion it will gradually come to rest. Only living beings, it was thought, could move without help of some external agency. Aristotle thought that the heav-enly bodies were pushed by Gods. Here on earth, animals can set themselves in motion and can cause motion in dead

matter. . . . Everything depends upon impulsion from the souls of living beings.

So long as this view prevailed, physics as an independent science was impossible, since the physical world was thought to be not causally self-contained. But Galileo and Newton between them proved that all the movements of the planets, and of dead matter on the earth, proceed according to the law of physics, and once started, will continue indefinitely. There is no need of mind in this process.[6]

At a later date the philosopher and mathematician Descartes "held that not only dead matter, but the bodies of animals also, are wholly governed by the laws of physics."[7] The French freethinkers and the eighteenth-century materialists took the next step by saying that all causes are material in nature, and that mental occurrences are inoperative by-products. We will see, however, that if we accept these views as part of our personal cosmology, certain implications result that are contrary to the words of the prophets and the scriptures.

Belief in a self-acting, self-perpetuating system in which all changes conform to natural law eliminates a belief that God has any power to direct or control matter.[8] Such a position is that of naturalism. Instead of believing that God is the author of all natural law and therefore ultimately controls all phenomena in the physical universe (theism), the naturalist believes that self-existing "Law" is the sovereign power in the universe and ultimately controls all phenomena.[9] According to this view, all causation is material (according to natural law) rather than mental (originating in the mind of God or some other living creature).

Burtt points out that the shift from theism (in medieval times) to naturalism (in modern times) was gradual. In the early history of science, many scientists held theistic views.[10] Their religious beliefs led them to conclude that God controls all matter by his power and that he commands this matter to behave in certain ways. To them God was sovereign and therefore the author of all natural laws. As scientists, they attempted to discover these laws by gathering facts empirically in an attempt to induce from them certain regularities in nature. Once these regularities (natural laws) were found, the scientists could better predict, control, and explain the phenomena in the universe around them. However, to them God was not just a super scientist or super engineer who discovered and worked with self-existing natural laws; rather, he was the Great Creator, who authored the laws they were attempting to discover. Thus, a description of how matter behaves would also be a description of the handiwork of God. This was the position of Alma when rebutting the position of Korihor: "Will ye say, Show unto me a sign, when ye have the testimony of all these thy brethren, and also all the holy prophets? The scriptures are laid before thee, yea, and all things denote there is a God; yea, even the earth, and all things that are upon the face of it, yea, and *its motion*, yea, and also all *the planets which move in their regular form do witness that there is a Supreme Creator.*" (Alma 30:44; emphasis added.)

If God had no power to command and direct matter, then Alma would not have given God credit for the orderly motion of the earth and other heavenly bodies. Alma's position is substantiated by the word of the Lord in modern revelation wherein the regular motion of the heavenly bodies is attributed to God's commands (law), which reach all matter through the Spirit of Christ:[11]

> Which truth shineth. This is the light of Christ. . . . Which light proceedeth forth from the presence of God to fill the immensity of space — the light which is in all things, which giveth life to all things, which is *the law by which all things are governed*, even the power of God who sitteth upon his throne. . . . And again, verily I say unto you, *he hath given a law unto all things, by which they move in their times and their seasons*; and their courses are fixed, even the courses of the heavens and the earth. . . . The earth rolls upon her wings, and the sun giveth his light by day, and the moon giveth her light by night, and the stars also give their light, as they roll upon their wings in their glory, in the midst of the power of God. . . . Behold, all these are kingdoms, and any man who hath seen any or the least of these hath seen God moving in his majesty and power. (D&C 88:7, 12-13, 42-43, 45, 47; emphasis added.)

The Nature of Humanity

In Russell's second statement, he not only advocated a self-acting and self-perpetuating universe, but also one that was inanimate. A universe that was self-acting and self-perpetuating, where all changes result from the operation of natural law, would of necessity be one where man was merely a physical machine. Such a machine would be controlled completely by natural law, leaving no room for a spirit within the physical body to interact with the body and influence its actions. Some early scientists such as Johannes Muller believed that humans were composed of more than a mere body that was a physical machine. However, some of Muller's own students made a pact among themselves to promote the idea that people's actions were the result of no forces other than the operation of natural law. They were eventually successful in promoting that view, which has now become a traditional way of thinking for many of our modern scientists,[12] especially in the field of behavioristic psychology.[13]

Coming back to Korihor, we find that his views pertaining to humanity were consistent with these naturalistic views. Korihor implied that people had no spirits when he said that "when a man was dead, that was the end thereof." (Alma 30:18.) Furthermore, in such a mechanical universe as that advocated by Korihor, there could be no place for such things as God's law given by his prophets. Consequently, Korihor taught that the words of the prophets were not from God but were mere traditions of men. We also find Korihor teaching that even if people did not live according to the words of the prophets, they still would not "offend some unknown being, who they say is God." (Alma 30:28.)

The Effects of Korihor's Naturalistic Doctrine

In such a naturalistic universe as that advocated by Korihor, where there were no laws of God to break, there could be no sin nor spiritual death that results from sin. Instead of being motivated in their behavior by a fear or love of God, people's actions would be motivated by a survival of the fittest, both physically and mentally, which was no crime. Holding such naturalistic views would influence people to believe that they were not accountable to a higher power for their actions. As a result, they would be led away into sin. Mormon comments on Korihor's teachings and their effect on the people of his day as follows: "Many more such things did he say unto them, telling them that . . . every man fared in this life according to the management of the creature; therefore every man prospered according to his genius, and that every man conquered according to his strength; and whatsoever a man did was no crime. And thus he did preach unto them, leading away the hearts of many, causing them to lift up their heads in their wickedness, yea, leading away many women, and also men, to commit whoredoms." (Alma 30:17-18.)

Since Korihor's universe held no room for a God, God's laws, or certain effects resulting from the breaking of these laws, to be consistent he would have to deny the fall of man which came as the result of the transgression of Adam and Eve. The scriptures describe how the transgression of a commandment of God in the Garden of Eden by our first parents affected not only them but all their posterity by causing them to become mortals subject to spiritual and temporal death. (Alma 42:2-14.) It seems that Korihor was denying the fall when he said: "Ye say that this people is a guilty and a fallen people, because of the transgression of a parent. Behold, I say that a child is not guilty because of its parents." (Alma 30:25.)

Ancient as well as modern scriptures teach that an atonement was needed to provide a remission of personal sins (on conditions of repentance) as well as to overcome the effects of the fall of Adam and Eve. (2 Ne. 9:1-13; Alma 42:12-16.) Again to be consistent with his other naturalistic views, Korihor would have had to deny a need for an atonement and of course a need for Christ to perform the atonement. Concerning the atonement, he said "that there could be no atonement made for the sins of men." (Alma 30:17.) He also stated that to "look forward and say ye see a remission of your sins . . . is the effect of a frenzied mind; and this derangement of your minds comes because of the traditions of your fathers, which lead you away into a belief of things which are not so." (Alma 30:16.) Since Korihor did not believe in sin or a need for an atonement to overcome the effects of sin, he claimed that the idea of a Christ slain for the sins of the world was a foolish tradition of the Nephites used by their priests to keep them in bondage: "Ye . . . say that Christ shall come. But behold, I say that ye do not know that there shall be a Christ. And *ye say also that he shall be slain for the sins of the world—*

and thus *ye lead away this people after the foolish traditions of your fathers*, and according to your own desires; and ye keep them down, even as it were in bondage, that ye may glut yourselves with the labors of their hands." (Alma 30:26-27; emphasis added.)

Consequently, he taught the people "that there should be no Christ" (Alma 30:12) and that to look forward to the coming of Christ was to yoke themselves "under a foolish and a vain hope" (Alma 30:13).

Why Korihor Was an Anti-Christ

It is now easy to see why Mormon labeled Korihor an Anti-Christ: Korihor was denying the truth of those doctrines that made it necessary that Jesus was (and is) the Christ. The role of Christ is twofold.[14] First, he is the Lord God of this world. He attained to this position in premortal life. (Abr. 3:19-21; D&C 38:1-3.) As the Lord God, his word is law to the physical elements, and by his word or power he created or organized this world and continues to sustain and uphold it. He also gives his word (or law) to people on earth, and they have a spirit within them with the capacity to receive and obey his word (or law) or to reject it. Even though each person has a physical body subject to natural law, the spirit within that body can control the body's outward behavior.[15]

Christ's second role is that of Savior or Redeemer. Because Jesus was born the Son of God and performed the atonement during his mortal ministry, he gained power to overcome the effect of people's breaking the very laws he gave in his role as the Lord God. (2 Ne. 2:10.) Hence, he gained power to overcome the effects of the fall as well as to overcome the effects of individual sin, if the person sincerely repents and strives to live the gospel. The purpose of creation was to give people joy, which comes when they overcome spiritual and temporal death through the atonement of Christ.[16] Korihor denied all this (Alma 30:22, 35), as do the "naturalists" of our day who hold similar viewpoints.[17]

In his final confrontation with Alma, Korihor exclaimed he would never believe in God unless he received a physical sign as a manifestation of God's power. Finally, the Lord allowed Alma to give him a sign, but it was to his condemnation: Korihor was struck dumb by the power of God. Korihor then confessed that his doctrines were false and were authored by the devil:

> Now when Alma had said these words, Korihor was struck dumb, that he could not have utterance, according to the words of Alma. . . . And Korihor put forth his hand and wrote, saying: I know that I am dumb, for I cannot speak; and I know that nothing save it were the power of God could bring this upon me; yea, and I also knew that there was a God. But behold, *the devil hath deceived me*; for he appeared unto me in the form of an angel, and said unto me: Go and reclaim this people, for they have all gone astray after an unknown God. And he said unto me: *There is no God; yea, and he taught me that which I should say. And I have taught his words*; and I taught them because they were pleasing unto the carnal mind; and I taught them, even until I had much success, insomuch that I verily believed that they were true; and for this cause I withstood the truth, even until I have brought this great curse upon me. (Alma 30:50, 52-53; emphasis added.)

Summary and Conclusions

If we accept the Book of Mormon as the word of God, the account of Korihor teaches us that the beliefs associated with the philosophy of naturalism are anti-Christ in nature. Science itself should not be anti-Christ, for its methodology should restrict scientists to making statements only about things that can be observed through the natural senses. Some scientists have taken theistic views while others have taken naturalistic views about the nature of the universe, but both groups have acted as philosophers, making statements that go beyond what can be confirmed publicly through the natural senses. According to C. S. Lewis, what is behind the things science observes cannot (and should not) be answered by the scientist if he or she is speaking as a scientist. Lewis comments on the role of science in solving the question of whether God created the universe and continues to uphold it, or whether it is merely an inanimate, self-perpetuating system with no God involved:

Wherever there have been thinking men both views turn up. And note this too. You cannot find out which view is the right one by science in the ordinary sense. Science works by experiments. It watches how things behave. Every scientific statement in the long run, however complicated it looks, really means something like, "I pointed the telescope to such and such a part of the sky at 2:20 A.M. on January 15th and saw so-and-so," or, "I put some of this stuff in a pot and heated it to such-and-such a temperature and it did so-and-so." Do not think I am saying anything against science: I am only saying what its job is. And the more scientific a man is, the more (I believe) he would agree with me that this is the job of sci-ence—and a very useful and necessary job it is too. But why anything comes to be there at all, and whether there is anything behind the things science observes—something of a different kind—this is not a scientific question. If there is "Something Behind," then either it will have to remain altogether unknown to men or *else make itself known in some different way.* The statement that there is any such thing, and the statement that there is no such thing, are neither of them statements that science can make. And real scientists do not usually make them.[18]

C. S. Lewis makes a good point. As a result of scientists using the methodology of science in the last few centuries, an enormous amount of valuable knowledge has been gained about the world around us, knowledge that can be confirmed by empirical observation. However, God has given us revelation through his prophets and through scripture, which reveal to us many things about the universe that cannot be observed in a scientific way. Sometimes what the philosophers say about our universe disagrees with what God has revealed. However, God will confirm to us that the knowledge he has given to us by the prophets and the scriptures is true. That confirmation can come to our spirits through the Holy Ghost if we sincerely ask for it.[19] God has said that part of our test here is to see if we will seek the truth through the power of the Holy Ghost: "Ye shall live by every word which proceedeth forth out of the mouth of God. For he will give unto the faithful line upon line, precept upon precept; and I will try you and prove you herewith." (D&C 98: 11-12.)

Consequently, if we seek and gain a confirmation through the power of the Holy Ghost that the Book of Mormon is true, we can use the contents of that book as a guide in detecting the beliefs of our modern generation that are anti-Christ in nature. It is our responsibility to not "put off the Spirit of God" (Alma 30:42) as did Korihor so that we may not "be seduced by evil spirits, or doctrines of devils, or the commandments of men; for some are of men, and others of devils." (D&C 46:7.)

NOTES

1. Edwin Arthur Burtt, *The Metaphysical Foundations of Modern Physical Science* (London: Routledge & Kegan Paul Ltd., 1950).

2. Bertrand Russell, *The Impact of Science on Society* (New York: Simon and Schuster, 1953), pp. 1-2.

3. *The Impact of Science on Society*, p. 6.

4. Russell held the extreme position of naturalism by advocating all three of these assumptions as being true. There are various other positions that are not quite so extreme. However, advocating any one of these assumptions as being true results in holding a position that is still not in accordance with the words of the scriptures and the prophets. For example, a "deist" believes that God created the universe to begin with but then withdrew, and that since then the universe has run by itself according to natural law. In such a universe there could be no miracles or revelations because there would be no divine intervention after the creation.

5. Alma 5:45-48. Joseph Smith stated that revelation comes "to our spirits precisely as though we had no bodies at all." (Joseph Smith, *Teachings of the Prophet Joseph Smith*, selected by Joseph Fielding Smith [Salt Lake City: Deseret Book Company, 1938], p. 355.) See also D&C 6:14-17, 22-24; 18:1-5; 29:7; Moroni 10:4-5.

6. *The Impact of Science on Society*, pp. 9-10.

7. *The Impact of Science on Society*, p. 10.

8. The Prophet Joseph Smith and the scriptures indicate that when God commands the elements, they obey his will. (Abr. 2:7; Moses 1:25; Hel.

12:7-17; D&C 133:23; *Teachings of the Prophet Joseph Smith*, pp. 197-98.) This earth had its origin first as a plan in the mind of God. (Abr. 3:24; 5:1-3.) He then spoke to or commanded the elements (D&C 38:3) by means of his spirit (D&C 29:30-32), and they obeyed him (Abr. 4:9-11, 18, 21, 25). They continue to obey him and are thus governed (D&C 88:7-13) or upheld by his power (*Teachings of the Prophet Joseph Smith*, pp. 55-56, 345.) In other words, what we *describe* the elements as doing (natural law) is nothing more than what God has *prescribed* them to do. Furthermore, God tells us that it is offensive to him to not acknowledge his hand in all things. (D&C 59:21.) A more detailed discussion on this subject is given by the author in "Creation, Fall, and Atonement," *Studies in Scripture, Vol. 7: 1 Nephi to Alma 29*, ed. Kent P. Jackson (Salt Lake City: Deseret Book Company, 1987), pp. 87-90, 98-100.

9. A more detailed discussion on the shift from theism to naturalism is given by the author in "What Is Man?" *Hearken O Ye People* (Sandy, Utah: Randall Book Company, 1984), pp. 134-42.

10. As an example, Burtt points out that both Robert Boyle and Isaac Newton held theistic beliefs. See *The Metaphysical Foundations of Modern Physical Science*, pp. 289-90.

11. Joseph Smith also gave God credit for the movement of the heavenly bodies when he said that "God set the sun, the moon, and the stars in the heavens, and gave them their laws, conditions and bounds, which they cannot pass, except by His commandments; they all move in perfect harmony in their sphere and order." (*Teachings of the Prophet Joseph Smith*, pp. 197-98.)

12. Edwin G. Boring, *A History of Experimental Psychology* (New York City: Appleton-Century-Crofts, 1957), p. 708.

13. A more detailed discussion of the naturalistic views on humanity is given by the author in "What Is Man?" pp. 133-39.

14. A more detailed discussion of the two roles of Christ is given by the author in "Jesus Is the Christ," *Studies in Scripture, Vol. 5: The Gospels*, ed. Kent B. Jackson and Robert L. Millet (Salt Lake City: Deseret Book Company, 1986), pp. 323-40.

15. As an example, Christ's spirit ruled over his body at all times. (Mosiah 15:5-7.)

16. 2 Nephi 2:10-13, 25; Alma 42:16; D&C 101:35-38; *Teachings of the Prophet Joseph Smith*, p. 255. A more detailed discussion on the subject of the joy that comes from overcoming spiritual and temporal death is given by the author in "The Fall of Man," *Principles of the Gospel in Practice* (Salt Lake City: Randall Book Co., 1985), pp. 48-58.

17. It should be recalled that the naturalist denies that there is "purpose" in the universe. Burtt summarizes Russell's naturalistic beliefs on this subject as follows: "To Russell, man is but the chance and temporary product of a blind and purposeless nature, an irrelevant spectator of her doings, almost an alien intruder on her domain. No high place in a cosmic teleology is his; his ideals, his hopes, his mystic raptures, are but the creations of his own errant and enthusiastic imagination, without standing or application to a real world interpreted mechanically in terms of space, time, and unconscious, though eternal atoms. His mother earth is but a speck in the boundlessness of space, his place even on the earth but insignificant and precarious, in a word, he is at the mercy of brute forces that unknowingly happened to throw him into being, and promise ere long just as unknowingly to snuff out the candle of his little day. Himself and all that is dear to him will in course of time become 'buried in a universe of ruins.' " (*The Metaphysical Foundations of Modern Physical Science*, p. 10.)

18. C. S. Lewis, *Mere Christianity* (New York: Macmillan, 1960), p. 32, emphasis added.

19. Moroni 10:4-5; D&C 6:14-17, 22-24; 18:1-4; James 1:5-6; Matt. 7: 7-11.

2

A FAITH UNTO SALVATION
(Alma 31-33)

RODNEY TURNER

The religion of the ancient Zoramites in the Book of Mormon is paralleled by much of the religion practiced in our modern world: it was false, superficial, undemanding, impotent, and Christless. Consequently, the message of God's prophets to that misguided people is as relevant now as it was over two thousand years ago. While religious illusions may serve us in time, they will fail us in eternity. Only a faith centered in things as they really are and as they really will be can produce the knowledge that saves. Such a faith was the topic of the message delivered to certain Zoramites by the prophet Alma in 74 B.C.

Four False Faiths

Alma's teachings and those of his companion, Amulek (Alma 34), can best be understood in the larger context of certain incorrect doctrines that arose from time to time among the Nephites beginning in the days of Jacob. These erroneous ideas had one thing in common: they denied the future coming of God to the earth in the person of Jesus Christ. The underlying question in them all was the same as it is now: How are we saved? The Book of Mormon describes five variant answers to this question. Four of them are false.

Of these four, the first was advocated by a man named Sherem,

---

Rodney Turner is professor of Church history and doctrine at Brigham Young University.

16

who lived in the sixth century B.C. He taught that the law of Moses was all-sufficient for salvation. (See Jacob 7:7.) Characteristically, Sherem was a learned, eloquent speaker who denied the possibility of prophecy but then proceeded to prophesy himself: "I know that there is no Christ, neither has been, nor ever will be." (Jacob 7:9.) Deceived by the devil, Sherem became Satan's servant and led many souls into apostasy. Struck down by God, and knowing that he was dying, he confessed: "I fear lest I have committed the unpardonable sin, for I have lied unto God; for I denied the Christ, and said that I believed the scriptures; and they truly testify of him." (Jacob 7:19.) The spirit of Sherem—denying prophets and prophecy—is with us today.

The second heresy arose some four hundred years later in 91 B.C. when a man named Nehor taught a pleasing doctrine of universal salvation without the need for repentance: "For the Lord had created all men, and had also redeemed all men; and, in the end, all men should have eternal life." (Alma 1:4; cf. 15:15.) Humanity's redemption required no sacrifice on God's part; he simply willed it. So Nehorism predestined everyone to heaven; hell was no problem.

The spirit of Nehorism is alive and well in many Christian churches where much sermonizing on God's unconditional love can be heard. Because God loves us, they say, sin is not as sinful as once thought. And if there is a hell—which is doubtful—it will be a vast improvement over the old fire-and-brimstone one of eternal burnings. This deceptive attitude was foreseen by Nephi: "There shall also be many which shall say: Eat, drink, and be merry; nevertheless, fear God—he will justify in committing a little sin; yea, lie a little, take the advantage of one because of his words, dig a pit for thy neighbor; there is no harm in this; and do all these things, for tomorrow we die; and if it so be that we are guilty, God will beat us with a few stripes, and at last we shall be saved in the kingdom of God." (2 Ne. 28:8.) In advocating a paid ministry, Nehor introduced priestcraft among the Nephites.[1] Opposed by an aged man named Gideon, a member of Alma's church, Nehor slew him and was executed for his murder. But Nehorism did not die with its founder; it wreaked great havoc among the Nephites for at least twenty more years.

The third, and probably the most charismatic, of the great heretics in the Book of Mormon was the anti-Christ Korihor.[2] He denied the existence of anything beyond the natural order.[3] God, Christ, prophecy, immortality, and judgment were products of false traditions and deranged minds. His advocacy of jungle law ("every man conquered according to his strength; and whatsoever a man did was no crime" — Alma 30:17) promoted rampant immorality among his eager followers. Korihor's descent from theism ("I always knew that there was a God" — Alma 30:52) into professed atheism and its frequent companion, libertinism ("I taught them because they were pleasing unto the carnal mind; and I taught them, even until I had much success, insomuch that I verily believed that they were true" — Alma 30:53) is a classic example of self-delusion. Like Sherem, Korihor demanded a sign and, like Sherem, was struck dumb. Thereafter, while begging food among another group of apostates, the Zoramites, he was trampled to death. Mormon concluded his account of this pathetic anti-Christ by observing: "Thus we see that the devil will not support his children at the last day, but doth speedily drag them down to hell." (Alma 30:60; cf. 2 Ne. 28:21.)

The fourth false faith was advocated by a man named Zoram[4] who, with his followers, had apostatized from Alma's church of Christ. Like Sherem, Nehor, and Korihor, the Zoramites denied that there would ever be an incarnated — flesh and bone — Christ. How could there be? God was "a spirit forever." (Alma 31:15.) They thanked their immaterial God for having "made it known unto us that there shall be no Christ." They were also grateful that God had "elected us that we shall be saved, whilst all around us are elected to be cast by thy wrath down to hell; for the which holiness, O God, we thank thee." (Alma 31:16-17.)

Their weekly group-devotion on the "Rameumptom," a prayer tower that dominated their synagogues, consisted of this single, formalized, self-congratulatory prayer. Having taken care of their spiritual obligations for the week, "they returned to their homes, never speaking of their God again until they had assembled themselves together again to the holy stand." (Alma 31:23.) Their choral exercise in vanity sufficed to appease their God and permitted them to freely indulge themselves. Having been predestined to holiness and salvation, they had no need for daily prayer or obedience to restrictive commandments. The issue of life after death had been fully and happily settled; they could get on with the things of this world. Such is the underlying assumption of every "Sunday religion." It renders God a practical irrelevance. He exists, but he need not be taken too seriously. The false doctrines of Sherem, Nehor, Korihor, and Zoram were both predictive and representative of those apostate religious beliefs—Christian and non-Christian—that shroud the world in spiritual darkness in these latter days.

True Faith

To combat the Zoramite heresy, and knowing that "preaching of the word . . . had had more powerful effect upon the minds of the people than the sword, or anything else, . . . therefore Alma thought it was expedient that they should try the virtue of the word of God." (Alma 31:5.) The battle between truth and error, righteousness and rebellion, was joined.

Spiritual Humility

Bad religion breeds bad societies. The Zoramites created a class system that ostracized their less fortunate brothers and sisters from the very synagogues they had built. But—as has been the case from time immemorial—it was these downtrodden souls who proved most responsive to the message of Alma and his companions.[5] Impoverished "as to things of the world," they are described as "poor in heart" or "lowly in heart." (Alma 32:3-4, 8.) That is, they were dispirited and quite hopeless.[6] Alma "beheld that their afflictions had truly humbled them, and that they were in a preparation to hear the word." (Alma 32:6.)

Spiritual humility—the recognition of one's dependence upon God for all things temporal and spiritual, coupled with a willingness to accept his law—is a precondition for true repentance. Some achieve this humility only after they have been "compelled to be humble" by those "slings and arrows of outrageous fortune" of which Hamlet soliloquized. Some do so only after they have been brought face-to-face with the stark truth about themselves and the God they defied, or never knew.

Some will never learn humility and, therefore, never repent even when they stand before God with a "perfect knowledge" of their guilt and uncleanness.[7] However, God's truth will prove irresistible, and they will acknowledge to their "everlasting shame that all his judgments are just." (Alma 12:15; cf. 2 Ne. 9:13-16.) President Spencer W. Kimball wrote one "disbeliever": "The time will come when there will be a surrender of every person who has ever lived on this earth ... and it will be an unforced surrender, an unconditional surrender. When will it be for you? ... It is not *if* you will capitulate to the great truth; it is *when,* for I know that you cannot indefinitely resist the power and pressure of truth."[8]

"Therefore," said Alma, "blessed are they who humble themselves without being compelled to be humble ... who would humble themselves, let them be in whatsoever circumstances they might." (Alma 32:16, 25.) Such spirits are in tune with the Holy Spirit. "Without compulsory means" (D&C 121:46), the intelligence, virtue, and truth in them draws them to the intelligence, virtue, and truth in God (see D&C 88:40). Perhaps they developed much of this affinity with the divine in their premortal existence, although undoubtedly it can be developed during mortality as well. Elder Bruce R. McConkie referred to this disposition as "the talent for spirituality. Those so endowed find it easy to believe the truth in this life."[9] Needless to say, the sooner genuine humility—"a broken heart and a contrite spirit" (2 Ne. 2:7)—is achieved, the better off one is.

Sign-Seekers

To be "compelled to know" is characteristic of the carnally minded. This disposition results from an empirical or rational mindset that accepts only what can be perceived through the physical senses or is deemed reasonable. (See Hel. 16:17-18.) But physical experiences and secular knowledge are the common property of the entire, disparate human race without regard to spirituality or moral character. A person may be a gifted artist, scientist, or philosopher, and a scoundrel at the same time. A university degree is not a prerequisite for salvation. Rather, we are saved only as we gain spiritual intelligence—light and truth, the glory of God. (See D&C 93:36.) Such knowledge comes only through faith and its resulting works. Paul wrote: "The natural man receiveth not the things of the Spirit of God: for they are foolishness unto him: neither can he know them, because they are spiritually discerned." (1 Cor. 2:14.) The sign-seeker is the natural man par excellence. For him, if a thing cannot be seen, heard, touched, tasted, or smelled, it does not exist. Thus such people demand "a sign from heaven" before they will acknowledge the reality of "things which are not seen." Alma asked: "Is this faith? Behold, I say unto you, Nay; for if a man knoweth a thing he hath no cause to believe, for he knoweth it." (Alma 32:18.) When certitude is obtained, faith is swallowed up in knowledge, becoming one with it. But, as we shall see, faith is indispensable in acquiring the knowledge that leads to salvation. To demand such knowledge in the absence of faith is to invite disaster. Those who do so will never obtain a fullness of either faith or knowledge.

The sign-seekers, the God-tempters, presume to put the Almighty on trial by challenging him to prove his own existence. Korihor typified them: "Except ye show me a sign, I will not believe." (Alma 30:48.) In their pride, the Korihors of this world set up the preconditions under which they may condescend to believe. But it is all a sham; their insistence on signs is not meant to foster faith but to justify doubt. And the seed of faith will never grow in the soil of doubt. Where there is a will to doubt, a heavenly sign or evidence will be ignored, rejected, or rationalized away. The Lord told young Joseph Smith: "Behold, if they will not believe my words, they would not believe you, my servant Joseph, if it were possible that you should show them all these things [obtained from the hill Cumorah] which I have committed unto you." (D&C 5:7; cf. Luke 16:31.) The rational mind will always reject what the hardened heart is unprepared to accept. That is why signs without faith are a barrier against, not a path to, God.

The last thing sign-seekers should seek is a sign. In insisting upon knowing before believing, they become their own worst enemy. "How much more cursed is he that knoweth the will of God and doeth it not, than he that only believeth, or only hath cause to believe, and falleth into transgression?" (Alma 32:19; cf. D&C 63:7, 11; 82:3.) The principle enunciated by Moroni—"Ye receive no witness until after the trial of your faith" (Ether 12:6)—is a blessing. Knowledge in excess of one's will and wisdom is a formula for disaster in all things. The world's understanding of nuclear energy far exceeds their ability to control it, because that knowledge does not rest upon a commitment to moral law. This condition accounts for the very real likelihood that we will yet be confronted with nuclear war. Power without principle is a scourge in every age.

Just as a wise parent keeps medicine or tools out of a child's reach, so does God withhold divine knowledge from the ill-prepared.[10] In his wisdom and mercy, he has ordained that faith must precede certitude so that, in the very process of exercising faith, the individual develops the spiritual maturity needed to possess divine knowledge in righteousness. Thus capacitated, such knowledge magnifies rather than diminishes one's relationship to God.

For example, the Lord promised the brother of Jared that if he developed sufficient faith he could be shown all things. The brother of Jared did so, "wherefore [Christ] showed him all things, for he could no longer be kept without the veil." (Ether 12:21.) Christ was bound by his own promise; he could not deny the brother of Jared the knowledge his faith had prepared him to receive. This is an eternal principle. Hence the Prophet Joseph Smith's remark: "God hath not revealed anything to Joseph, but what He will make known unto the Twelve, and even the least Saint may know all things *as fast as he is able to bear them.*"[11]

Faith versus Knowledge

In scripture, faith and belief are frequently employed as interchangeable terms.[12] In its broadest sense, faith is belief in the existence, virtue, validity, or efficacy of something or someone, seen or unseen, past, present, or future.[13] It may be a good faith or a bad faith; it may be constructive or destructive. It all depends upon the nature of the person or thing that is its object. However, Alma delimited faith to belief in what is real and deserving of trust—the doctrine of Christ. Hence, he spoke of "things which are not seen, *which are true.*" (Alma 32:21; italics added.)

Alma begged the Zoramites to "exercise a particle of faith, yea, even if you can no more than desire to believe, let this desire work in you." (Alma 32:27.) The "desire to believe" becomes the motivation for the "trial of faith," which eventually produces a "perfect knowledge" or verification of what was, at first, only an unproven possibility. When the desire to believe is combined with effort, faith is born, and when faith is born, saving works follow.

Alma used the example of planting a seed (his own testimony of Christ — Alma 33:1) in the hope of growing a tree, the fruit of which would be everlasting life (Alma 32:27-43). As each step of the "experiment" is verified by observed results, there is no further need to exercise faith in what has become an accomplished fact. For example, when the "seed" germinates, there is no longer need to have faith that it *will* germinate: "Yea, your knowledge is perfect *in that thing*, and your faith is dormant; and this because *you know*, for ye know that the word hath swelled your souls, and ye also know that it hath sprouted up, that your understanding doth begin to be enlightened, and your mind doth begin to expand." (Alma 32:34; italics added.)

While each successfully accomplished phase of the experiment is replaced with certitude or perfect knowledge *of that phase*, faith is still needed in carrying out each *subsequent* phase of the experiment. So initial faith produces initial knowledge, which, in turn, produces more faith, which then leads to even more knowledge, and so on until one's knowledge is perfect or complete pertaining to the *entire* experiment.

This same process was advocated by Jesus when he said: "If any man will do [God's] will, he shall know of the doctrine, whether it be of God, or whether I speak of myself." (John 7:17.) This is simply the scientific method raised to the spiritual plane: we do in order to know. As we live the gospel, we reap an ever greater harvest of faith and knowledge until, like God himself, our faith and our knowledge become perfect in all things. For those who aspire to that divine state, the faith-to-knowledge process must continue into eternity until they obtain "a fulness of truth, yea, even of all truth." (D&C 93:26.) Like Adam and Eve, they will have become as the Gods who forever partake of both the tree of life and the tree of knowledge. Such is that "perfect day" called exaltation. (See D&C 50:24.)

Hope

As faith is not knowledge, but the means to knowledge, so faith is not hope, but the basis of hope: "If ye have faith ye hope for things which are not seen, which are true." (Alma 32:21.)[14] Faith and hope are inseparable; one does not exist without the other. (See Moro. 7:41-42.) Faith in the redemptive power of Christ produces the hope of everlasting life, "the heavenly gift." (Ether 12:8.) Once that hope is realized, it is no longer hoped for; it is possessed. Paul wrote: "We are saved by hope: but hope that is seen [realized] is not hope: for what a man seeth, why doth he yet hope for?" (Rom. 8:24.) However, if the "tree of life"—which grows from a testimony of Christ—never matures, "it is because your ground [soul] is barren, and ye will not nourish the tree." (Alma 32:39.) No matter how fervent one's faith in the beginning, if the person becomes neglectful, apathetic, or rebellious, faith dies. And when faith dies, hope dies with it. But as Alma assured the Zoramites, if, with "an eye of faith,"[15] and with great diligence and patience, we nourish the word, "[we] shall pluck the fruit . . . which is most precious . . . and . . . feast upon this fruit even until [we] are filled, that [we] hunger not, neither shall [we] thirst." (Alma 32:42.)

The Prophetic Witness

Alma's general teachings on faith became increasingly specific as he brought his message to its climax. Driven from their synagogues, the despised Zoramites felt that they could no longer worship God. (See Alma 32:2, 3, 5; 33:2.) Somewhat perplexed by Alma's message, they asked two questions: (1) Should they believe in but one God? and (2) How were they to begin exercising faith?

Alma responded by first quoting two ancient prophets of Israel, Zenos and Zenock. Zenos taught that the real issue was not *where* or *when* one prays—it can be any place, any time—but *how*, and *to whom*, one prays. Zenos stressed that prayers are heard and mercy is extended through the Son of God. Said he: "Thou hast turned thy judgments [the demands of justice] away from me, *because of thy Son.*" (Alma 33:11; italics added.) Zenock testified that Israel "will not understand thy mercies which thou hast bestowed upon them *because of thy Son.*" (Alma 33:16; italics added; see 34:7.)[16] Moses taught the same doctrine: the brazen serpent symbolized the saving power of the God of Israel.[17] "But few understood the meaning of those things, and this because of the hardness of their hearts." (Alma 33:20.) Nevertheless, every true prophet understood and testified of the Son of God. (See Jacob 7:11; 3 Ne. 20:24.) Their combined testimonies of the promised Messiah constituted the "seed" the Zoramites were to plant in their hearts. "And as it beginneth to swell even so nourish it by your faith. And behold, it will become a tree, springing up in you unto everlasting life." (Alma 33:23.) Where can we worship? Everywhere. When should we worship? Always. Whom should we worship? The only true God.[18]

Conclusion

Prominent among the many truths taught by Alma are the following: God is not an amorphous spirit ruling with arbitrary indifference over human affairs. He responds to our prayers and is profoundly involved in our lives, so much so that he sent his Son into the world to rescue us from endless temporal and spiritual death.

Prayer is not a weekly ritual but a daily necessity. It is not a means of evading our responsibilities; rather, it is an expression of commitment to them. Disdain of others renders prayer a vain, hypocritical exercise in self-delusion. If we would have God hear our cries, we cannot be deaf to the pleas of those around us.

True faith is not centered in ourselves but in the Lord; not in our virtues but in his. We believe in ourselves because we believe in him. Saving faith—unlike the credulity of the Zoramites, ancient and modern—is not a static, lifeless, attitude of self-complacency requiring nothing and giving nothing. Rather, true faith is dynamic and demanding. It is a lifetime process of spiritual growth wherein we work out our salvation "with fear before God." (Alma 34:37; cf. Philip. 2:12.) "Faith precedes the miracle" of revelation. To know—as God knows—the hidden things of time and eternity, we must first become like him. Only as we are transformed through faith are we capacitated to receive the blessings and responsibilities of spiritual knowledge.

Faith in Jesus Christ, the Redeemer of mankind, is the key to salvation and a knowledge of all things. Those who walk the strait and narrow way with "an eye of faith" shall be perfected in all the knowledge of God: "And to them will I reveal all mysteries, yea, all the hidden mysteries of my kingdom from days of old, and for ages to come, will I make known unto them the good pleasure of my will concerning all things pertaining to my kingdom. Yea, even the wonders of eternity shall they know, and things to come will I show them, even the things of many generations." (D&C 76:7-8.) Thus, from the tiny seed of mortal faith in the Son of Man will come an immortal knowledge of God and his unimaginable mysteries. It only remains for us to plant that seed and nourish it with diligence.

NOTES

1. "Priestcrafts are that men preach and set themselves up for a light unto the world, that they may get gain and praise of the world; but they seek not the welfare of Zion." (2 Ne. 26:29.)

2. Korihor is the only person called anti-Christ in the Book of Mormon. (See Alma 30:6, 12.)

3. The contemporary philosophies of naturalism, existentialism, and secular humanism take the same position. See chapter 1 in this volume.

4. Zoram's lineage is not given, but he quite possibly descended from Laban's servant of the same name. (See 1 Ne. 4:35; Alma 30:59; 31:1; 54:23.)

5. Alma was accompanied by his two sons Shiblon and Corianton, three sons of Mosiah (Ammon, Aaron, and Omner), and Amulek and Zeezrom. (See Alma 31:32.)

6. It is commonly assumed that the phrase "poor in spirit" (Matt. 5:3) refers to the humble and spiritually rich. However, as used by Alma and Jesus, the phrase refers to those who are impoverished spiritually.

7. See Joseph Smith, *Teachings of the Prophet Joseph Smith*, selected by Joseph Fielding Smith (Salt Lake City: Deseret Book Company, 1938), p. 358.

8. *Ensign*, September 1978, p. 8. Italics in original.

9. Bruce R. McConkie, *The Millennial Messiah* (Salt Lake City: Deseret Book Company, 1982), p. 234.

10. For the most part, the Lord provides *evidences* rather than *proofs* of spiritual matters. For example, the Book of Mormon does not constitute a proof of its own teachings. Hence, Moroni's admonition to the reader to ask God "if these things are not true." (Moro. 10:4.)

11. *Teachings of the Prophet Joseph Smith*, p. 149; italics added.

12. For example, see 3 Nephi 19:20, 28. The gospel of John consistently uses the word "believe" rather than the word "faith."

13. In the vast majority of instances in scripture, faith is defined in terms of what is real or true; however, a few passages refer to a vain faith, meaning one that is centered in something or someone that is false, non-existent, or unjustifiable. (See 3 Ne. 1:8; Moro. 7:44; D&C 104:55; 1 Cor. 15:14.)

14. Like the words of Alma, Paul's oft-quoted words in JST Hebrews 11:1 define faith as belief in the existence of unseen or unobtained realities that can be hoped for because of Christ. For example, faith in Christ's atonement is the basis for the hope of a future remission of sins.

15. The "eye of faith" sees eternal verities that lie beyond mortality and the natural order. Lacking that "eye," we are blind to eternal and spiritual realities.

16. Zenos and Zenock were prophets in Israel before 600 B.C. Their writings are on the plates of brass but not in the Old Testament. (See 1 Ne. 19:10, 12, 16; Jacob 5:1; 6:1; Alma 34:7; Hel. 8:19-20; 15:11; and 3 Ne. 10:16.) It is obvious from their testimonies that "plain and precious" truths are missing from the Old Testament as well as the New Testament. The result is the distorted view of the religion of ancient Israel current among biblical scholars. Israel was taught that God's Son was to come to earth and atone for the sins of the world. Her sins are all the more reprehensible because of this knowledge.

17. See Numbers 21:9; 1 Nephi 17:41; 2 Nephi 25:20; Helaman 8:14-15.

18. The Book of Mormon makes it clear that the Son of God (Jehovah, the Holy One of Israel, the Messiah, the Redeemer, Jesus Christ, etc.) is subordinate to his literal Father. However, by "investiture of authority" the Son serves under his Father in a dual capacity and bears a joint title: Father and Son. "And they are one God, yea, the very Eternal Father of heaven and earth." (Mosiah 15:4; cf. Ether 3:14.) It is this "one God" to whom the Zoramites—and all people—are to look for salvation. This "one God" is emphasized throughout holy writ.

3

THE INFINITE ATONEMENT OF GOD
(Alma 34–35)

RODNEY TURNER

A major doctrine of the Book of Mormon is that as a result of Adam's transgression, "all mankind became a lost and fallen people." (Alma 12:22.)[1] The whole world was lost to God, and only God could redeem it from its fallen state. (See 1 Ne. 10:6.) The message with which Amulek climaxed Alma's preceding discourse (Alma 31-33) was that God—in the person of Jesus Christ—would bring about that imperative redemption.

Zoramite Religion

Amulek's audience consisted of Zoramites—a Nephite faction that had apostatized from the church of God and turned to the worship of idols. They believed that God (who was "a spirit forever") had elected them to be saved "whilst all around [them were] elected to be cast by [God's] wrath down to hell." (Alma 31:15-17.) This predestinarian doctrine implied that, for all practical purposes, God was independent of all moral considerations: he could forgive sins and save souls—or not—as he chose, without regard to justice, mercy, or any other divine principle. That being the case, a Redeemer was not really needed, and there never would be one.

It was the rejection of the message of the prophets concerning the future coming of a divine Redeemer that was at the heart of the

Rodney Turner is professor of Church history and doctrine at Brigham Young University.

28

Zoramite apostasy. Like much erroneous doctrine, it did not stem from faulty logic but from incorrect premises. Wrong assumptions produce wrong conclusions. The syllogistic argument of the Zoramites — like many theological propositions — was logically valid but materially false.[2]

Although Christ is spoken of in the Book of Mormon as "the Lord God Omnipotent" (Mosiah 5:15), yet he does not function as an absolutely omnipotent being. If he did, the Zoramite argument would have been correct and there would have been no inescapable need for an atoning sacrifice. But the Almighty works in harmony with the various systems of law he has established. (See D&C 88:36-38.) That is why he cannot lie (Ether 3:12), "look upon sin with the least degree of allowance" (Alma 45:16), grant mercy without repentance, or save a sinner in his sins (Alma 11:37; 42:24). Thus, it is more accurate to say that God rules as a *pen*-omnipotent being rather than as an absolute monarch.

Testimony of the Prophets

In whom were the Zoramites to believe — a predestinarian God who arbitrarily saved or damned as he chose, or a God who respected human agency and governed with justice, equity, and mercy? Amulek addressed their dilemma. He reminded them that they were not ignorant of the truth: "These things were taught unto you bountifully before your dissension from among us." (Alma 34:2.) But failing to nourish the "seed" of testimony, they had failed to harvest its intended fruit. Continuing Alma's analogy (Alma 32:28), Amulek invited the Zoramites: "Have so much faith as even to plant the word in your hearts, that ye may try the experiment of its goodness." Only by doing so could they determine "whether the word [the truth] be in the Son of God, or whether there shall be no Christ." (Alma 34:4-5.) Amulek had done this; he knew the answer to that critical question.

To the testimonies of Alma, Zenos, Zenock, and Moses, Amulek added his own: "I do know that Christ shall come." (Alma 34:8.) He *knew* because he had *experienced* a witness from the Lord to that effect. He did not merely rationalize, conjecture, hypothesize, or assume such a being; he knew by direct revelation that there would be a Christ. So certain, so absolute is such knowledge, that any denial of it is the ultimate lie called the sin against the Holy Ghost. The Prophet Joseph Smith said that one guilty of this sin "has got to say that the sun does not shine while he sees it; he has got to deny Jesus Christ when the heavens have been opened to him, and to deny the plan of salvation with his eyes open to the truth of it."[3] While the apostate Zoramites claimed that God had told them that there would be no Christ (Alma 31:16), their unsupported lie was refuted by the Spirit of truth. This Spirit enables the prophets — and those sent by them — to "seal both on earth and in heaven [the spirit world], the unbelieving and rebellious." (D&C 1:8; cf. 2 Ne. 11:3; 27:14; 33:10-15.)

The Nature of Fallen Humanity

Amulek did not mince words; his testimony was categorical and emphatic: "According to the great plan of the Eternal God there must be an atonement made, or else all mankind must unavoidably perish; yea, all are hardened; yea, all are fallen and are lost, and must perish except it be through the atonement which it is expedient should be made." (Alma 34:9.) Amulek's description of humanity as hardened, fallen, and lost must be understood in context. The Book of Mormon does not teach an Augustinian-like doctrine of human depravity. This now largely rejected concept defined humans as creatures of God who, through willful rebellion, became essentially incapable of any virtuous thought or act.

While rejecting this extreme doctrine, the Book of Mormon does describe mankind as "carnal, sensual, and devilish, by nature." (Alma 42:10; Mosiah 16:3.) That is, because of the Fall, people tend to yield to the undisciplined, unsanctified appetites and passions of the flesh.[4] Just as gravity abets poor physical posture, so does the Fall abet poor moral and spiritual posture. Those who cater to their fleshly appetites become "devilish" because they subject themselves to the will of the devil. (See Mosiah 16:3.)

But Augustine's doctrine of human depravity differs from the Book of Mormon doctrine of the Fall on two important points. First, Augustine viewed mortals as *creatures* of God whose nature was "a mean between the angelic and the bestial."[5] As such, mortals at their best could only aspire to "the company of the angels," who were themselves but creatures of God. Thus humanity's immortal horizon was circumscribed by their literal creaturehood.[6]

Secondly, humanity's depravity was total, their *whole* being—soul and flesh—was in revolt against God: "For the soul, revelling in its own liberty, and scorning to serve God, was itself deprived of the command it had formerly maintained over the body. And because it [the soul] had willfully deserted its superior Lord, it no longer held [controlled] its own inferior servant; neither could it hold the flesh subject, as it would always have been able to do had it remained itself subject to God. . . . And thus, from the bad use of free will, there originated the whole train of evil, which, with its concatenation of miseries, convoys the human race from its depraved origin, as from a corrupt root, on to the destruction of the second death, which has no end, those only being excepted who are freed by the grace of God."[7]

The Book of Mormon does not support this view. It is not the *whole* soul—spirit and flesh—that is corrupt and "an enemy to God" (Mosiah 3:19), but only the person's *fallen mortal nature*—a nature *inherited* through Adam's necessary transgression. Through the atonement of Christ, this *initially corrupt* nature may be overcome, sanctified, and glorified. Therefore, humanity's condemnation is not that as mortals they were born carnal, sensual, and devilish,[8] but that they choose to *remain* so when given the opportunity to repent and overcome that condition. For, contrary to Augustine, the gospel is not designed to restore some people to an acceptable creature state as immortal angels, but to endow all who fully repent with the very nature of God—both in spirit and in flesh. Those who do so achieve a fullness of eternal life.

The Infinite Atonement of Christ

The "great plan of the Eternal God" was formulated in the eternities. It was not a spur-of-the-moment reaction to unforeseen problems arising from Adam's transgression. All was foreordained; all was *planned.* The critical elements in that eternal plan were moral agency, the Fall, the Atonement, the resurrection, and the judgment. Moral agency led to the Fall, and the Fall made the three-fold mission of Christ (atonement, resurrection, and judgment) imperative. The Almighty does not rule by mere fiat, nor does he ignore the moral imbalance in the universe caused by the cumulative sins of mankind.

Yet some who reject the atonement of Christ argue, "How can one mortal die for the sins of all mortals?" The answer is, he cannot. No mortal, however virtuous, can atone for the sins of another, let alone the sins of all mankind. (See Alma 34:11-12.) Why not? Because as a result of Adam's transgression, "*all* mankind became a lost and fallen people." (Alma 12:22; italics added.) If *all* are lost, who can save them? Only an infinite Being—free of the spiritual consequences of the Fall—could do so. Only a God could atone for the sins of the world. Only by God satisfying the righteous demands of divine justice could the truly penitent be saved by divine mercy. (See Alma 34:15-16; 42:13-15, 22-25.) Therefore, "God himself shall come down among the children of men, and shall redeem his people." (Mosiah 15:1.) "God himself atoneth for the sins of the world." (Alma 42:15.)

Lest the idolatrous Zoramites assume that the God called Christ would be a mere mortal, Amulek explained: "It shall not be a *human* sacrifice; but it must be an *infinite* and eternal sacrifice." (Alma 34:10; italics added; cf. 42:15.) In the Book of Mormon, we read of God's infinite goodness, mercy, and grace. (See 2 Ne. 9:7; 25:16.) In other words, all that pertains to God is infinite, even as the adjectives eternal, endless, and everlasting describe his divine nature. (See D&C 19:10-13.) Therefore, the Atonement was an infinite act because it was performed by an infinite Being. The nature of the act reflected the nature of the Actor.

The Prophet Joseph Smith taught that the atonement of Jesus Christ was efficacious not only for mankind on this earth, but for the human family on other earths as well. In his poetic parallel of Doctrine and Covenants 76:23-24, the Prophet wrote of the worlds the Saviour had organized:

> Whose inhabitants, too, from the first to the last,
> Are sav'd by the very same Saviour of ours;
> And, of course, are begotten God's daughters and sons
> By the very same truths and the very same powers.[9]

The Book of Mormon is silent on this doctrine. It treats the Atonement only in terms of Adam's posterity on this earth: "He [Christ] suffereth the pains of all men, yea, the pains of every living creature, both men, women, and children, who belong to the family of Adam." (2 Ne. 9:21.) That Jesus Christ performed an infinite atonement is beyond dispute, but how far-reaching it was pertaining to all the worlds that were, are, and will be is, as yet, unrevealed.[10]

Because of the Fall, the laws and commandments of God save no one. To the contrary, they tend to condemn everyone.[11] Yet with the Lord's help, his laws are livable. The Savior "kept the law of God, and remained without sin, showing thereby that it is in the power of man to keep the law and remain also without sin."[12]

Justice is the essence of law: we reap what we sow. Alma called this principle "the plan of restoration." (Alma 41:2.) And, said he, "restoration is to bring back *again* evil for evil . . . good for that which is good." (Alma 41:13; italics added.) That is, we are personally accountable for how we use the gift of moral agency. In harmony with this principle, Amulek asked: "Now, if a man murdereth, behold will our law, *which is just*, take the life of his brother? I say unto you, Nay. But the law requireth the life of him who hath murdered." (Alma 34:11-12; italics added.)

Speaking of the Mosaic order, Amulek declared Christ to be "the whole meaning of the law, every whit pointing to that great and last sacrifice; and that great and last sacrifice will be the Son of God, yea, infinite and eternal." (Alma 34:14.) Sacrifice began with Adam as an ordinance of the fullness of the gospel and was continued under Moses as an aspect of the "preparatory gospel," which included the Mosaic law. (See Moses 5:5-7; D&C 84:26-27.)

However, "the law of Moses availeth nothing except it were through the atonement of his blood." (Mosiah 3:15; cf. Alma 26:16.) Without Christ, the law was a shadow without substance. More to the point, without Christ humanity stood naked and helpless before the justice of God no matter how faithfully the law might have been observed. It is the Redeemer's atoning sacrifice—an act of infinite mercy—that provides the essential motivation for the faith taught by Alma and Amulek. For in the absence of God's mercy, why should anyone have faith? Life would still be a dead-end street leading to death, hell, and the devil. (See 2 Ne. 9:7-9; Jacob 7:12.) Thus God's mercy justifies human faith. And faith, in turn, begets the hope of eternal life. This hope is justified by the works of divine love that complete the triangle of salvation: faith, hope, and charity. (See Alma 34:27-29; Moro. 7:38-48.)

The Night of Darkness and the Day of Mercy

In the final analysis, people have but two choices: to be saved in the kingdom of God or to be damned in the kingdom of the devil; there is no third alternative. (See 2 Ne. 2:27-29; Alma 41:4.) Whatever the choice, it will be made *this side* of eternity *before* the last judgment. Hence, Amulek's warning: "Now is the time and the day of *your* salvation; ... *this life* is the time for men to prepare to meet God."[13] (Alma 34:31-32; italics added.) When the sun sets on the day of probation, "then cometh the night of darkness wherein there can be *no labor* performed." (Alma 34:33; italics added; cf. Alma 41:5, 7; 3 Ne. 27:33.) That "night" is the time when "it is everlastingly too late" (Hel. 13:38) to perform the labors of repentance. "For the Spirit of the Lord will not *always* strive with man." (2 Ne. 26:11; italics added.)

Alma was told by an angel that at death the righteous entered "a state of happiness, which is called paradise," while the wicked were consigned to a state of misery or "outer darkness." (Alma 40:12-13.) This black-or-white description of the post-mortal state was something of a generalization. It did not explicitly cover that gray host of spirits who—while not totally bereft of the Spirit of the Lord—were nevertheless unredeemed.[14]

Amulek taught: "That same spirit which doth possess your bodies at the time that ye go out of *this life*, that same spirit will have power to possess your *body* in that eternal world." (Alma 34:34; italics added.) "This life" means "this probationary state" (Alma 42:10), and "that eternal world" is the post-resurrection, *not* the spirit, world. "That same spirit" is one's distilled, fundamental self, stripped of all the transitory, superficial baggage acquired in mortality. It is what the soul really is in its fixed, resurrected state, rather than what it appeared to be at any given moment in its fluid, probationary state.[15] What it really is determines what it really desires. These desires, free of all mitigating entanglements, constitute the soul's own self-judgment. (See Alma 41:3-7.)[16]

The explicit teachings of Alma and Amulek quoted above must, therefore, be understood in the time frame of those who lived *before* the Savior initiated his appointed ministry to the unredeemed in the spirit world. Until that hour there was "a great gulf" (Luke 16:26) between those in "paradise" and those in "outer darkness." The latter were, relatively speaking, "in darkness, and a state of awful, fearful looking for the fiery indignation of the wrath of God upon them." (Alma 40:14.) Some thirty-five hundred years before Alma's day, Enoch learned that the unrepentant who perished in the world-wide Flood would be "in torment" in a "prison" prepared for them by the Lord.[17] (See Moses 7:38-39; cf. 6:29.) There they, and all like them, remained until Jesus personally inaugurated the spirit world dispensation of the gospel. Messengers were commissioned by the then-disembodied Son of God to bring the message of salvation "to those who had died in their sins, without a knowledge of the truth, or in transgression, having rejected the prophets." (D&C 138:32.)[18]

Thanks to the merciful Redeemer, eternity — the "night of darkness wherein there can be no labor performed" — was seemingly held back, and the probationary "day of salvation" extended even to the second resurrection! This post-mortal gospel dispensation enables those who repent after death to come forth from their prison of torment and despair and stand on the right hand of God — the hand of salvation.[19] Thus the gates of hell do not prevail against Christ and his priesthood. The vast majority of mankind will pass through those gates and be saved in the "many mansions" comprising the immortal kingdom of God! (See D&C 76:111.)

But to forever reject Christ is to forever forfeit mercy. In that event, it is "as though there had been no redemption made." (Alma 12:18; cf. verse 32.) Justice exercises total dominion, and mercy stands mute. Such is the fate of those children of perdition who, never repenting, are never redeemed. They are known as the "filthy still"[20] who are sealed up to Satan and suffer the fullness of the second death. (See 2 Ne. 9:15-16; Alma 12:16-17; 34:35.)

The rest of mankind—whatever their sins—will eventually repent: "And after they have *paid the penalty of their transgressions*, and are washed clean, shall receive a reward according to their works, for *they are heirs of salvation.*" (D&C 138:59; italics added; cf. 76:43-44, 88.)[21] And so beginning with the Book of Mormon, God's great plan of happiness for all of his children has been revealed, line upon line, in this, the dispensation of the fullness of times!

Epilogue

Upon completing their mission, Alma, Amulek, and their fellow companions left Antionum and journeyed northward to the land of Jershon—the home of the people of Ammon, the Lamanite converts who had taken the name Anti-Nephi-Lehies. (Alma 23:17.) They were soon joined by those Zoramites who, because they accepted the teachings about Christ, had been driven out by their leaders who sought to perpetuate priestcraft. The people of Ammon fed and clothed the wretched Zoramites and even provided them with inheritances.

Ironically, Alma's mission of peace provoked a war in 74 B.C. Infuriated by the Ammonites' acts of charity, the unbelieving Zoramites not only joined the Lamanites in preparing for war but actually became Lamanites. (Alma 43:4.) Their descent into even greater spiritual darkness bore out an earlier observation by Amulek: "They that will harden their hearts, to them is given the lesser portion of the word until they know nothing concerning his mysteries; and then they are taken captive by the devil, and led by his will down to destruction. Now this is what is meant by the chains of hell." (Alma 12:11.)

Under oath never to take up arms again (Alma 24:18), the people of Ammon temporarily left Jershon to the defending Nephite armies—whom they materially supported—and withdrew to the land of Melek, west of the Sidon river. However, the converted Zoramites remained to support the Nephite armies in defending the land of Jershon. The "chief captains" of the Lamanite armies were Amalekites and Zoramites—fanatical enemies of their own Nephite people. But within the year—and with devastating losses to the Lamanites—the Nephites, led by young general Moroni and "inspired by a better cause" (Alma 43:45), proved victorious.

Meanwhile, Alma and his associates returned to Zarahemla, "having been instruments in the hands of God of bringing many of the Zoramites to repentance." (Alma 35:14.) But during the war, Alma "could not rest." (Alma 43:1.) With his three sons, Helaman, Shiblon, and Corianton, he went forth for the last time to declare the truth. Then, after giving final instructions to his sons, prophesying the eventual destruction of the Nephite nation, and reaffirming America's law of inheritance, "he departed out of the land of Zarahemla, as if to go into the land of Melek. And it came to pass that he was never heard of more." (Alma 45:10-18.) Thus passed from the scene two of the Lord's most faithful witnesses, Alma and Amulek.

Conclusion

The heart of the plan of salvation is the infinite atoning sacrifice of the Son of God. Without him, there is no salvation for anyone. His merits, combined with faith and its ordained works, open the door to an appropriate mansion in the kingdom of God for all who call upon his name either in this world or in the world to come.

The Lord's witnesses, both divine and human, leave humanity without excuse. Nephi wrote: "Wherefore, by the words of three, God hath said, I will establish my word. Nevertheless, God sendeth more witnesses, and *he proveth all his words.*" (2 Ne. 11:3; italics added; cf. D&C 6:28.) To their own testimonies, Alma and Amulek added those of Zenos, Zenock, and Moses. All such prophetic testimonies are quickened, made alive, by the over-arching witness of the Holy Spirit. (See Alma 30:44; 31:34-36; 34:30, 33, 38.) "When a man speaketh by the power of the Holy Ghost the power of the Holy Ghost carrieth it unto the hearts of the children of men. But behold, there are many that harden their hearts against the Holy Spirit, that it hath no place in them." (2 Ne. 33:1-2.)

The sum and substance of the prophet Amulek's discourse on the infinite atonement of the Son of God is, "That ye contend no more against the Holy Ghost, but that ye receive it, and take upon you the name of Christ; that ye humble yourselves even to the dust, and worship God, in whatsoever place ye may be in, in spirit and in truth." (Alma 34:38.) Peace of mind, lasting happiness, and salvation in the presence of God the Father are assured to all who heed this counsel.

NOTES

1. Exactly why one man and woman's transgression led to everyone's transgression is not explicitly revealed in scripture. However, God is just; we are no more accountable to him for someone else's acts in one estate than we are in another. Possibly, the Fall affected all people because all people — exercising their agency — became willing co-partners in Adam's foreordained fall. That is, humanity covenanted to accept the Fall's temporary negative consequences (spiritual and physical death) so as to obtain its ultimate blessings (immortality and eternal life).

2. If the major premise of a syllogism is false, regardless of how valid the reasoning, the conclusion will be materially — that is to say, factually — false. The major premise of the Zoramites (God saves whom he chooses) was false, therefore the conclusion (Christ is unnecessary) was factually incorrect. Logic determines the soundness or validity of one's reasoning, but it cannot, of itself, establish its factual correctness.

3. Joseph Smith, *Teachings of the Prophet Joseph Smith*, selected by Joseph Fielding Smith (Salt Lake City: Deseret Book Company, 1938), p. 358.

4. It is in this sense that mankind is "conceived in sin." (Moses 6:55; cf. Ps. 51:5.) That is, whereas the human spirit — a child of God — was conceived by divine parents in a holy estate, its mortal tabernacle was brought by mortal parents into an unholy, imperfect estate.

5. *The City of God*, chapter 21.

6. While the Book of Mormon also speaks of man as a creature, it is always in the context of his *fallen* physical nature, not of his relationship to God as an immortal spirit or soul. The doctrine that man is the literal spirit offspring of divine parents was apparently made known to Joseph Smith subsequent to the publication of the Book of Mormon.

7. *The City of God*, chapters 13 and 14.

8. Speaking of little children, an angel of the Lord told king Benjamin that "as in Adam, *or by nature*, they fall, even so the blood of Christ atoneth for their sins." (Mosiah 3:16; italics added.)

9. See Bruce R. McConkie, *Mormon Doctrine*, 2nd ed. [Salt Lake City: Bookcraft, 1966], p. 66.

10. It is understood that Christ redeems every earth he has organized under the Father's direction. The question is whether this is literally all existing earths, or only a limited number. Elder Bruce R. McConkie defined the word "infinite" quantitatively as well as qualitatively: "The atonement of Christ, being literally and truly infinite, applies to an infinite number of earths." (Bruce R. McConkie, *Mormon Doctrine*, p. 65.)

11. Only Jesus Christ lived the law of God with perfectness. "For all have sinned, and come short of the glory of God." (Rom. 3:23; cf. 4:15; Gal. 2:16; 3:10-13.)

12. *Lectures on Faith* (Salt Lake City: Deseret Book Company, 1985), no. 5, par. 2.

13. Amulek was addressing a people who knew of Christ and had the opportunity to repent and come unto him. Such are expected to do so and be faithful until the end of "the life of the mortal body." (Mosiah 4:6.)

14. The extent to which Alma and Amulek understood the doctrine of post-mortal repentance and salvation is unknown. Their silence on the matter does not prove that they were unaware of it. The stark dichotomy described by Alma may have been designed to make clear the issue of life and death facing his wayward son Corianton, and all mankind. (See Alma 39:3-8; 42:29-30; 2 Ne. 2:27.) The Lord has deliberately employed some extreme terminology so that "it might work upon the hearts of the children of men, altogether for my name's glory." (D&C 19:7; cf. 43:25.)

15. Alma, the four sons of Mosiah, and the Apostle Paul are examples of people whose conduct at one period of their lives belied their true worth. Indeed, the doctrine of salvation of the dead is predicated upon the assumption that a "mighty change" of heart (Alma 5:14) is possible for some even beyond the grave.

16. The teachings of Alma and Amulek are directed *only* to those having a knowledge of Christ and his commandments. They do not apply to any little children or to any adults who lived and died in ignorance of God's will (without his law). These two classes are automatically redeemed (saved) by virtue of the power of the Atonement. See 2 Nephi 9:25-27; Moroni 8:19-22.

17. All who reject Christ are sent to this "prison." See D&C 76:73-74, 82-85, 106; JST 1 Peter 3:20; 4:6.

18. See also John 5:25; JST 1 Peter 3:18-20; 4:6; D&C 138:20-22, 29-37.

19. See Moses 7:57; Isaiah 42:7; 61:1; D&C 128:22.

20. See 2 Nephi 9:16; Mormon 9:14; D&C 29:44; 88:35.

21. In scripture, salvation is not always synonomous with exaltation. To be saved is one thing; to be exalted, another. There is no "gospel of the second chance." Elder Melvin J. Ballard stated Church doctrine when he said: "In this day any man or woman who has had a good chance to have heard the Gospel to receive it and embrace it and enjoy its blessings and privileges, who lived during their life in absolute indifference to these things, ignoring it, and neglected it, need not hope or anticipate that when they are dead the work can be done for them and they gain Celestial Glory." (*The Three Degrees of Glory* [Salt Lake City: Deseret Book Company, n.d.], p. 23.) In any given case, only God can determine what constitutes a "good chance" to receive and live the gospel. Regardless of their eternal state, all who are saved in any heaven or degree of glory are "heirs of salvation." Those who inherit the telestial kingdom are specifically spoken of as "heirs of salvation." (D&C 76:88.)

4

ALMA'S COUNSEL TO HIS SONS
(Alma 36–38)

CLARK V. JOHNSON

Inherent within the gospel is the divine power given by God to act in his name. God restored this authority to the Prophet Joseph Smith through John the Baptist; Peter, James, and John; and Elijah. (JS–H 1:69; D&C 13; 27:12; 110:16.)[1] Once a man holds the Melchizedek Priesthood and receives in the temple with his wife those covenants and ordinances available, he has the divine right to preside over his family. This means that he may importune the Lord for inspiration and then bless and counsel his family. King Benjamin taught his people: "Ye will not suffer your children that they go hungry, or naked; neither will ye suffer that they transgress the laws of God, and fight and quarrel one with another." (Mosiah 4:14.) In this dispensation the Lord stated, "I have commanded you to bring up your children in light and truth." (D&C 93:40.) He then instructed Frederick G. Williams, Sidney Rigdon, Joseph Smith, Jr., and Newell K. Whitney to go home and teach their families. (D&C 93:41-49.) The scriptures contain several examples of fathers seeking inspiration and instructing their children.

Alma and His Sons

Alma is an example of a father who counseled his sons. He explained to them: "The Spirit of the Lord doth say unto me: Command

---

Clark V. Johnson is associate professor of Church history and doctrine at Brigham Young University.

thy children to do good." (Alma 39:12.) Under the guidance of the Spirit, Alma approached each of his sons differently as he urged them to keep the commandments, as he taught them the doctrines of the gospel, and as he bore them his testimony.

Alma promised his sons Helaman and Shiblon that if they kept the commandments they would "prosper in the land." (Alma 36:1; 38:1.) Unlike Eli in the Old Testament, who apparently did not discipline his sons sufficiently for their misconduct, Alma confronted Corianton about his lack of diligence in keeping the commandments. (Alma 39:2; 1 Sam. 2:22-25, 27-34.) Whether Alma taught his sons collectively or individually in a personal interview cannot be determined. Yet even though the approach in addressing each son was different, his discussions have one thing in common: They are Christ-centered. (Alma 36; 37:9, 43-47; 38:8-9; 39:15.)

Unlike his brothers Shiblon and Corianton, Helaman did not accompany his father on the mission to the Zoramites. (Alma 31:7.) Alma encouraged his eldest son, Helaman, to place his trust in God. He promised Helaman that God would support him in his trials, troubles, and afflictions. (Alma 31:7; 36:3.) He referred to the scriptures to teach Helaman that God sustains his children if they worship him and keep his commandments. He challenged him to remember the bondage of their ancestors and that God had supported them in their afflictions. He also referred to the enslavement of ancient Israel. Alma reminded Helaman that God had delivered Israel from the Egyptians by allowing them to pass through the Red Sea safely, while destroying Pharaoh's army. (Alma 36:2, 28-29.) The promise to each group was prosperity. Israel did prosper physically in the land, as Abraham, Isaac, and Jacob prospered both physically and spiritually as they achieved eternal life. (D&C 132:28, 36-37.)

Alma concluded his remarks to Helaman by referring to the "shadow" and "type" found within the scriptures. Reminding Helaman of the history of his father Lehi, Alma said, "They tarried in the wilderness, or did not travel a direct course . . . because of their transgressions."[2] (Alma 37:42.) The reason for their wanderings was their lack of faith. The Liahona worked only according to their faith and obedience. Alma taught "that these things are not without a shadow; for as our fathers were slothful to give heed to this compass (now these things were temporal) they did not prosper; even so it is with things which are spiritual." (Alma 37:43.) Thus, the Liahona or "shadow" served the same purpose to Lehi's family that the brazen serpent had served to ancient Israel. (1 Ne. 17:41; Num. 21:4-9.) The Liahona was a "shadow" or "type" that strengthened their faith and led them to Christ.

Alma promised Helaman that the words of Christ "carry us beyond this vale of sorrow [earth life] into a far better land of promise [eternal life]." (Alma 37:45.) Hence, the promised land has a two-fold interpretation. First, it is a physical place to live, where God blesses his children temporally. Second, it has spiritual significance in which God blesses his children with experiences to lead them to eternal life. Alma concluded his interview by admonishing his son not to be slothful because of the easiness of the way, but to "look to God and live." (Alma 37:46-47.)

Shiblon was a faithful missionary and had endured many hardships. During his mission, he was imprisoned and stoned by the Zoramites. (Alma 38:3-4.) Alma commended this faithful son for his "steadiness" and "faithfulness" during a time of persecution. (Alma 38:2.) He also gave special counsel to this son who had brought him "great joy." (Alma 38:3.) Alma cautioned Shiblon to beware of pride, not to boast of his own wisdom, to be diligent and temperate, to use boldness, but not overbearance, to bridle his passions, to refrain from idleness, and to pray. (Alma 38:10-13.) He instructed him to acknowledge the power of God in his prayers, and to remember his own weaknesses, to pray for his brethren, and to "acknowledge [his] unworthiness before God at all times." (Alma 38:14.)

Alma's Testimony

Alma loved his sons and wanted only the best in life for each of them. As he bore his testimony to them he said, "I would not that ye think that I know of myself," for "*if I had not been born of God I should not have known these things.*" (Alma 36:4-5; emphasis added.) He continued to explain that he and the sons of Mosiah had sought to destroy the church of God. (Alma 36:6; Mosiah 27:8-10.)

They were stopped by an angel who promised their destruction if they continued, and they fell to the earth in fear. (Alma 36:7-9.) Alma noted that he did not hear the rest of the words spoken by the angel, but he remembered all his sins, and was "tormented with the pains of hell." (Alma 36:11, 13.) He asserted that he did not want to be brought into the presence of God, for he was ashamed, and he knew he was unworthy. It was at this moment that he remembered the teachings of his father "concerning the coming of one Jesus Christ, a Son of God, to atone for the sins of the world." (Alma 36:17.) He said, "I cried within my heart: O Jesus, thou Son of God, have mercy on me, who am in the gall of bitterness." (Alma 36:18.) From that moment on Alma did not remember his sins, but he knew joy, and then he said, "Methought I saw, even as our father Lehi saw, God sitting upon his throne, surrounded with numberless concourses of angels, in the attitude of singing and praising their God; yea, and my soul did long to be there." (Alma 36:22; 1 Ne. 1:8-15; Isa. 6:1-6.) He ended his testimony by pointing out that after this experience he had sought continually to teach the people the truth.

Most people do not gain a testimony by having experiences with angels. Almost all testimonies come through prayer, as did that of Enos. Enos said: "My soul hungered; and I kneeled down before my Maker, and I cried unto him in mighty prayer. . . . There came a voice unto me, saying: Enos, thy sins are forgiven thee, and thou shalt be blessed. And I, Enos, knew that God could not lie; wherefore, my guilt was swept away." (Enos 1:4-6.) Elder Bruce R. McConkie wrote:

> Any accountable person can gain a testimony of the gospel by obedience to that law upon which the receipt of such knowledge is predicated. This is the formula: 1. He must desire to know the truth of the gospel, of the Book of Mormon, of the Church, or of whatever matter is involved. 2. He must study and learn the basic facts relative to the matter involved. "Search the scriptures." (John 5:39). "Search these commandments," (D&C 1:37). 3. He must practice the principles and truths learned, conforming his life to them. "My doctrine is not mine, but his that sent me. If any man will do his will, he shall know of the doctrine, whether it be of God, or whether I speak of myself" (John 7:16-17). 4. He must pray to the

Father in the name of Christ, in faith, and the truth will then be made manifest by revelation "by the power of the Holy Ghost. And by the power of the Holy Ghost ye may know the truth of all things" (Moroni 10:3-5; 1 Corinthians 2).[3]

Many times a testimony comes through fulfilling the challenge Moroni issued to those who have read the Book of Mormon. He promised those who read the book a special witness from the Holy Ghost regarding its veracity. (Moroni 10:4-5.) Testimonies are borne about many things and are expressed in many different ways. Latter-day Saints are expected to receive revelation. Elder McConkie pointed out that "every devoted, obedient, and righteous person on the earth has and does receive revelation from God. Revelation is the natural inheritance of all the faithful. . . . The saints are expected (because they have the gift of the Holy Ghost) to gain personal revelation and guidance rather than to run to the First Presidency or some other church leaders to be told what to do."[4]

When Alma related his witness to Shiblon, he only alluded to his conversion, which he had told in great detail to Helaman, and then, he testified boldly of Jesus Christ. (Alma 38:6-9.) To his son Corianton, Alma testified powerfully, while teaching him the doctrines of the kingdom. (Alma 39-42.)

Alma's Charge to His Sons

During his interviews with his sons, Alma challenged each to keep the commandments, to be an example, and to teach the gospel to the people. (Alma 37:47; 38:15; 42:31.) However, he gave Helaman additional responsibilities.

Alma entrusted Helaman with the sacred records: the plates of brass, the twenty-four plates belonging to the Jaredites, and the records of the Nephites, as well as the interpreters or Urim and Thummim, and the Liahona. (Alma 37:24.)

The records that Alma and his predecessors kept served two purposes. First, they had been used to teach the Nephites and the Lamanites. Alma stated, "Were it not for these things that these records do contain, which are on these plates, Ammon and his brethren could not have convinced so many thousands of the Lamanites of the incorrect tradition of their fathers." These records brought the Lamanites to the knowledge of the Lord and caused them "to rejoice in Jesus Christ their Redeemer." (Alma 37:8-9.) Second, speaking prophetically he said that these records will show God's "power unto future generations." (Alma 37:14, 18-19.)

With the responsibility of keeping the sacred artifacts safe, Helaman was also admonished to write and continue the record. (Alma 37:2, 47.) Likewise, a modern father might entrust to one of his children journals, papers, and diaries belonging to previous generations. From such records may come spiritual witnesses to enrich the lives of living family members as well as future generations.

Conclusions

The Book of Mormon contains several father-son encounters: Father Lehi with Laman, Lemuel, Sam, Nephi, Jacob, and Joseph; Alma the Elder and Mosiah with their sons; and Mormon and Moroni. But none is more soul-searching than the counsel given to Helaman, Shiblon, and Corianton by Alma. Each of these fathers, like Alma, had one thing in mind, the welfare of his children. Alma counseled his sons about physical and spiritual matters. He encouraged them to put their trust in God, to keep his commandments, to pray, to keep records, to be an example, and to teach the gospel to others. And, like the others, he blessed them. Modern-day scripture instructs us · to "set in order" our own homes. (D&C 93:43.) Nothing is more beautiful than Mormon's farewell to his son, Moroni. After instructing his faithful son one final time, Mormon, echoing the desire of every father, wrote, "Behold, my son, I recommend thee unto God." (Moro. 9:22.)

NOTES

1. See also Joseph Smith, *Teachings of the Prophet Joseph Smith*, selected by Joseph Fielding Smith (Salt Lake City: Deseret Book Company, 1938), pp. 158, 323, 337-38.

2. Lehi and his family wandered eight years in the wilderness. (1. Ne. 17:4.)

3. Bruce R. McConkie, *Mormon Doctrine*, 2nd ed. (Salt Lake City: Bookcraft, 1966), pp. 786-87.

4. *Mormon Doctrine*, pp. 644-45.

5

THE PATH OF REPENTANCE
(Alma 39)

ROBERT L. MILLET

Alma discovered, to his horror, that his son Corianton had been guilty of sexual sin during his mission to the Zoramites; he had become involved with a harlot named Isabel, a woman of degraded character and morals who had contributed to the downfall of many men. In the words of Alma, Corianton had yielded to moral temptation for several reasons, reasons that should cause the Saints of the twentieth century to take note:

1. He had become haughty, had yielded to feelings of self-sufficiency. He had begun to boast in his own strength (Alma 39:2), to rely less and less on the arm of the Lord and more and more on the arm of flesh. In our day, Corianton might have been heard to say repeatedly, "I can handle it!" Corianton learned through a painful process that no man or woman has sufficient strength to resist the enticements of the father of lies. Alma had pleaded almost a decade earlier with a rebellious people: "Cast off your sins, and [do] not procrastinate the day of your repentance; but *humble yourselves before the Lord*, and *call on his holy name*, and watch and pray continually, that ye may not be tempted above that which ye can bear." (Alma 13:27-28; emphasis added.)

2. Corianton had forsaken his ministry (Alma 39:3), had left his duty station. He was not where he had been assigned to be. One who sings "I'll go where you want me to go, dear Lord," must not then

Robert L. Millet is associate professor of ancient scripture at Brigham Young University.

be guilty of desertion, of negligence and waywardness when the assignment comes. "No man," the Savior declared, "having put his hand to the plough, and looking back, is fit for the kingdom of God." (Luke 9:62.)

3. He had begun to associate with the wrong kinds of people; he eventually surrendered to the allurements and pressures to conform to the ways of the worldly. But, Alma scolded, because others gave in to sin was no reason for him to do the same: "This was no excuse for thee, my son. Thou shouldst have tended to the ministry where-with thou wast entrusted." (Alma 39:3-4.)

The Seriousness of Sexual Transgression

Alma then placed all things in perspective by stressing the seriousness of this immoral practice: he explained that only two sins were greater abominations in the sight of God—the sin against the Holy Ghost, and murder or the shedding of innocent blood. In speaking of the former sin, he taught: "If ye deny the Holy Ghost when it once has had place in you, and ye know that ye deny it, behold, this is a sin which is unpardonable." (Alma 39:6.)

"All manner of sin and blasphemy shall be forgiven unto men," Jesus warned, "but the blasphemy against the Holy Ghost shall not be forgiven unto men, . . . neither in this world, neither in the world to come." (Matt. 12:31-32.) These are they who "know [God's] power, and have been made partakers thereof, and suffered themselves through the power of the devil to be overcome, and to deny the truth and defy [God's] power—they are they who are the sons of perdition, . . . vessels of wrath," enemies to the cause of truth, "having denied the Holy Spirit after having received it, and having denied the Only Begotten Son of the Father, having crucified him unto themselves and put him to an open shame." (D&C 76:31-35.)[1] Joseph Smith declared:

> All sins shall be forgiven, except the sin against the Holy Ghost; for Jesus will save all except the sons of perdition. What must a man do to commit the unpardonable sin? He must receive the Holy Ghost, have the heavens opened unto him, and know God, and then sin against Him. After a man has

sinned against the Holy Ghost, there is no repentance for him. He has got to say that the sun does not shine while he sees it; he has got to deny Jesus Christ when the heavens have been opened unto him, and to deny the plan of salvation with his eyes open to the truth of it; and from that time he begins to be an enemy.[2]

The sin against the Holy Ghost is *unpardonable* because it is not covered by the atoning blood of Christ and because no amount of personal suffering on the part of the sinner can atone for the pernicious deed.

"Whosoever murdereth against the light and knowledge of God, it is not easy for him to obtain forgiveness," Alma warned. (Alma 39:6.) "A murderer," Joseph Smith explained, "one that sheds innocent blood, cannot have forgiveness."[3] Murder is thus referred to as an *unforgivable* sin, a heinous crime against humanity, an offense not covered by the atoning blood of Christ and for which deliverance from hell in the world of spirits is possible only after much personal suffering. "There are sins unto death," wrote Elder Bruce R. McConkie, "meaning spiritual death. There are sins for which there is no forgiveness, neither in this world nor in the world to come. There are sins which utterly and completely preclude the sinner from gaining eternal life. Hence there are sins for which repentance does not operate, sins that the atoning blood of Christ will not wash away, sins for which the sinner must suffer and pay the full penalty personally."[4]

Sexual immorality ranks third in order of serious offenses before God because it, like murder, deals with life. One who tampers with virtue prematurely or inappropriately — outside of marriage — tampers with the powers of life. Elder Boyd K. Packer has taught: "There was provided in our bodies — and this is sacred — a power of creation, a light, so to speak, that has the power to kindle other lights. This gift was to be used only within the sacred bonds of marriage. Through the exercise of this power of creation, a mortal body may be conceived, a spirit enter into it, and a new soul born into this life." Further, this power "is a gift from God our Father. In the righteous exercise of it as in nothing else, we may come close to him." On the other hand, "God has declared in unmistakable language that misery and sorrow will follow the violation of the laws of chastity.... Crowning glory awaits you if you live worthily. The loss of the crown may well be punishment enough. Often, very often, we are punished as much by our sins as we are for them."[5]

A Pattern for Repentance

It would appear that much of Corianton's problem was borne of doctrinal ignorance and misunderstanding, particularly concerning the appropriateness of justice and punishment for sin. (See Alma 41:1; 42:1.) It is fitting, then, that Alma should instruct his son about repentance and point the way back to the path of peace and happiness.

First, having stressed the seriousness of the offense, Alma sought now to ensure that Corianton was experiencing godly sorrow for sin, the kind of sorrow that is an essential element of true repentance. In short, Alma desired that his son experience appropriate guilt—no more than is requisite, but surely no less than is needful to bring about change. Alma observed: "I would to God that ye had not been guilty of so great a crime. I would not dwell upon your crimes, to harrow up your soul, if it were not for your good." (Alma 39:7; compare 2 Cor. 7:10.) Alma later remarked: "And now, my son, I desire that ye should let these things trouble you no more, and only let your sins trouble you, with that trouble which shall bring you down unto repentance." (Alma 42:29.) Alma knew only too well the awful agony associated with grievous sin; on the other hand, he understood as few others do how intense pain could be turned to consummate joy, how suffering could make saints out of sinners. Appropriate guilt can and does have a sanctifying effect: it alerts the offender to the spiritual chasm between himself and his Maker and motivates him thereafter to a godly walk and conduct.

"Now my son," Alma continued, "I would that ye should repent and forsake your sins, and go no more after the lusts of your eyes, but cross yourself in all these things." (Alma 39:9.) For Corianton to "cross himself" was for him to turn away from evil inclinations, to deny himself of worldly lusts, to work at cross purposes from the natural man, to forsake worldly paths, and to chart and navigate a course of righteousness. (See 3 Ne. 12:30.) "As well as establishing worthy goals, charting the course prevents one from living an un-planned, haphazard life—a tumbleweed existence."[6] Those desirous of keeping themselves from sinful practices must often change associations, places, and attitudes toward life. Corianton was specifically advised to lean upon his older brothers—Helaman and Shiblon— for support, to look to their example and seek their counsel. "Ye stand in need to be nourished by your brothers," Alma said. (Alma 39:10.)

Because Corianton's abominable deeds rang so loudly in the ears of the Zoramites, the words of the Nephite missionaries did not have the spiritual appeal they might otherwise have had. "How great iniquity ye brought upon the Zoramites," Alma chastened the errant son, "for when they saw your conduct they would not believe in my words." (Alma 39:11.) It was thus incumbent upon Corianton—a major part of his repentance and a key to forgiveness—to make restitution where possible. "Turn to the Lord with all your mind, might, and strength; that ye lead away the hearts of no more to do wickedly; but rather return unto them, and acknowledge your faults and that wrong which ye have done." (Alma 39:13.) President Joseph F. Smith asked: "Does repentance consist of sorrow for wrong doing?" "Yes," he answered, "but is this all? By no means."

> True repentance only is acceptable to God, nothing short of it will answer the purpose. Then what is true repentance? True repentance is not only sorrow for sins, and humble penitence and contrition before God, but it involves the necessity of turning away from them, a discontinuance of all evil practices and deeds, a thorough reformation of life, a vital change from evil to good, from vice to virtue, from darkness to light. Not only so, but to make restitution, so far as it is possible, for all the wrongs we have done, to pay our debts, and restore to God and man their rights—that which is due to them from us. This is true repentance, and the exercise of the will and all the powers of body and mind is demanded, to complete this glorious work of repentance; then God will accept it.[7]

Indeed, Corianton learned, as do we all, that repentance consists of a major realignment of priorities, a turn from the fleeting, and an acceptance of the permanent. "Seek not after riches nor the vain things of this world," a tender father thus counseled, "for behold, you cannot carry them with you." (Alma 39:14.)

No discussion of repentance would be complete without a focus upon the power and saving grace available through the redemptive work of Jesus Christ. And thus it is that Alma set forth in plain and unmistakable language the significance of the timeless and eternal sacrifice available through the blood of him who is man's Advocate with the Father. Alma's testimony (see Alma 39:17-18) is in harmony with that of John the Revelator: Jesus Christ is the Lamb slain from the foundation of the world (Rev. 13:8). The Book of Mormon provides a restoration of a vital and precious truth, a verity largely absent from the biblical record: the knowledge that Christian prophets have taught Christian doctrine and administered Christian ordinances since the beginning of time. Our Lord's atonement reaches from creation's dawn to millennial splendor; the children of God from Eden to Armaggedon can have their sins remitted in the name of the Holy One of Israel. That is, the atonement applies to "not only those who believed after he came in the meridian of time, in the flesh, but all those from the beginning, even as many as were before he came, who believed in the words of the holy prophets, . . . as well as those who should come after, who should believe in the gifts and callings of God by the Holy Ghost." (D&C 20:26-27.)

The Return of the Prodigal

Corianton's sin was abhorrent to God and the people of God. It hindered the work of the Lord among the Zoramites and caused deep pain and sorrow for those who knew and loved him. But it was not an unpardonable nor an unforgivable sin. Though it is true that the Holy One cannot look upon sin with the least degree of allowance, it is also true that "he that repents and does the commandments of the Lord shall be forgiven." (D&C 1:31-32; see also Alma 45:16.) God the Father is anxious for the return of his children to the path of righteousness and peace, perhaps infinitely more so than we can now perceive. Elder Orson F. Whitney held out this hope for the parents of wandering or wayward children:

> You parents of the wilful and the wayward: Don't give

them up. Don't cast them off. They are not utterly lost. The shepherd will find his sheep. They were his before they were yours—long before he entrusted them to your care; and you cannot begin to love them as he loves them. They have but strayed in ignorance from the Path of Right, and God is merciful to ignorance. Only the fulness of knowledge brings the fulness of accountability. Our Heavenly Father is far more merciful, infinitely more charitable, than even the best of his servants, and the Everlasting Gospel is mightier in power to save than our narrow finite minds can comprehend.[8]

President J. Reuben Clark observed: "I feel that [the Lord] will give that punishment which is the very least that our transgression will justify. . . . I believe that when it comes to making the rewards for our good conduct, he will give the maximum that it is possible to give."[9]

Alma was not only a concerned father; he was a prophet of God and the president of the Church. His was the gift of discernment and the spirit of prophecy and revelation. He was thus able to judge whether Corianton's repentance was genuine and when his heart was right before God. Knowing these things, it is touching to read these words of Alma to his son: "And now, O my son, ye are called of God to preach the word unto this people. And now, my son, go thy way, declare the word with truth and soberness, that thou mayest bring souls unto repentance, that the great plan of mercy may have claim upon them. And may God grant unto you even according to my words. Amen." (Alma 42:31.) We have every reason to believe that Corianton's repentance was complete, that he "crossed himself" and forsook sinful practices, places, and people, and that he qualified to return to the ministry and to full fellowship among the household of faith. We read of Corianton's labors a year or so later: "Thus ended the nineteenth year of the reign of the judges over the people of Nephi. Yea, and there was continual peace among them, and exceedingly great prosperity in the church because of their heed and diligence which they gave unto *the word of God, which was declared unto them by* Helaman, and Shiblon, and *Corianton*, and Ammon and his brethren, yea, and by all those who had been ordained by the holy order of God." (Alma 49:29-30, emphasis added.)[10] Truly salvation is free (2 Ne. 2:4), freely available, and the Lord's hand is extended to all, such that "whosoever will come may come and partake of the waters of life freely" (Alma 42:27; cf. Isa. 55:1-2).

NOTES

1. There is a sense in which those who have "shed innocent blood" are guilty of the sin against the Holy Ghost. That person who becomes a son of perdition crucifies Christ anew. (Compare Heb. 6:4-6.) "He gets the spirit of the devil—the same spirit that they had who crucified the Lord of Life—the same spirit that sins against the Holy Ghost." (*Teachings of the Prophet Joseph Smith*, selected by Joseph Fielding Smith [Salt Lake City: Deseret Book Company, 1976], p. 358.) "The blasphemy against the Holy Ghost, which shall not be forgiven in the world nor out of the world, is in that *ye commit murder wherein ye shed innocent blood*, and *assent unto my death*." (D&C 132:27; emphasis added.) See also Bruce R. McConkie, *Doctrinal New Testament Commentary*, 3 vols. (Salt Lake City: Bookcraft, 1965-73), 3:116, 345; *The Mortal Messiah: From Bethlehem to Calvary*, 4 vols. (Salt Lake City: Deseret Book Company, 1979-81), 2:216; *A New Witness for the Articles of Faith* (Salt Lake City: Deseret Book Company, 1985), p. 233.

2. *Teachings of the Prophet Joseph Smith*, p. 358.

3. Ibid., p. 339.

4. *A New Witness for the Articles of Faith*, p. 231.

5. Boyd K. Packer, *Conference Report*, April 1972, pp. 136-38.

6. Spencer W. Kimball, *The Miracle of Forgiveness* (Salt Lake City: Bookcraft, 1969), pp. 233-34.

7. Joseph F. Smith, *Gospel Doctrine* (Salt Lake City: Deseret Book Company, 1971), pp. 100-101.

8. *Conference Report*, April 1929, p. 110.

9. From "As Ye Sow . . . ," Address at Brigham Young University, May 3, 1955.

10. Later in the story we read of Corianton busily engaged in the work of the Lord. (See Alma 63:10.)

6

JUSTICE, MERCY, AND THE LIFE BEYOND
(Alma 40–42)

ROBERT L. MILLET

It is in the context of a serious father-and-son discussion — counsel by Alma to his errant son, Corianton — that we are able to read some of the deepest and most profound doctrine in the Book of Mormon. Because life is at best tenuous; because death is an ever-present reality; and because all men and women must eventually put off this mortal coil and engage a new existence that is, for the most part, strange and unknown, a theological discussion of life after life is welcomed and appreciated. The prophet Alma, recognizing that resurrection — the inseparable union of spirit and body — did not immediately follow death, inquired of the Lord about the state of the soul between death and the resurrection. An angel, a citizen himself of the world of spirits, taught Alma about the nature of the afterworld. And it is through Alma's explanation of these things to his son that we become privy to sacred and solemn matters.

Between Death and Resurrection

Before discussing the doctrine of resurrection and the law of restoration — the principle that all people will be raised to that level of glory commensurate with the lives they lived in mortality — Alma turned his attention to a discussion of the postmortal spirit world, a matter he had "inquired diligently of the Lord to know." (Alma 40:9.)

Robert L. Millet is associate professor of ancient scripture at Brigham Young University.

He explained that, according to what he had been taught by an angel, "the spirits of all men, as soon as they are departed from this mortal body, yea, the spirits[1] of all men, whether they be good or evil, are taken home to that God who gave them life." (Alma 40:11.) "Then shall the dust return to the earth as it was," said the Preacher, "and the spirit shall return unto God who gave it." (Eccl. 12:7.) Both of these scriptural preachers were speaking in broadest terms and should not be interpreted to mean that the spirit—at the time of death—goes into the immediate presence of the Lord. President Brigham Young explained that to speak of the spirit returning to the God who gave it means that "when the spirits leave their bodies they are in the presence of our Father and God" in the sense that they "are prepared then to see, hear and understand spiritual things."[2] To go into the "presence" of God is not necessarily to be "placed within a few yards or rods, or within a short distance of his person."[3] President George Q. Cannon explained: "Alma, when he says that 'the spirits of all men, as soon as they are departed from this mortal body, . . . are taken home to that God who gave them life,' has the idea, doubtless, in his mind that our God is omnipresent—not in His own personality but through His minister, the Holy Spirit. He does not intend to convey the idea that they are immediately ushered into the personal presence of God. He evidently uses that phrase in a qualified sense."[4]

The transition from time into eternity is immediate. As the physical self breathes its last breath, the spirit self passes through a veil separating this world from the next. At this point the spirit experiences what might be called a "partial judgment."[5] Those who have been true and faithful to their trust in mortality, Alma explained, are received into *paradise*, "a state of rest, a state of peace, where they shall rest from all their troubles and from all care, and sorrow." (Alma 40:12.) As I have written elsewhere, "those things which burdened the obedient—the worldly cares and struggles, the vicissitudes of life—are shed with the physical body. Paradise is a place where the spirit is free to think and act with a renewed capacity and with the vigor and enthusiasm which characterized one in his prime. Though a person does not rest per se from the work associated with the plan of salvation . . . , at the same time he is delivered from those cares and worries associated with a fallen world and a corrupt body."[6]

Those, on the other hand, who have been wicked on earth—who gave themselves up to the lusts and lasciviousness of the flesh—shall be received into that portion of the spirit world called *hell* or *outer darkness*,[7] a place of "weeping, and wailing, and gnashing of teeth, and this because of their own iniquity, being led captive by the will of the devil." (Alma 40:13.) Joseph Smith explained: "The great misery of departed spirits in the world of spirits, where they go after death, is to know that they come short of the glory that others enjoy and that they might have enjoyed themselves, and they are their own accusers."[8] On another occasion the Prophet taught: "A man is his own tormenter and his own condemner. Hence the saying, They shall go into the lake that burns with fire and brimstone. The torment of disappointment in the mind of man is as exquisite as a lake burning with fire and brimstone. I say, so is the torment of man."[9] Hell or outer darkness is both a place—a part of the world of spirits where suffering and sorrow and repentance take place—and a state—a condition of the mind associated with remorseful realization. The righteous remain in paradise and the wicked in hell until the time of their resurrection. (Alma 40:14.)[10]

The Doctrine of Resurrection

No doctrine provides a more powerful assurance and comfort to the bereaved than the doctrine of resurrection—the verity that all who have taken physical bodies through birth shall survive death, shall receive those bodies again in the resurrection. Resurrection is a doctrine as old as the world: it is not a creation of the first-century Christians, nor a belief spawned by the Jews in Babylonian captivity. It was taught to Adam, discussed by Enoch, and testified of by Abraham. Any people through the ages who have gained the understanding of the ministry of the Messiah, who have come to know by revelation of the coming of Jesus Christ, have likewise gained the understanding that Christ would break the bands of death and open the door for all others to be likewise raised from death to life in glorious immortality. It was just so with the Nephites. Alma, the noble patriarch, sought to inform and inspire his son on this fundamental principle of the Christian religion.[11]

"The soul shall be restored to the body," Alma explained, "and the body to the soul; yea, and every limb and joint shall be restored to its body; yea, even a hair of the head shall not be lost; but all things shall be restored to their proper and perfect frame." (Alma 40:23; cf. 11:43.)[12] Joseph Smith provided additional insight into the nature of the resurrection when he said: "As concerning the resurrection, I will merely say that all men will come from the grave as they lie down, whether old or young; there will not be 'added unto their stature one cubit,' neither taken from it; all will be raised by the power of God, having spirit in their bodies, and not blood."[13]

A prophetic successor, Joseph F. Smith, observed: "The body will come forth as it is laid to rest, for there is no growth or development in the grave. As it is laid down, so will it arise, and changes to perfection will come by the law of restitution. But the spirit will continue to expand and develop, and the body, after the resurrection will develop to the full stature of man."[14]

Alma's discussion of the first resurrection (Alma 40:16-20) is slightly difficult to follow. At first it appears that Alma was suggesting that the first resurrection consists of the resurrection of all persons — righteous and wicked — who had lived before Christ. (See Alma 40:16.) Abinadi had clearly stated, however, that the first resurrection would be made up of "the prophets, and all those that have believed in their words, or all those that have kept the commandments of God." (Mosiah 15:22.) That is to say, from Abinadi's and Alma's chronological perspective, the first resurrection would be made up of the righteous dead — "an innumerable company of the spirits of the just" (D&C 138:12) — from Adam to Christ. From our perspective in the final dispensation, with information revealed to Joseph Smith, we know that the first resurrection will resume at the time of the Second Coming; the Savior will bring with him the hosts of the righteous from the meridian of time to the time of his coming. Finally Alma did give his opinion on the matter — an opinion that is in fact accurate and appropriate — that "the souls and the bodies are reunited, *of the righteous*, at the resurrection of Christ, and his ascension into heaven." (Alma 40:20; emphasis added.) [15]

The Lord has stated in a modern revelation that "the resurrection from the dead is the redemption of the soul." (D&C 88:16.) Death is not the end. The grave shall not have won the victory. The prophetic promise is sure. Joseph Smith declared: "All your losses will be made up to you in the resurrection, provided you continue faithful. By the vision of the Almighty I have seen it." [16]

The Doctrine of Restoration

The resurrection, Alma explained, is but a part of a larger system of restoration: not only shall spirit and body be inseparably united, but all things shall hereafter be restored to the way they were here. In short, our station and reward hereafter shall be directly related to the manner in which we managed our time and spiritual resources while in this life. It is thus ludicrous to suppose that one could hope for a glorious resurrection and transcendent reward hereafter when his or her thoughts and actions in this life were shoddy and superficial. What was to Paul the Law of the Harvest ("whatsoever a man soweth, that shall he also reap" — Gal. 6:7) was to Alma the Law of Restoration. "The plan of restoration," he observed, "is requisite with the justice of God; for it is requisite that all things should be restored to their proper order." Further, "it is requisite with the justice of God that men should be judged according to their works; and if their works were good in this life, and the desires of their hearts were good, that they should also, at the last day, be restored unto that which is good," what we would know as exaltation in the highest heaven. "And if their works are evil they shall be restored unto them for evil." (Alma 41:2-4.)

Wickedness here never was and never will be happiness here or hereafter. Carnality here never was and never will be spirituality here or hereafter. Charting a course contrary to God and his plan in this life can never lead to spiritual union and joy with him in the life to come. (See Alma 41:10-11.) Moroni focused the attention of his readers upon the stark reality of the Law of Restoration in these words: "Do ye suppose that ye shall dwell with [God] under a consciousness of your guilt? Do ye suppose that ye could be happy to dwell with that holy Being, when your souls are racked with a consciousness of guilt that ye have ever abused his laws? Behold, I say unto you that ye would be more miserable to dwell with a holy and just God, under a consciousness of your filthiness before him, than ye would to dwell with the damned souls in hell." (Morm. 9:3-4.) A modern revelation thus stated that "they who are not sanctified through the law which I have given unto you, even the law of Christ, must inherit another kingdom, even that of a terrestrial kingdom, or that of a telestial kingdom."

> For he who is not able to abide the law of a celestial kingdom cannot abide a celestial glory. And he who cannot abide the law of a terrestrial kingdom cannot abide a terrestrial glory. And he who cannot abide the law of a telestial kingdom cannot abide a telestial glory; therefore he is not meet for a kingdom of glory. Therefore he must abide a kingdom which is not a kingdom of glory.
>
> They who are of a celestial spirit [in mortality] shall receive [in the resurrection] the same body which was a natural body; even ye shall receive your bodies, and your glory shall be that glory by which your bodies are quickened. Ye who are quickened by a portion of the celestial glory shall then receive of the same, even a fulness. And they who are quickened by a portion of the terrestrial glory shall then receive of the same, even a fulness. And also they who are quickened by a portion of the telestial glory shall then receive of the same, even a fulness. (D&C 88:21-24, 28-31.)

In summary, "that which ye do send out [the life we live, the deeds we do] shall return unto you again, and be restored; therefore, the word restoration more fully condemneth the sinner, and justifieth him not at all." (Alma 41:15.)

Justice and Mercy: The Delicate Balance

To demonstrate the necessity and timelessness of justice and to show that there are always consequences for our transgressions, Alma recounted the story of the fall of Adam and Eve. The fall brought on the justice of God and resulted in physical and spiritual death, both of which were necessary in the eternal plan of the Father. "Now behold," Alma continued, "it was not expedient that man should be reclaimed from this . . . death, for that would destroy the great plan of happiness." (Alma 42:8.) Jacob had noted earlier that "death hath passed upon all men, to fulfil the merciful plan of the great Creator." (2 Ne. 9:6.) It was necessary for the justice of a God to be meted out in order for the mercy of a God to be extended; as the fall is the father of the atonement, so justice paves the way for mercy. (See Alma 42:1-13.)

The balance of justice and mercy is achieved only in and through a God, only in and through a being in whom there is a perfect balance, through him who is both infinitely just and merciful. The balance is achieved only by him who is sinless and upon whom justice has no claim, through him who has no need of pardoning mercy. Elder Boyd K. Packer beautifully illustrated the role of Christ as Mediator in the following parable:

> There was once a man who wanted something very much. It seemed more important than anything else in his life. In order for him to have his desire, he incurred a great debt.
>
> He had been warned about going into that much debt, and particularly about his creditor. But it seemed so important for him to do what he wanted to do and to have what he wanted right now. He was sure he could pay for it later.
>
> So he signed a contract. He would pay it off some time along the way. He didn't worry too much about it, for the due date seemed such a long time away. He had what he wanted now, and that was what seemed important.
>
> The creditor was always somewhere in the back of his mind, and he made token payments now and again, thinking somehow that the day of reckoning really would never come.
>
> But as it always does, the day came, and the contract fell due. The debt had not been fully paid. His creditor appeared and demanded payment in full.
>
> Only then did he realize that his creditor not only had the power to repossess all that he owned, but the power to cast him into prison as well.

"I cannot pay you, for I have not the power to do so," he confessed.

"Then," said the creditor, "we will exercise the contract, take your possessions, and you shall go to prison. You agreed to that. It was your choice. You signed the contract, and now it must be enforced."

"Can you not extend the time or forgive the debt?" the debtor begged. "Arrange some way for me to keep what I have and not go to prison. Surely you believe in mercy? Will you not show mercy?"

The creditor replied, "Mercy is always so one-sided. It would serve only you. If I show mercy to you, it will leave me unpaid. It is justice I demand. Do you believe in justice?"

"I believed in justice when I signed the contract," the debtor said. "It was on my side then, for I thought it would protect me. I did not need mercy then, nor think I should need it ever. Justice, I thought, would serve both of us equally as well."

"It is justice that demands that you pay the contract or suffer the penalty," the creditor replied. "That is the law. You have agreed to it and that is the way it must be. Mercy cannot rob justice."

There they were: One meting out justice, the other pleading for mercy. Neither could prevail except at the expense of the other.

"If you do not forgive the debt there will be no mercy," the debtor pleaded.

"If I do, there will be no justice," was the reply.

Both laws, it seemed, could not be served. They are two eternal ideals that appear to contradict one another. Is there no way for justice to be fully served, and mercy also?

There is a way! The law of justice *can* be fully satisfied and mercy *can* be fully extended — but it takes someone else. And so it happened this time.

The debtor had a friend. He came to help. He knew the debtor well. He knew him to be shortsighted. He thought him foolish to have gotten himself into such a predicament. Nevertheless, he wanted to help because he loved him. He stepped between them, faced the creditor, and made this offer:

"I will pay the debt if you will free the debtor from his

63

contract so that he may keep his possessions and not go to prison."

As the creditor was pondering the offer, the mediator added, "You demanded justice. Though he cannot pay you, I will do so. You will have been justly dealt with and can ask no more. It would not be just."

And so the creditor agreed.

The mediator turned then to the debtor. "If I pay your debt, will you accept me as your creditor?"

"Oh yes, yes," cried the debtor. "You save me from prison and show mercy to me."

"Then," said the benefactor, "you will pay the debt to me and I will set the terms. It will not be easy, but it will be possible. I will provide a way. You need not go to prison."

And so it was that the creditor was paid in full. He had been justly dealt with. No contract had been broken.

The debtor, in turn, had been extended mercy. Both laws stood fulfilled. Because there was a mediator, justice had claimed its full share, and mercy was fully satisfied.[17]

The scriptures affirm that "there is one God, and one mediator between God and men, the man Christ Jesus." (1 Tim. 2:5.) Mercy comes because of the atonement. Mercy is extended to the penitent. (Alma 42:23.) Those who accept Christ as their Benefactor and pay the appropriate price of repentance are delivered from the demands of justice and come to know that freedom and peace available only through him who is the Way, the Truth, and the Life. (John 8:31-32.)

Can God Cease to Be God?

In seeking to dramatize the absolute necessity for God's justice to be meted out where appropriate, Alma spoke to Corianton of a most unusual hypothetical situation. "According to justice," he said, "the plan of redemption could not be brought about, only on conditions of repentance of men in this probationary state, yea, this preparatory state; for except it were for these conditions, mercy could not take effect except it should destroy the work of justice. Now the work of justice could not be destroyed; if so, *God would cease to be God*." Alma explained further that "there is a law given, and a punishment affixed, and a repentance granted; which repentance, mercy claimeth; otherwise, justice claimeth the creature and executeth the law, and the law inflicteth the punishment; if not so, the works of justice would be destroyed, and *God would cease to be God*." (Alma 42:13, 22, emphasis added; see also v. 25.) Some have taken these verses to mean that it is indeed possible for God to cease to be God; that if he should, by some bizarre means, fail to function in perfectness, he would be unseated and removed from his place of preeminence; that the forces in the universe would demand his abdication from the heavenly throne. Such ideas are to some quite stimulating. They are, nonetheless, erroneous and misleading.

Joseph Smith taught and the scriptures boldly and repeatedly attest to the fact that God is omnipotent, omniscient, and, by the power of his Holy Spirit, omnipresent. The Prophet taught that "God is the *only supreme governor and independent being* in whom all fulness and perfection dwell; . . . without beginning of days or end of life; and that in him every good gift and every good principle dwell; and that he is the Father of lights; *in him the principle of faith dwells independently*, and he is the object in whom the faith of all other rational and accountable beings center for life and salvation."[18] Joseph Smith also stated:

> It is . . . necessary, in order to the exercise of faith in God unto life and salvation, that men should have the idea of the existence of the attribute justice in him; for without the idea of the existence of the attribute justice in the Deity, men could not have confidence sufficient to place themselves under his guidance and direction; for they would be filled with fear and doubt lest the judge of all the earth would not do right, and thus fear or doubt, existing in the mind, would preclude the possibility of the exercise of faith in him for life and salvation. But when the idea of the existence of the attribute justice in the Deity is fairly planted in the mind, it leaves no room for doubt to get into the heart, and the mind is enabled to cast itself upon the Almighty without fear and without doubt, and with the most unshaken confidence, believing that the Judge of all the earth will do right.[19]

The fact of the matter is that God will not nor cannot cease to be God. His title, his status, and his exalted position are forever fixed and immutable. Exalted beings simply do not apostatize! They do not slip! It is contrary to their divine nature to lie or cheat or be impartial. God is not dependent on others for his Godhood, nor can he be impeached. Nor need the Saints of God spend a particle of a second worrying and fretting about the Almighty falling from grace. For members of the Church to do so, in fact—as the Prophet has suggested—is to err in doctrine as to the true nature of God and thus fall short of that dynamic faith which leads to life and salvation. Alma's hypothetical case is just that—purely hypothetical. He is arguing toward the impossible to demonstrate the logical certainty of his position—that mercy cannot rob justice. It is as if Alma had said: "To suppose that one can break the laws of God with impunity; to suppose that one can live a life of sin and have the atonement of Christ—the mercy of the Lord—rob justice of its due, is to suppose that which *cannot* be. It is as absurd as to suppose that God could cease to be God!" Truly, Alma explained, "*God ceaseth not to be God*, and mercy claimeth the penitent, and mercy cometh because of the atonement. . . . For behold, justice exerciseth all his demands, and also mercy claimeth all which is her own; and thus, none but the truly penitent are saved." (Alma 42:23-24; emphasis added.)

NOTES

1. Alma repeatedly used the word *soul* to refer to the spirit (see vv. 7, 9, 11, 14, 15, 17, 18, 21, 23). This, of course, is a different usage from the more specific definition of soul (the spirit and the body) contained in D&C 88:15; see also 2 Nephi 9:13.

2. *Journal of Discourses*, 26 vols. (London: Latter-day Saints' Book Depot, 1854-86), 3:368.

3. Orson Pratt, ibid., 16:365.

4. George Q. Cannon, *Gospel Truth*, 2 vols. in one, comp. Jerreld L. Newquist (Salt Lake City: Deseret Book Company, 1987), p. 58.

5. This expression is used by Joseph F. Smith (see *Gospel Doctrine* [Salt Lake City: Deseret Book Company, 1971], pp. 448-49) and is probably

what Alma was describing in Alma 40:15 as an initial consignment to happiness or misery before the actual resurrection.

6. Robert L. Millet and Joseph Fielding McConkie, *The Life Beyond* (Salt Lake City: Bookcraft, 1986), p. 18. For a discussion of the Savior's statement to the thief on the cross, "To day shalt thou be with me in paradise" (Luke 23:43), see *The Life Beyond*, pp. 19-20, 168.

7. With but few exceptions, *outer darkness* refers to hell, the place of suffering and sadness and confrontation in the spirit world. (See Alma 34:33; 40:13-14; 41:7; D&C 38:5; 138:22, 30, 57; Isa. 49:9.) "So complete is the darkness prevailing in the minds of these spirits, so wholly has gospel light been shut out of their consciences, that they know little or nothing of the plan of salvation, and have little hope within themselves of advancement and progression through the saving grace of Christ." (Bruce R. McConkie, *Mormon Doctrine*, 2nd. ed. [Salt Lake City: Bookcraft, 1966], pp. 551-52.)

8. Joseph Smith, *Teachings of the Prophet Joseph Smith*, selected by Joseph Fielding Smith (Salt Lake City: Deseret Book Company, 1938), pp. 310-11.

9. Ibid., p. 357.

10. The entire spirit world, and not just that portion designated as hell, is appropriately called a "spirit prison." (See D&C 45:17; 138:15, 18, 50; Moses 7:55-57; *Teachings of the Prophet Joseph Smith*, p. 310; Orson Pratt, *Journal of Discourses*, 1:289-90; Brigham Young, *Journal of Discourses*, 3:95; Bruce R. McConkie, *Ensign*, August 1976, p. 11.) Paradise will be vacated and its residents released to a glorious resurrection at the second coming of Christ. Hell comes to an end at the time of the second resurrection, at the end of the Millennium.

11. Joseph Smith explained that "the fundamental principles of our religion are the testimony of the Apostles and Prophets, concerning Jesus Christ, that He died, was buried, and rose again the third day, and ascended into heaven; and all other things which pertain to our religion are only appendages to it." (*Teachings of the Prophet Joseph Smith*, p. 121; cf. 1 Cor. 15:1-4.)

12. Joseph Smith distinguished between the fundamental and nonfundamental elements of the body. "There is no fundamental principle," he taught, "belonging to a human system that ever goes into another in this world or in the world to come; I care not what the theories of men are. We have the testimony that God will raise us up, and he has the power to do it. If anyone supposes that any part of our bodies, that is, the fundamental parts thereof, ever goes into another body, he is mistaken." (*History of the*

Church of Jesus Christ of Latter-day Saints, 2nd ed. rev., edited by B. H. Roberts [Salt Lake City: The Church of Jesus Christ of Latter-day Saints, 1932-51], 5:339.)

13. *Teachings of the Prophet Joseph Smith*, pp. 199-200.

14. *Improvement Era*, June 1904, pp. 623-24; see also *Gospel Doctrine*, pp. 23, 447-48. President Smith's son, Joseph Fielding Smith, commented on these words as follows: "President Smith was in full accord with Amulek and Alma. He taught that the body will be restored as stated in Alma 11:42-45 and 40:22-23. While he expresses the thought that the body will come forth as it was laid down, he also expresses the thought that it will take time to adjust the body from the condition of imperfections. This, of course, is reasonable, but at the same time the length of time to make these adjustments will not cover any appreciable extent of time.

"President Smith never intended to convey the thought that it would require weeks or months of time in order for the defects to be removed. These changes will come naturally, of course, but *almost instantly.* We cannot look upon it in any other way." (Joseph Fielding Smith, *Doctrines of Salvation*, 3 vols., comp. Bruce R. McConkie [Salt Lake City: Bookcraft, 1954-56], 2:293-94.)

15. "It is evident Alma's understanding of the extent of the resurrection at the time the Savior came forth from the dead was limited, therefore he stated only his opinion." (Joseph Fielding Smith, *Answers to Gospel Questions*, 5 vols., compiled by Joseph Fielding Smith, Jr. [Salt Lake City: Deseret Book Company, 1957-66], 1:36; see also *Doctrines of Salvation*, 2:300.)

16. *Teachings of the Prophet Joseph Smith*, p. 296.

17. *Conference Report*, April 1977, pp. 79-80.

18. *Lectures on Faith* (Salt Lake City: Deseret Book Company, 1985), 2:2.

19. Ibid., 4:13. In a limited meaning of the phrase, therefore, God *can* cease to be God in the mind of mortals, but never in an absolute sense. That is to say, if people do not understand that God Almighty possesses all attributes in perfection, they cannot exercise saving faith in him — he ceases to be God to them!

7

INSPIRED BY A BETTER CAUSE
(Alma 43–51)

H. Dean Garrett

Mormon, as the compiler of the Book of Mormon, was faced with the challenge of determining what to include in his abridged record. In making his decisions, he was guided by two factors. The first was the charge given him by the Lord to write those things "which have been commanded." (3 Ne. 26:12.) The second influence was Mormon's understanding of the times and the conditions under which the records would come forth in the last days. Thus directed, Mormon deliberately selected those events and discourses from the original plates that best met the needs his future book would serve.

His account of the record of Alma is a good illustration of Mormon's methodology. In the first part of this book, he dedicated considerable space to the missionary labors of Alma and the four sons of Mosiah. However, in recording the events of their missions, he announced that he was changing his emphasis: "Now we shall say no more concerning their preaching, except that they preached the word, and the truth, according to the spirit of prophecy and revelation; and they preached after the holy order of God by which they were called. And now I return to an account of the wars between the Nephites and the Lamanites in the eighteenth year of the reign of the judges." (Alma 43:2-3.)

This was a curious decision for Mormon to make. If the Book of Mormon was intended to be used by a church greatly involved in

---

H. Dean Garrett is assistant professor of Church history and doctrine at Brigham Young University.

missionary work, would it not be more beneficial for the readers of the book to be instructed in the missionary experiences of Alma and the sons of Mosiah? Why write about the wars of the Nephites?

An analysis of the composition of the Book of Mormon might lead us to an answer to such questions. Sixty-four percent of the history covered from 1 Nephi to Mormon 6, comprising 220 pages, is found in Alma 1 to 3 Nephi 10, surely an inordinate amount of space for a diminutive amount of history.[1] A unique historical pattern is found in this section of the Book of Mormon. In Alma 1-42, Mormon emphasized priestcraft, materialism, social-economic inequality, and other social problems. This period is followed in Alma 43-63 by a period of war and civil disruptions. This dissension led to a corruption of civil government (as described in the book of Helaman) and to the eventual collapse of the government (see 3 Nephi 1-10). At this point, the Savior visited the people.

A similar pattern of social problems, priestcrafts, materialism, wars, government corruption, and disrupted life is prophesied for the last days leading to the Savior's second coming. (D&C 45:16-48; D&C 87; Mormon 8:26-41.) As indicated, Mormon and his successor, Moroni, saw our day (see Mormon 8:27-31) and took from the history and prophecies of the Nephites those events that would best help the readers of their record in the day in which it would come forth. Since Mormon knew of the wars and chaos that would characterize the last days, he abbreviated his account of the missionary efforts of Alma and the sons of Mosiah and emphasized the challenges created by war and social turmoil, along with the reaction of the righteous to those challenges.

Motivations for War

A study of the Nephite-Lamanite wars provides helpful insights into the motivations of people or nations at war. In Alma 43, Mormon related how the Zoramites joined the Lamanites (under Zerahemnah) and an apostate group of Nephites called Amalekites to war against the Nephites. Because the Amalekites and Zoramites were "of a more wicked and murderous disposition than the Lamanites," Zerahemnah placed them as "chief captains" over his armies. (Alma 43:6.) In doing this, the Lamanite leader wished to "preserve their hatred towards the Nephites" and to "stir up the Lamanites to anger against the Nephites." His personal design was to "usurp great power over them [the Lamanites], and also that he might gain power over the Nephites by bringing them into bondage." (Alma 43:7-8.) It appears that Zerahemnah's motivation for going to war was his hatred of the Nephites and his thirst for power.

On the other hand, the Nephites entered this war with a far different attitude. It was their desire to "support their lands and their houses, and their wives, and their children, that they might preserve them from the hands of their enemies; and also that they might preserve their rights and their privileges, yea, and also their liberty, that they might worship God according to their desires." (Alma 43:9.) Because of the Lamanites' hatred toward them and because of the evil desires of their apostate allies, the Nephites knew they would suffer much death and an insufferable bondage if they fell prey to their enemies.

The major motivation of each of these groups determined the approach each took in preparing for war and in actually fighting. The Lamanites gathered themselves with anger, while the Nephites responded with resolve and preparation.

The leader of the Nephites, Moroni, "had prepared his people with breastplates and with arm-shields, yea, and also shields to defend their heads, and also they were dressed with thick clothing." (Alma 43:19.) The Lamanites, on the other hand, had their weapons of war, but they were naked, except for a "skin which was girded about their loins." (Alma 43:20.) The Nephites also prepared for battle by spying on the foe and by seeking direction from the prophet Alma.

The motivation that people have for going to war often dictates the manner in which the conflict is pursued. Even though the Lamanites were not prepared to battle a more physically prepared foe, nevertheless they "did fight exceedingly; yea, never had the Lamanites been known to fight with such exceedingly great strength and courage, no, not even from the beginning. And they were inspired by the Zoramites and the Amalekites, who were their chief captains and leaders, and by Zerahemnah, who was their chief captain, or their chief leader and commander; yea, they did fight like dragons." (Alma 43:43-44.) The Nephites, however, were inspired by a greater cause. They "were not fighting for monarchy nor power but they were fighting for their homes and their liberties, their wives and their children, and their all, yea, for their rites of worship and their church." (Alma 43:45.)

The Nephites were fighting for a higher cause—"their duty which they owed to their God." (Alma 43:46.) They were fighting under a God-given mandate that declared: "Inasmuch as ye are not guilty of the first offense, neither the second, ye shall not suffer yourselves to be slain by the hands of your enemies." And again, the Lord said: "Ye shall defend your families even unto bloodshed. Therefore for this cause were the Nephites contending with the Lamanites, to defend themselves, and their families, and their lands, their country, and their rights, and their religions." (Alma 43:46-47.) This motivation produced a faith in the Nephites that allowed them to fight with valor, for when they began to fear and were about to flee the fierceness of the Lamanites, a reminder of their cause from Moroni allowed them to turn on the Lamanites with power. (See Alma 43:48-50.) On the other hand, when the Lamanites saw the power of the Nephites, they were filled with fear and "were struck with terror." (Alma 43:53.)

The account of this war clarified an important concept: there might be a justifiable reason for going to war. That reason should not include the motivation to gain power, nor control, nor should it be out of anger or hatred. The Lord simply stated that if the Nephites were not guilty of the first or second offense, they should not allow themselves to be slain by their enemies. (Alma 43:46.) This same counsel was given to the early saints through the Prophet Joseph Smith. In the Doctrine and Covenants, section 98, the Lord gave this command: "Now, I speak unto you concerning your families—if men will smite you, or your families, once, and ye bear it patiently and revile not against them, neither seek revenge, ye shall be rewarded; but if ye bear it not patiently, it shall be accounted unto you as being meted out as a just measure unto you." (D&C 98:23-24.) The Lord further instructed the saints that if they bore these attacks the third and fourth times, their rewards would be increased. However, if their enemies escaped the vengeance of God, then a warning voice should be raised that if the enemy came against them again, the Lord would have "delivered thine enemy into thine hands." (D&C 98:29.) If the saints spared the enemy, they would be blessed, but if "thou rewardest him according to his works thou art justified; if he has sought thy life, and thy life is endangered by him, thine enemy is in thine hands and thou art justified." (D&C 98:31.)

The Lord applied this same law to nations, with the injunction that "if any nation, tongue, or people should proclaim war against them, they should first lift a standard of peace unto that people, nation, or tongue." (D&C 98:34.) If that people or nation did not accept the standard of peace, then the same procedures would be followed the second and third time. After this procedure was followed, the Lord would "justify them in going out to battle against that nation, tongue, or people. And I, the Lord, would fight their battles." (D&C 98:36-37.) This law of war was given to Nephi, Joseph, Jacob, Abraham, "and all mine ancient prophets and apostles." (D&C 98:32.)

The Lord commanded his people to "renounce war and proclaim peace" (D&C 98:16), but he does give a nation the right to go to war. President David O. McKay suggested the following righteous reasons for war:

> I still say that there are conditions when entrance into war is justifiable, and when a Christian nation may, without violation of principles, take up arms against an opposing force. Such a condition, however, is not a real or fancied insult given by one nation to another. When this occurs proper reparation may be made by mutual understanding, apology or by arbitration. Neither is there justifiable cause found in a desire or even a need for territorial expansion. The taking of territory implies the subjugation of the weak to the strong—the application of the jungle law. Nor is war justified in an attempt to enforce a new order of government, or even to impel others to a particular form of worship, however better the government or eternally true the principles of the enforced religion may be.[2]

An example of this philosophy is found in the Book of Mormon when Mormon, the abridger, was acting as the military leader for the

Nephites. After great victories over the Lamanites, the Nephites began to "boast in their own strength, and began to swear before the heavens that they would avenge themselves of the blood of their brethren who had been slain by their enemies. And they did swear by the heavens, and also by the throne of God, that they would go up to battle against their enemies, and would cut them off from the face of the land." (Morm. 3:9-10.)

This attitude did not reflect the "law of war" as defined by the Lord. Thus Mormon "did utterly refuse from this time forth to be a commander and a leader of this people, because of their wickedness and abomination" (Morm. 3:11), even though Mormon had led the Nephites in battle many times. Furthermore, "when they had sworn by all that had been forbidden them by our Lord and Savior Jesus Christ, that they would go up unto their enemies to battle, and avenge themselves of the blood of their brethren, behold the voice of the Lord came unto me, saying: Vengeance is mine, and I will repay; and because this people repented not after I had delivered them, behold, they shall be cut off from the face of the earth." (Morm. 3:14-15.)

A message to the people of the latter days from the war period of the Book of Mormon would be that if there must be war, then it must be entered for the right reasons and under proper circumstances if people desire the blessings of God. Writing to Zerahemnah, Captain Moroni made this interesting observation: "Ye see that God will support, and keep, and preserve us, so long as we are faithful unto him, and unto our faith, and our religion; and never will the Lord suffer that we shall be destroyed except we should fall into transgression and deny our faith." (Alma 44:4.)

In a day when prophecies note that there will be wars and rumors of wars (JS–M 1:28-29), there are some who question their role in supporting a government that is preparing for war. As nations prepare from time to time to go to war, what should be an individual's role? Must one support the government? Is one morally responsible to take sides? Mormon pointed out in the Book of Alma that perhaps the side is not as important to one's personal salvation as the motivation.

The Fight for Liberty

Mormon continued the account of the wars of the Nephites by interjecting a prophecy of Alma. Alma, before his final departure, told his son Helaman that the Nephites would dwindle in unbelief until a final destruction of his people took place. (See Alma 45:10-16.) As Helaman and his brethren tried to organize the people, "there arose a dissension among them, and they would not give heed to the words of Helaman and his brethren." (Alma 45:23.) This reaction to the attempts of Helaman to establish righteousness laid a foundation for internal dissent. Those who would not give heed to "Helaman and his brethren were gathered together against their brethren." (Alma 46:1.) This dissension allowed a man by the name of Amalickiah to create a movement to make him king over the Nephites. There were many in the church who accepted the flatteries of Amalickiah and therefore broke away from the Church. "And thus were the affairs of the people of Nephi exceedingly precarious and dangerous, notwithstanding their great victory which they had had over the Lamanites, and their great rejoicings which they had had because of their deliverance by the hand of the Lord." (Alma 46:7.) It does not take long for a people who are full of pride to "forget the Lord their God" and "be led away by the evil one." (Alma 46:8.) One wicked individual can cause great wickedness to take place among such a people. (See Alma 46:9.)

On the other hand, one righteous person can make a difference in such a setting. Captain Moroni reacted to this situation by making a banner (the Title of Liberty) on which he wrote this reminder: "In memory of our God, our religion, and freedom, and our peace, our wives, and our children." (Alma 46:12.) He prayed fervently to the Lord for "the blessings of liberty to rest upon his brethren, so long as there should a band of Christians remain to possess the land." (Alma 46:13.) This became such an important time for Moroni that he challenged all his supporters to "enter into a covenant that they will maintain their rights, and their religion, that the Lord God may bless them." (Alma 46:20.)

The battle that followed forced Amalickiah and his people into the wilderness. The Amalickiahites who were taken captive were given the option of joining the people of Moroni by entering into the covenant with them. Those Amalickiahites who "would not enter into a covenant to support the cause of freedom, that they might maintain a free government, he caused to be put to death; and there were but few who denied the covenant of freedom." (Alma 46:35.)

The Amalickiahites who had fled joined forces with the Lamanites; and, through treachery and murder, Amalickiah became the king of the Lamanites. It was still his design to control the Nephites, and thus a great battle ensued. The righteous Nephites turned to God in preparation for this war. Mormon observed that the wicked Nephites "became more hardened and impenitent, and more wild, wicked and ferocious than the Lamanites." (Alma 47:36.) This battle for the Nephite nation, which lead to much dissension among the Nephites, was due to their own wickedness. Mormon stated: "For it has been their quarrelings and their contentions, yea, their murderings, and their plunderings, their idolatry, their whoredoms, and their abominations, which were among themselves, which brought upon them their wars and their destructions." (Alma 50:21.) No matter who the leader was, this wickedness caused some to seek an overthrow of freedom, to replace the government with a monarchy. Thus they had the kingmen trying to seize power, and the ensuing battle between the kingmen and the freemen took place. (See Alma 50-51.)

This dissension so weakened the Nephites that "while Moroni was thus breaking down the wars and contentions among his own people, and subjecting them to peace and civilization" (Alma 51:22), the Lamanites again attacked and tried to overpower the Nephites. Mormon showed, by his account, that wickedness brought dissent, and dissent brought the threat of destruction from outside forces. The only way that the Nephites could stay free was to stay righteous.

Edmund Burke echoed these same feelings when he stated:

> Men are qualified for civil liberty in exact proportion to their disposition to put moral chains upon their own appetites, in proportion as their love to justice is above their rapacity, in proportion as their soundness and sobriety of understanding is above their vanity and presumption, in proportion as they are more disposed to listen to the counsels of the wise and good, in preference to the flattery of knaves. Society cannot exist, unless a controlling power upon will and appetite be placed somewhere; and the less of it there is within, the more

there must be without. It is ordained in the eternal constitution of things, that men of intemperate minds cannot be free. Their passions forge their fetters.[3]

The Individual and War

Can righteousness be maintained and happiness be found in an atmosphere of wars and rumors of war? Can righteous people remain righteous under such circumstances? Mormon gave us insights into the answers to these questions by describing how the Nephites struggled through this period. He made this intriguing observation about the Nephites who were preparing for war: "And those who were faithful in keeping the commandments of the Lord were delivered at all times, whilst thousands of their wicked brethren have been consigned to bondage, or to perish by the sword, or to dwindle in unbelief, and mingle with the Lamanites. But behold there never was a happier time among the people of Nephi, since the days of Nephi, than in the days of Moroni." (Alma 50:22-23.)

Yet the challenges and struggles that come with war come to the individual. Can a righteous, peaceful individual maintain those qualities in an atmosphere of hatred, along with an environment where life is not respected nor God revered? The answer to this question is also found in this section of the Book of Mormon. We are given the example of Captain Moroni. He did not want to shed blood, but he loved peace and desired to keep the commandments. Yet he spent most of his adult life in war. His profession appeared to be that of a military leader. He took good men into battle, and he had to watch many of them suffer and die.

Even with this life-style, he still remained righteous. Mormon gave this description of him: "If all men had been, and were, and ever would be, like unto Moroni, behold, the very powers of hell would have been shaken forever; yea, the devil would never have power over the hearts of the children of men." (Alma 48:17.)

Moroni remained righteous, strong, and powerful even in an environment where death, suffering, pain, and hatred became the norm. The question can then be asked, "Can a Latter-day Saint be righteous in a military environment?" The answer, based on Moroni's experience, is yes.

Conclusion

The Book of Mormon was designed to prepare its readers to survive the problems of the latter days. Book of Mormon prophets stated that this book would be brought forth when there would be wars and other social problems. Elder Marion G. Romney made this observation: "Latter-day Saints know that this earth will never again, during its telestial existence, be free from civil disturbance and war."[4] This being true, if people of these latter days have any hope, it will be founded in righteousness. We must be careful that we do not follow the pattern of the Book of Mormon people who had more faith in their own armaments than they had in God. A modern-day general, Omar N. Bradley, once warned: "We have grasped the mystery of the atom and rejected the Sermon on the Mount. . . . Ours is a world of nuclear giants and ethical infants. We know more about war than we know about peace, more about killing than we know about living."[5]

In our society today, we find that we are well prepared for war. In our preparation, however, we have lost the spiritual strength to prevent it.

President Dwight D. Eisenhower observed: "Every gun made, every warship launched, every rocket fired signifies, in the final sense, a theft from those who hunger and are not fed, those who are cold and are not clothed. This world in arms is not spending money alone. It is spending the sweat of its laborers, the genius of its scientists, the hopes of its children. . . . This is not a way of life at all, in any true sense. Under the cloud of threatening war, it is humanity hanging from a cross of iron."[6]

The cry in these days is for righteousness. If there is to be hope for a peaceful future, it will be because people repent and serve the Lord. The First Presidency, in a Christmas message to the world, made this plea:

> We are dismayed by the growing tensions among the nations, and the unrestricted building of arsenals of war,

including huge and threatening nuclear weaponry. Nuclear war, when unleashed on a scale for which the nations are preparing, spares no living thing within the perimeter of its initial destructive force, and sears and maims and kills wherever its pervasive cloud reaches.

While recognizing the need for strength to repel any aggressor, we are enjoined by the word of God to "renounce war and proclaim peace." We call upon the heads of nations to sit down and reason together in good faith to resolve their differences. If men of good will can bring themselves to do so, they may save the world from a holocaust, the depth and breadth of which can scarcely be imagined. We are confident that when there is enough of a desire for peace and a will to bring it about, it is not beyond the possibility of attainment.[7]

It is the duty of every Latter-day Saint to live righteously enough to be an influence for peace. However, if the time comes that they have to fight "for their homes and their liberties, their wives and their children, and their all, yea, for their rites of worship and their church" (Alma 43:45), then they must be prepared to respond in righteousness and with purity of heart.

NOTES

1. See H. Dean Garrett, "The Book of Mormon on War," *A Symposium on the Book of Mormon* (Salt Lake City: Church Education System, 1986), pp. 47-53, for a more thorough discussion of this concept.

2. *Conference Report*, April 1942, p. 72.

3. *The Works of the Right Honorable Edmund Burke* (Boston: Little, Brown, and Company, 1889), pp. 51-52.

4. "Peace in This World," *Improvement Era*, June 1967, p. 77.

5. Cited in Louis Fischer, *The Life of Mahatma Ghandi* (New York: Harper & Brothers, Publishers, 1950), p. 349.

6. *Peace with Justice, Selected Addresses of Dwight D. Eisenhower* (New York: Columbia University Press, 1961) pp. 37-38.

7. "From the First Presidency," *Church News*, 20 Dec. 1980, p. 3.

8

RIGHTEOUS OATHS, REPROOF, AND RECONCILIATION
(Alma 52–63)

SPENCER J. CONDIE

The concluding chapters of the book of Alma are not only an exciting account of ingenious military strategies but also a spiritual saga in which humble followers of Christ encounter in exquisite detail "an opposition in all things." (2 Ne. 2:11.) This is the a story of a people with deep, abiding faith despite unrestrained wickedness in the world in which they lived. These chapters reassure us that there are still promises to keep, notwithstanding the fact that others may engage in deception, intrigue, and even murder to gain greater power. This is the unusual story of larger-than-life military leaders who loved their troops more than themselves and who loved liberty more than life.

One of the great lessons of the Nephite-Lamanite war, and perhaps all wars, was that "many had become *hardened*, because of the exceedingly great length of the war; and many were *softened* because of their afflictions, insomuch that they did humble themselves before God, even in the depth of humility." (Alma 62:41; emphasis added.)

Alma's successor as chief judge, Nephihah, died, and his son Pahoran "was appointed chief judge and governor over the people." (Alma 50:37-40.) Citizens who have inherited a long, traditional, constitutionally based form of government take for granted the smooth transition of leadership from one leader to another. But in

---

Spencer J. Condie is professor of ancient scripture at Brigham Young University.

many societies, even today, the death of a ruler or the transition from a military rule to a more civilian form of government sometimes creates a leadership vacuum filled only after revolution and bloodshed. Unless the transition is considered legitimate by the opposition, political turmoil will likely result.

Such was the political climate in 67 B.C. Notwithstanding the ever present external threat of Lamanite invasions, the Nephites became divided among themselves, and a revolutionary movement of so-called "king-men" sought to alter the laws of the land in order to remove the duly appointed Pahoran from the judgment seat. (Alma 51:2-5.)

The matter was put to a vote, and "the voice of the people came in favor of the freemen, and Pahoran retained the judgment-seat" (Alma 51:7). But order in the land of Zarahemla was short-lived, because the dreaded king of the Lamanites, Amalickiah, "had gathered together a wonderfully great army" (Alma 51:11) and quickly took possession of the heavily fortified cities of Nephihah, Lehi, Morianton, Omner, Gid, and Mulek (Alma 51:25-27). But the fearless leader of one of the Nephite armies, Teancum, successfully resisted the forces of Amalickiah and bravely stole into the Lamanite camp at night and thrust a javelin into the Lamanite leader's heart. (Alma 51:33-34.) Shortly thereafter, the king's equally bloodthirsty brother, Ammoron, was appointed to be a king over the Lamanites.

Teancum concluded that it would be impossible to attack the Lamanites in their fortified cities, so the chief captains of the Nephite armies held a council of war and developed a plan to "decoy the Lamanites out of their strongholds." (Alma 52:17-21.) Teancum led a token force near the seashore while Moroni led his forces into the wilderness. The Lamanites pursued Teancum in vain while Moroni marched back to take the city of Mulek. (Alma 52:22-26.)

In the meantime, Captain Lehi marched against the weary Lamanites with a fresh Nephite army that joined forces with Moroni's army. A furious battle ensued. Jacob, the head of the Lamanites, was slain, and Moroni himself was wounded. The chief captains of the Lamanites "came forth and threw down their weapons," but those who would not surrender voluntarily were taken as prisoners. (Alma

52:27-40.) The Nephites used these prisoners of war to dig trenches around the city of Bountiful and to build a "breastwork of timbers" around the ditches to fortify the city.

Just as the tides of fortune seemed to be turning in a favorable direction, while Moroni was away from Zarahemla, the Lamanites had caused great dissensions among the Nephites and had taken possession of several cities on the west sea, south. (Alma 53:8-9.)

The Nephite armies had regained the city of Mulek and fortified the land of Bountiful. In the process they were now confronted with the simultaneous problems of regaining their other lost cities, dealing with the dissension and intrigue between the king-men and freemen back at headquarters, watching over an ever-increasing number of prisoners of war, and protecting the Ammonites who had taken an oath never again to fight. Who could assume responsibility for leading and defending this people amidst such apparently insurmountable problems?

A Profile of Captain Moroni

The record describes Moroni as "a strong and a mighty man," "a man of a perfect understanding," "a man that did not delight in bloodshed," "a man whose soul did joy in the liberty and the freedom of his country." (Alma 48:11.) "If all men had been, and were, and ever would be, like unto Moroni, behold, the very powers of hell would have been shaken forever; yea, the devil would never have power over the hearts of the children of men." (Alma 48:17.)

Moroni had been appointed chief captain only two years previously at the age of twenty-five. (Alma 43:17.) He was a very astute strategist and tactician and was absolutely fearless, a style of leadership involving considerable risks as he, himself, was wounded in battle. (Alma 52:35.) In describing the desirable qualities of a great leader, Hugh Nibley cites Moroni's character traits as the epitome of the consummate leader. Said Nibley: "Leaders are movers and shakers, original, inventive, unpredictable, imaginative, full of surprises that discomfit the enemy in war and the main office in peace."[1]

Yes, indeed, Moroni was righteous, intelligent, creative, and courageous. But what of his communication skills? May it be said of

Captain Moroni that he was seldom, if ever, misunderstood. A case in point is the letter he wrote to Ammoron in response to an offer to exchange prisoners. The Lamanites had not only taken captive Nephite soldiers, but their wives and children as well. Thus, it was an enticing offer to exchange prisoners. But Moroni would agree only on his own terms: a Nephite family for each Lamanite prisoner. (Alma 54:11.)

To underscore the intensity of his feelings about Ammoron's aggressive attempts to take the Nephite lands through bloodshed, Moroni wrote: "I would tell you concerning that awful hell that awaits to receive such murderers as thou and thy brother have been" (Alma 54:7), and "it supposeth me that thou art a child of hell" (Alma 54:11). Then, just in case Ammoron did not catch the full flavor of his message, Moroni added the afterthought: "Behold, I am in my anger." (Alma 54:13.)

Here was the right man, in the right place, at the right time! Moroni's integrity would not allow him to bargain cheaply the lives of the Nephite families in question, especially without an assurance from Ammoron that he would no longer seek to destroy the Nephites (Alma 54:13), and so Moroni refused Ammoron's offer to exchange prisoners (Alma 55:1-2).

Never one to shrink from his duty to free the Nephite prisoners of war, Moroni identified a Lamanite convert within his own ranks whom he sent by night to the city of Gid, where the Lamanites were guarding numerous Nephite prisoners. This courier, whose name was Laman, took with him a few other men and some bottles of strong wine. Upon reaching the Lamanite camp, the Nephite platoon indicated that they had just escaped from the Nephite camp. The Lamanites were only too happy to welcome them and to drink their specially prepared wine. (Alma 55:4-13.)

As soon as the Lamanite guards had had their fill of wine and had sunk into a drunken slumber, Laman's platoon returned to report to Captain Moroni. Moroni's troops returned to the city of Gid and quietly armed the Nephite prisoners while the Lamanites slept. In the morning the Lamanites awakened to discover that they were surrounded. Perhaps with tongue in cheek, the chronicler of these events wrote: "In these circumstances they found that it was not expedient that they should fight with the Nephites." (Alma 55:23.)

Again we are reminded that Moroni "did not delight in murder or bloodshed, but he delighted in the saving of his people from destruction." (Alma 55:19.) So it was that the Lamanite prisoners' lives were spared, and they were subsequently put to work fortifying the city of Gid. (Alma 55:25.)

As mentioned previously, protracted war can either harden or soften a people, coarsen or refine them, create cynicism or build faith. As for the Nephites, they "were not slow to remember the Lord their God in this their time of affliction." (Alma 55:31.)

Promises to Keep

As internal dissensions among the Nephites added fuel to the already raging fires of war with the Lamanites, the need for additional valiant Nephite warriors became critical. And so it was that the faithful people of Ammon, Lamanite converts who had been the beneficiaries of Nephite protection for several years, felt such an acute sense of obligation to assist in the war effort that they were about to break the oath they had taken never to bear arms and shed the blood of another. (See Alma 24.) "But behold, as they were about to take their weapons of war, they were overpowered by the persuasions of Helaman and his brethren, for they were about to break the oath which they had made." (Alma 53:14.)

Long before the age of notarized signatures, of quintuplicate copies of contracts with countless qualifications and exceptions, there was a time when a verbal oath had all the pulling power necessary to bind someone to his word. The commitment to oaths among the people of the Book of Mormon is everywhere evident, from the reciprocal promises between Nephi and Zoram (1 Ne. 4:33-37) to the refusal of Zerahemnah, the Lamanite leader, to take an oath "which we know that we shall break" (Alma 44:8), to the people of Morianton who, "upon their covenanting to keep the peace," were once again allowed to return to their lands (Alma 50:36).

Whether made by the righteous or the wicked, an oath was a sacred promise to be kept inviolate under any and all circumstances.

Few examples of broken oaths are recorded in the entire Book of Mormon, and these breaches occurred under very unusual mitigating circumstances. (See Mosiah 19:20–20:24.)

Hugh Nibley has provided enlightening evidence of the great binding power of oaths in the ancient Arab world.[2] Henry Sumner Maine, in his classic treatise on Ancient Law, also cites examples of binding verbal oaths from Roman Law and more recent Anglo-Saxon jurisprudence.[3] Indeed, our own contemporary courtroom oath "to swear the truth, the whole truth, and nothing but the truth" is not to be taken lightly (as indicted perjurers have painfully discovered).

How could the Nephites resolve their current dilemma? They had a critical shortage of troops and were encumbered by an obligation to protect the faithful Ammonites who had taken an oath not to bear arms. The Ammonites "had many sons, who had not entered into a covenant that they would not take their weapons of war to defend themselves against their enemies. . . . And they entered into a covenant to fight for the liberty of the Nephites." (Alma 53:16-17.)

Two Thousand Heroic Mothers

There are about two thousand mothers whose names remain unknown but whose faithful stripling sons helped to alter the course of Nephite history. Helaman was selected to lead them and described his young "sons" as being "exceedingly valiant for courage, and also for strength and activity . . . men who were true at all times in whatsoever thing they were entrusted. Yea, they were men of truth and soberness, for they had been taught to keep the commandments of God and to walk uprightly before him." (Alma 53:20-21.) Helaman further shared the observation that "they had been taught by their mothers, that if they did not doubt, God would deliver them. And they rehearsed unto me the words of their mothers, saying: We do not doubt our mothers knew it." (Alma 53:47-48.)

The age of these young warriors is not stated, but Helaman once referred to them as "men" (Alma 53:20), sometimes as "striplings" (Alma 53:22; 56:57), other times as his "little sons" (Alma 56:30 and 56:39), but most frequently as "my sons" (Alma 56:10, 27, 44, 46, 57:22). Regardless of the young men's ages, their parents' permission to leave home was certainly not given without sacrifice. Their numbers began with an even two thousand but eventually increased to two thousand and sixty. (Alma 57:6.)

Just as the mothers reared sons of great faith and courage, the fathers sacrificed in delivering provisions to their sons. (Alma 56:27.) Though the Ammonite fathers would not bear arms, they gave "a large portion of their substance" in support of the Nephite armies. (Alma 43:13.)

Helaman and his "little sons" were under the command of Antipus, who ordered them to divert the attention of the Lamanites by marching to a neighboring city near the seashore. As the Lamanites began to pursue the stripling warriors, Antipus's troops marched in hot pursuit of the Lamanites. Just as the weary troops "were about to fall into the hands of the Lamanites," Helaman's little army came to the rescue, surrounding the enemy. As the dust settled, the Nephites were clearly victorious, and the Lamanites were taken prisoner. (Alma 56:30-54.)

With typical paternalistic concern, Helaman surveyed his army and was overjoyed to discover that not a single one of his stripling soldiers had "fallen to the earth." (Alma 56:56.)

Shortly thereafter, Helaman's army received, in addition to fresh provisions, sixty more Ammonite sons to strengthen their numbers. (Alma 57:6.) Through a fortuitous set of circumstances, the supply line to the Lamanites was interrupted by the Nephites, and for want of food the Lamanites surrendered the city of Cumeni. Now the troops of Helaman were overburdened with an excessive number of prisoners to guard, and they were ultimately compelled to slay many of those who persisted in fighting, while the other prisoners were escorted by a contingent of Helaman's troops back to the land of Zarahemla. (Alma 57:7-16.)

Meanwhile, Ammoron's army had received new provisions, and "a numerous army of men" had engaged the remaining stripling soldiers in a desperate battle. In the moment of greatest despair, those who had escorted the prisoners to Zarahemla returned to the battlefield and successfully drove the Lamanites back to the city of Manti. This time, the census of wounded revealed that two hundred of

Helaman's army "had fainted because of the loss of blood; nevertheless, according to the goodness of God . . . there was not one soul of them who did perish," notwithstanding the fact that, without exception, every stripling had been wounded. (Alma 57:25.) Referring once again to their unshakable faith, Helaman described his sons as "young, and their minds are firm, and they do put their trust in God continually." (Alma 57:27.)

The joy of previous victories was short lived, however. Helaman wrote in an epistle to Moroni that their supply line had been most unreliable for several months, and that they "were about to perish for the want of food." (Alma 58:7.) But in their hour of affliction, Helaman wrote that "we did pour out our souls in prayer to God, that he would strengthen us and deliver us out of the hands of our enemies . . . and it came to pass that the Lord our God did visit us with assurances that he would deliver us." (Alma 58:10-11.)

Although greatly outnumbered by the Lamanites, Helaman again employed a strategy of dividing and conquering. One of the Nephite captains, Gid, led his troops into the wilderness on the right, while Teomner and his troops entered the wilderness on the left.

As the Lamanites attacked Helaman's army, the armies of Gid and Teomner cut off the Lamanite spies, hurried to the Lamanite-occupied city of Manti, and overwhelmed the guards who had been left behind. Helaman led his troops in the direction of Zarahemla, and while the Lamanites slept, the striplings changed course and continued marching toward the city of Manti, thus taking possession of it before the Lamanites returned. (Alma 58:16-29.)

After recounting their successes in a letter to Moroni, Helaman then broached the subject of an unreliable supply line, suspecting "that there is some faction in the government, that they do not send more men to our assistance," adding with typical faith: "We trust God will deliver us." (Alma 58:36-37.)

Reproof and Reconciliation

Upon receiving Helaman's request for aid, Moroni, ever the great advocate for his army, "immediately sent an epistle to Pahoran," asking for reinforcements. (Alma 59.) When the city of Nephihah was lost because the expected help never arrived, Moroni sent another epistle to Pahoran, expressing his anger with the seeming indifference of the government. (Alma 60.)

The 121st section of the Doctrine and Covenants contains some of the greatest counsel in holy writ regarding the proper exercise of authority. The Lord revealed to the Prophet Joseph Smith that "no power or influence can or ought to be maintained by virtue of the priesthood, only by persuasion, by long-suffering, by gentleness and meekness, and by love unfeigned; by kindness, and pure knowledge.... Reproving betimes with sharpness, when moved upon by the Holy Ghost." (D&C 121:41-43.)

Some readers may be surprised at the sharpness of Moroni's epistle to Pahoran, the leader of the land. It may be well to examine Moroni's letter within the context in which it was written. Moroni had served as chief captain of the Nephite armies for more than a dozen years, and he was weary of war. Secondly, he was writing as an advocate for Helaman and his army. Thirdly, he told Pahoran that they would not complain if their afflictions had been confined to "hunger, thirst, and fatigue" (Alma 60:3), but his greatest concern was the unnecessary "slaughter among our people" (Alma 60:5).

Congruent with the Lord's counsel to be patient and long-suffering, Moroni had suffered various afflictions for over twelve years. But now his emotions were brimming with anger, and he did, indeed, reprove Pahoran with sharpness. There is one crucial element that Moroni overlooked: pure knowledge. That is to say, before reproving with sharpness it is well to have all the facts straight. The suspicions of Helaman and Moroni about the intrigue and dissension on the home front were all well founded; however, Moroni's aspersions against Pahoran were not grounded in truth.

Nevertheless, the magnanimous, charitable Pahoran received Moroni's scorching letter in the spirit in which it should have been written and accepted it with joy and a forgiving heart.

Another important element of the Lord's counsel on exercising power and authority involves "reproving *betimes* with sharpness." Many English-speaking people assume that the meaning of this archaic word, *betimes*, means "frequently" or "sometimes," but this is not the case. *Betimes* means literally "before it is too late." It is significant in this context that Pahoran responds to Moroni's letter by saying, "I do joy in receiving your epistle, for *I was somewhat worried concerning what we should do*, whether it should be just in us to go against our brethren." (Alma 61:19; emphasis added.)

One gathers the impression that Pahoran, perhaps like the great high priest Eli of old, knew full well that remedial action should be taken but lacked the motivation to follow through until the message was sent in an unmistakable fashion that could not be misunderstood. Not until he received Moroni's sharp message did Pahoran make the firm resolve to clean house on the home front in order to be unified against the Lamanite armies.

Even while castigating Pahoran in his letter, Moroni nonetheless addressed the loftier side of Pahoran's character as he challenged him to "come out and show unto me a true spirit of freedom." (Alma 60:25.) Moroni's sharp epistle was the catalyst in overcoming Pahoran's indecisiveness.

Strength Through Unity

After Moroni received Pahoran's gracious reply, "his heart did take courage." He began to march toward the land of Gideon, and "thousands did flock unto his standard, and did take up their swords in the defence of their freedom." (Alma 62:1-5.) As Moroni and Pahoran united their forces, "they became exceedingly strong" and successfully rooted out the king-men, the internal dissenters who would have toppled the government from within. After being placed on trial in accordance with the laws of the land, "those king-men, whosoever would not take up arms in the defence of their country, but would fight against it, were put to death." (Alma 62:6-9.)

As Pahoran and Moroni's troops engaged the Lamanites in battle, they influenced the defeated Lamanites "to enter into a covenant that they would no more take up their weapons of war against the Nephites." (Alma 62:16.) Underscoring the binding power of verbal promises, those who made this covenant were sent to live with the Ammonites in peace.

A series of dramatic, successive victories occurred as the ranks of Moroni and Pahoran were joined by the armies of Lehi and Teancum. Filled with exceeding anger toward Ammoron, Teancum stealthily cast a javelin into Ammoron's heart just as he had done with Ammoron's brother, Amalickiah. But this time he was pursued and slain. (Alma 62:35-36.) A mighty warrior had fallen.

With the demise of Ammoron, the Nephites were able to drive the Lamanites from the land, and peace was at least temporarily restored. Pahoran returned to his rightful place in the chief judgment-seat. Helaman began again "to preach unto the people the word of God," and the church was reestablished throughout the land. (Alma 62:44-46.) Captain Moroni relinquished his military command to his son, Moronihah, and retired in peace. (Alma 62:43.)

And the Nephite people "did pray unto the Lord their God continually, insomuch that the Lord did bless them, according to his word, so that they did wax strong and prosper in the land." (Alma 62:51.)

An Exceedingly Curious Man

Two years following the death of Helaman and the year following Moroni's death, "an exceedingly curious man" by the name of Hagoth built and launched a large ship "into the west sea, by the narrow neck which led into the land northward." (Alma 63:5.) John L. Sorenson builds a rather persuasive case for locating this launching point at the Gulf of Tehuantepec in Mesoamerica. His careful reasoning is well worth consideration.[4]

After taking several provisions and people with him, Hagoth returned the next year to build other ships and to take "many more people" and provisions with him to the land northward. "And it came to pass that they were never heard of more." (Alma 63:7-8.)

Students of Polynesian cultural history have sought to examine a possible link between Hagoth's voyages and the origins of the peoples of the South Pacific. R. Lanier Britsch has concluded that any such relationship "is not clear,"[5] and Sorenson contends that available anthropological information neither confirms nor refutes it.[6] Still, Church leaders have taught from time to time that Polynesians are descendants of Lehi, through Hagoth's voyages or other such travels of the Nephites and Lamanites.[7]

NOTES

1. Hugh Nibley, *Brigham Young Univeristy Summer Commencement Address*, August 19, 1983.

2. Hugh Nibley, *Lehi in the Desert and the World of the Jaredites* (Salt Lake City: Bookcraft, 1952), pp. 117-18, 196.

3. Sir Henry Sumner Maine, *Ancient Law* (New York: H. Holt and Co., 1885).

4. John L. Sorenson, *An Ancient American Setting for the Book of Mormon* (Salt Lake City: Deseret Book Company, and Provo, Utah: Foundation for Ancient Research and Mormon Studies, 1985) pp. 265-68.

5. R. Lanier Britsch, "Maori Traditions and the Mormon Church," *New Era*, June 1981, pp. 38-46.

6. Sorenson, *An Ancient American Setting*, p. 269.

7. See W. A. Cole and E. W. Jensen, *Israel in the Pacific* (Salt Lake City: Genealogical Society of Utah, 1961), p. 388; *Conference Report*, April 1962, p. 112; *Church News*, May 10, 1958, p. 2.

9

THEIR OWN WORST ENEMIES
(Helaman 1–6)

DANIEL C. PETERSON

Chapters 1-6 of Helaman cover fully thirty years and offer us a fairly good glimpse into how Mormon the editor worked. This section of the Book of Mormon is largely an example of what is often termed "annalistic" writing. "Annals," a type of historical record-keeping with many Near Eastern parallels, feature a narrative of events listed year by year. This is precisely what we find in these chapters. With only a single exception, every one of the thirty years extending from the fortieth year of the judges up to the sixty-ninth (from 52 to 23 B.C) is explicitly mentioned in these chapters. Sometimes, it is true, the year is cited very briefly, with only the most perfunctory indication of the state of the Nephites or of some event that occurred. Consider, for example, Helaman 3:1-2: In these verses, Mormon tells us very briefly that 49 B.C was characterized by a small problem with pride which was settled in that same year, and that the years 48 and 47 saw little or no contention. Likewise, Helaman 3:32-33 chronicles very briefly the years 43-40 B.C, which saw the Nephites decline from "peace and exceedingly great joy" to a cancerously growing pride, and Helaman 4:1-10 carries us from 38 to 31 B.C.[1]

We know already from the title page of the Book of Mormon that it is "an abridgment of the record of the people of Nephi," and we know that it was Mormon himself who was responsible for most of the condensation. It is possible, almost, to picture him at his task:

Daniel C. Peterson is assistant professor of Arabic at Brigham Young University.

He sits at a sort of writing table, surrounded by centuries of the records of his people. (Perhaps, given his central role in the violent events of his time, he does most of his writing in stolen moments in a military commander's field tent.) As he reads through the chronicles that have come to him, he knows he can include only a small portion in his abridgment. Therefore, under the inspiration of the Lord, he chooses what he thinks important and interesting, making occasional comments on the material he selects. However, he is too honest, too conscientious and thorough, to simply leave whole periods out of the record. Thus, for example, when he comes to his sources for the years 43-40 B.C., he finds a host of events and details that he cannot put into his book. But he can draw a lesson from them, and in this case the moral he distills from his source-chronicles is the evil of pride.

Rarely did Mormon go into an event or a sermon in great detail. Much of the record briefly summarizes what must have been a vast archive of source materials. (This is, of course, one of the frustrations of those who would read the Book of Mormon as an archaeological guidebook or as a geographical manual—such historical, archaeological, and geographical details as exist in it are there incidentally and sketchily. Mormon was serious about his assignment.)

Sedition and Invasion

Two spectacular events dominate the first chapter of the book of Helaman—a succession crisis accompanied by an assassination, and a successful but short-lived Lamanite seizure of the central Nephite lands. However, neither of these events proved as significant in the long term as the rise of a terrorist group that came to be called the "Gadianton robbers."

In 52 B.C., the great chief judge Pahoran I, who had presided over the Nephites during the recent period of wars, was dead. He left behind him a number of sons, among whom three—Pahoran, Paanchi, and Pacumeni—offered themselves as candidates to succeed their father. Each had his supporters, but Pahoran was chosen to occupy the judgment seat. Pacumeni gave up his claims and fell in behind the leadership of his brother, but Paanchi and his faction refused to reconcile themselves to their defeat. Instead, they began to plot a *coup d'état*. This was, of course, something that the government could not tolerate, and Paanchi was arrested and condemned to death. (And, although the record does not explicitly say so, it is likely that he was, in fact, executed.)

Furious over the failure of their attempt at sedition, a group of Paanchi's partisans dispatched an assassin, one Kishkumen, to eliminate their triumphant rival. Pahoran II, whose reign can have lasted at the most only a few months, was murdered as he sat upon the judgment seat, apparently while giving audience.[2]

Successful, Kishkumen escaped and returned to those who had sent him. The conspirators then swore an oath of silence. Intriguingly, the Nephite record tells us that it was a religious oath, "swearing by their everlasting Maker." (Hel. 1:11.) This seems odd to those of us unaccustomed to thinking of murder as a religious act. But the very word *assassin* was given to us by a religious sect of the medieval Near East who bore it as a name. The "Assassins" carried out daring murders for many years from mixed religious and political motives.[3] And it would seem, from the story of Cain and Abel as recorded in the book of Moses, that such "religious" oaths go back to the very beginning of human history. (See Moses 5:29.) Indeed, the Book of Mormon declares that the origin of such murderous conspiracies can be traced back to Lucifer through Cain, "who was a murderer from the beginning." (Ether 8:15; cf. Hel. 6:26-30.) Following their strange, quasi-religious meeting, the successful conspirators dispersed to their various ordinary pursuits, blending into Nephite society in such a way that the government could find only some of them. So religiously—if we may use that word—did they keep their oaths, that many of the group, including Kishkumen himself, remained at large.

In that same year, Pacumeni, the last of the three sons of Pahoran the First who had contested the judgment seat, was chosen to govern the Nephite nation. His reign was destined, however, to be just as short as that of his assassinated brother. The king of the Lamanites, perhaps sensing that the turmoil at the heart of the Nephite govenment offered him a major opportunity for success, chose the year 51 B.C. for a major invasion. It may be remembered that this king, named

Tubaloth, was not really a Lamanite. Rather, he was the son of Ammoron, the brother and successor of the notoriously unscrupulous Nephite adventurer, Amalickiah.[4] Tubaloth had chosen yet another dissenter from the Nephites, by the name of Coriantumr, to lead his warriors. It was certainly a common practice of those who would lead the Lamanites into battle against the Nephites to choose apostates as their assistants. (See, for an example of this, Alma 43:6-7.) These apostates could be counted upon to feel a powerful hatred for the Nephites, which made them very useful to the great manipulators who appear with such appalling frequency in the pages of the Book of Mormon.

Tubaloth's apparent guess that the Nephites' contentions had given him an opening was quite correct. Security in the Nephite heartland was almost nonexistent, owing to the breakdown in the government. Moronihah, the supreme commander of the Nephite armies, evidently faced with a shortage of troops, had chosen to place those that were available to him on the perimeter of Nephite territory. That is, they were stationed all about the lands of the Nephites, on the borders. Under the circumstances, this was the reasonable thing to do. But it also had its risks, since, as in the case of the notorious Maginot line in World War II, any invader who could get past the initial resistance at the border would find few obstacles from that point on.

And that is precisely what happened. Coriantumr launched a kind of *blitzkrieg*, piercing the Nephite border defenses, and seized the capital city of Zarahemla. The conquest was quick and, for the moment, total. Pacumeni, the chief judge, was killed. Perhaps somewhat astonished himself at the scope of his victory, Coriantumr then marched toward the other chief Nephite city, Bountiful. En route, he mopped up what disorganized opposition he encountered — the Nephites having been taken so completely by surprise that they did not even have time to mobilize a challenge to him.

But Coriantumr would not reach Bountiful. As Hugh Nibley points out, his drive "had been successful because it was completely unexpected; and it had been unexpected because it was utterly foolish."[5] It was utterly foolish because, having penetrated the Nephite defense on the circumference and seized the center of the land, Coriantumr was now, by the very nature of his own success, surrounded. Moronihah and his loyal subordinate officer, Lehi, caught the Lamanite intruders from before and behind, and, following a bloody battle in which Coriantumr was killed, left them no alternative but surrender. It was a humiliating defeat.

The Nephites must surely have breathed a massive sigh of relief at this point. If so, they were premature. For the remnants of the conspiracy that had killed Pahoran II were still at large, and, having previously tasted success, were apparently little disposed to go into retirement. While Coriantumr's daring invasion had been spectacular, it was to have little if any lasting effect; the future belonged, rather, in a very real sense, to the conspiracy that had begun the year before.

Gadianton

In the aftermath of the Lamanite invasion of 51 B.C., the Nephite government began to reconstitute itself. With all of the politically active sons of Pahoran I now dead, the choice of the people fell upon Helaman, the son of Helaman, to lead them. There was another, though, who wanted to rule. One Gadianton, who, like so many of the great agitators in the Book of Mormon, "was exceedingly expert in many words" (Hel. 2:4), at this point insinuated himself into the leadership of the old Paanchist conspiracy. If they would put him on the judgment seat, he said, he would reward them with power and authority.[6] They agreed to make the attempt. And, although they would never be successful in Gadianton's lifetime, so complete was his control over them and so completely were they identified with him that ever afterward they were known among the Nephites as "Gadianton's robbers."

Kishkumen, therefore, their tried and tested instrument in the case of Pahoran II, was dispatched to assassinate Helaman. But the new chief judge had not forgotten about the seditionists still on the loose among his people, and he had inaugurated a partially successful plan to infiltrate their organization. As Kishkumen proceeded toward the judgment seat to reprise his earlier triumph, he was stabbed to death by one of Helaman's operatives, who then ran to the chief judge to alert him to the developing situation. (The smooth way in which Kishkumen is taken care of—in total silence; see Hel. 2:9—makes us suspect that this "servant" of Helaman's was more than an ordinary domestic helper or government office-worker. Indeed, he may well have been the ancient equivalent of a professional intelligence specialist.[7])

Helaman's men were, however, unable to apprehend the wily Gadianton and his partisans. When Kishkumen did not return within the expected time, Gadianton did not wait around to be caught. Instead, he and his followers escaped from the city into the wilderness, where they and their successors would operate frequently in the next several centuries—offering a textbook illustration of guerrilla warfare.[8] They did not fade away. "More of this Gadianton shall be spoken hereafter," wrote Mormon. "And behold, in the end of this book [by which he meant the Book of Mormon as a whole] ye shall see that this Gadianton did prove the overthrow, yea, almost the entire destruction of the people of Nephi." (Hel. 2:12-13.)

A Season of Emigration to the North

Helaman 3 records that many people left the land of Zarahemla in 46 B.C. and made their way into the land to the north. (In this northward emigration, they were following the precedent that had been set a decade earlier by Hagoth and his people. See Alma 63:4-10.) They traveled a great distance to a region of "large bodies of water and many rivers." (Hel. 3:4.)[9] This area had previously sustained a large population that the Nephites identified with the earlier people known as the Jaredites (see Ether 1:1), and it had (in a situation we today can well imagine) been stripped of its timber.[10] Thus, given the fact that they could not rely upon wood for their construction materials, these colonists resorted to working with cement, although they also imported wood from the south and attempted, as a long-term solution to the problem, to reforest the land. (Hel. 3:7-10.)

Meanwhile, back in the central Nephite lands, the affairs of the people alternately prospered and decayed. In 43 B.C., for example, peace had been established and the church was flourishing. Referring to this time, Mormon noted that such blessings were—and always had been—open to all. "Thus," he wrote, "we may see that the Lord is merciful unto all who will, in the sincerity of their hearts, call upon his holy name. Yea, thus we see that the gate of heaven is open unto all, even to those who will believe on the name of Jesus Christ, who is the Son of God. Yea, we see that whosoever will may lay hold upon the word of God, which is quick and powerful, which shall divide asunder all the cunning and the snares and the wiles of the devil, and lead the man of Christ in a straight and narrow course across that everlasting gulf of misery which is prepared to engulf the wicked—and land their souls, yea, their immortal souls, at the right hand of God in the kingdom of heaven, to sit down with Abraham, and Isaac, and with Jacob, and with all our holy fathers, to go no more out." (Hel. 3:27-30.) There was never any need in Nephite history—and there is none in our own time—for the suffering and misery that inevitably accompany wickedness. Yet we are prey to the same temptations as our ancestors. One of the hopes of the scriptural writers who so frankly recorded the sins and errors of their own times was that we of a latter day might profit from their experiences, and, in many cases, avoid repeating them. (See, for example, Morm. 9:31 and Ps. 78:5-8.)

How are we to avoid falling into the same snares as did many of those before us? In his entry for 41 B.C., Mormon gave us a large portion of the answer to that question. In that year, class distinctions began again to appear within the church, and some members of the church gave themselves over to pride and arrogance, and to mistreating the more humble among their brothers and sisters. But amidst all the pain and despite all the discomfort that must have attended this situation, these humble saints remained faithful to God and to their covenants. We are told that "they did fast and pray oft, and did wax stronger and stronger in their humility, and firmer and firmer in the faith of Christ, unto the filling their souls with joy and consolation, yea, even to the purifying and the sanctification of their hearts, which sanctification cometh because of their yielding their hearts unto God." (Hel. 3:35.) Thus, in the face of adversity and perhaps even pain, the Lord's true saints drew yet closer to him, through fasting, prayer, and humble obedience. His true saints do so today, as well.

"Except the Lord Keep the City . . . "

For the year 38 B.C., Mormon's abridgment refers briefly to the rise of contention within the church, which became so severe that it eventually resulted in violence and bloodshed. "And the rebellious part were slain and driven out of the land, and they did go unto the king of the Lamanites. And it came to pass that they did endeavor to stir up the Lamanites to war against the Nephites." (Hel. 4:2-3.)

However, the Lamanites had been beaten too many times in the memory of many still living to be very enthusiastic about yet another assault on the Nephites; they were, in fact, "exceedingly afraid." (Hel. 4:3.) The great war narrated in the Book of Alma had ended in utter Lamanite defeat only a little more than two decades earlier, and the spectacular campaign led by Coriantumr had concluded disastrously just thirteen years before. And both of these military catastrophes had been set in motion by dissenters from the Nephites, who often seemed more than willing to fight their erstwhile brethren down to the last drop of Lamanite blood. Thus, the Lamanites did not respond favorably to the incitements of this particular group of dissenters.

But yet another wave of apostates arrived in Lamanite territory in the following year, and, with them fanning the flames kindled by the earlier group, the resistance of the Lamanites began to weaken. Finally, in 35 B.C., the Lamanites again launched an invasion of Nephite territory. By the next year, they had taken Zarahemla, the Nephite capital. Moronihah and his armies attempted a counterattack, but by 31 B.C. they had managed to recover only half of their original possessions.

It is at this point that Mormon, himself a great military commander, interrupted his narrative to offer some observations on the reasons behind the Nephites' inability to respond effectively to this invasion. It is highly interesting, however, that his remarks not only do not center on military strategy and tactical considerations, but indeed do not raise such issues at all. Rather, he wrote, the cause of the Nephites' weakness was their wickedness—a wickedness that extended even into the church of God. "And it was because of the pride of their hearts, because of their exceeding riches, yea, it was because of their oppression to the poor, withholding their food from the hungry, withholding their clothing from the naked, and smiting their humble brethren upon the cheek, making a mock of that which was sacred, denying the spirit of prophecy and of revelation, murdering, plundering, lying, stealing, committing adultery, rising up in great contentions, and deserting away into the land of Nephi, among the Lamanites — and because of this their great wickedness, and their boastings in their own strength, they were *left* in their own strength." (Hel. 4:12-13, emphasis added.)[11]

Mormon, of course, was sufficiently astute as a military strategist to know what it would mean for the Nephites to be left to merely their own strength. They had been vastly outnumbered by the Lamanites for many generations. If it came to a struggle of numbers, there could be only one outcome. Even the contemporary Nephites, wicked as they were, could see the disastrous implications of their course: "And they saw that they had become weak, like unto their brethren, the Lamanites, and that the Spirit of the Lord did no more preserve them; and they saw that the Lamanites were exceedingly more numerous than they, and except they should cleave unto the Lord their God they must unavoidably perish. For behold, they saw that the strength of the Lamanites was as great as their strength, even man for man." (Hel. 4:24-26.)

The greatness of Mormon, as well as of Moroni, consisted at least partially of the fact that, competent as the Nephites were, they continued to recognize that the Lord is the ultimate arbiter of human affairs. And they never became so obsessed with military tactics and technology as to forget that it is a nation's moral and spiritual resources that will most surely and fundamentally determine its fate. "Except the Lord keep the city," wrote the Psalmist, "the watchman waketh but in vain." (Ps. 127:1.)[12]

Roots, Not Branches

Nephi, son of Helaman, knew, fully as well as would the later chronicler Mormon, that the fundamental problem of the Nephites at this period was spiritual rather than military.[13] For this reason, he decided to devote all his energies to a spiritual solution. In that same year, 30 B.C., he resigned the judgment seat and, with his brother Lehi, undertook full-time preaching of the gospel.

The task was urgent if the Nephites were to be saved from themselves. "For as their laws and their governments were established by the voice of the people, and they who chose evil were more numerous than they who chose good, therefore they were ripening for destruction, for the laws had become corrupted." (Hel. 5:2.) This was precisely the situation King Mosiah II had foreseen as a frightening but remote possibility six decades earlier, when he abolished the monarchy and established the Nephite system of judges. The laws of the Nephites, he had said, were correct and divinely given. Further, he had said, placing the direction of the nation in the hands of a more representative form of government would tend to ensure the continuation of those laws in their correct form, since the majority of the people were unlikely to choose evil over good. But, he had continued, "if the time comes that the voice of the people doth choose iniquity, then is the time that the judgments of God will come upon you." (Mosiah 29:25-27.) And now, probably within the lifetimes of some who had heard him give that historic address, his fears had been realized.[14]

The two brothers, Nephi and Lehi, began their missionary tour at the city of Bountiful and went through a number of the settlements still under Nephite rule. Finally, they entered the territories that had been under Lamanite control since the war of four years earlier. There, in occupied Zarahemla, they preached with such power that they were able to win over many of the Nephite dissenters who had stirred up that war in the first place. But their success did not end with that. They were also able to convert fully eight thousand of the Lamanites who had settled in the former Nephite lands.

Perhaps heartened by this almost unprecedented success, Nephi and Lehi crossed over into Lamanite country itself, into the old land of Nephi. There, however, the reception was rather more chilly. They were captured by a Lamanite army and were almost immediately cast into prison under sentence of death. (After all, they were Nephites, hereditary enemies of the Lamanites — and very prominent ones at that.)

But when their keepers came to fetch them for execution, the Lord intervened. "Nephi and Lehi were encircled about as if by fire, even insomuch that they durst not lay their hands upon them." (Hel. 5:23.) Encouraged by this, the brothers began to preach to their would-be killers — accompanied by earthquakes, a preternatural "cloud of darkness," and a voice from heaven. Quite evidently, the Lord was working here in a major way, for purposes important to him. And, indeed, his intervention in this instance would be of major historical importance, as succeeding chapters of Helaman make clear.[15]

In the face of this supernatural display, the Lamanites were immobilized. Fortunately, one of the apostate Nephites was nearby. Such apostates could be the most bitter and implacable of enemies to the truths of God, but they were also capable — as in the case of this man, one Aminadab — of dredging up from deep in their memories the childhood teachings that would allow them to receive the gospel and teach it to others.[16] Aminadab was able to answer the now earnest inquiries of the Lamanites, and to explain to them how they could be delivered from the cloud of darkness that had engulfed them.

Calling upon the Lord, the newly humbled Lamanites were delivered — and not only so, but they were visited by angels and commended by the heavenly voice. This powerful experience created an instant missionary force of three hundred eager converts. Within a short time, "the more part of the Lamanites were convinced of them." (Hel. 5:50.)

The Tables Turned

Nephi and Lehi had apparently had little success preaching among the Nephites, but they had triumphed spectacularly with the Lamanites and their sympathizers. There ensued now a period that explodes the oversimplified view of the Book of Mormon held by some who do not know it well. For them, the book is a long but uncomplicated tale of white-hatted Nephites and black-hatted Lamanite villains. Certainly, however, for the period under discussion here nothing could be further from the truth.

Helaman 6 describes a time when the Lamanites were righteous, and the Nephites wicked. The Lamanites even sent missionaries among their former enemies and were able, at least temporarily, to bring many of them to the truth and to repentance. And their prosperity was not simply spiritual. With many Nephites and Lamanites converted to the Lord, peace was established, barriers to free trade fell, and—as a predictable consequence—the entire land became prosperous. (Hel. 6:7-9.)[17]

Wealth, however, carries with it major risks to the spiritual well-being of those who possess it. It can, in fact, come to possess *them*. Sometimes, oddly, those who have more than enough of worldly goods can become more obsessed with them than those who must struggle just to make ends meet. So it was with the Nephites at this time. "They began to set their hearts upon their riches." (Hel. 6:17.) They resurrected the old conspiratorial oaths and plans of Gadianton's band. The Lamanites were horrified at this new outbreak of Gadiantonism and made every effort to eradicate it. The Nephites, on the other hand, took to the new possibilities for organized evil with notable enthusiasm. By 24 B.C., their government was firmly in the hands of a revolutionary sect that had taken its immediate beginning in the political turmoil of a quarter of a century earlier.

Chapters 1-6 of Helaman end, thus, on a rather depressing note. From the gospel of Christ, the Nephites had turned to a set of practices and doctrines originating with his archenemy. Of these, Mormon wrote, "They were put into the heart of Gadianton by that same being who did entice our first parents to partake of the forbidden fruit—yea, that same being who did plot with Cain, that if he would murder his brother Abel it should not be known unto the world. And he did plot with Cain and his followers from that time forth." (Hel. 6:26-27; cf. Moses 5:29-33, 47-51.)

Nevertheless, Mormon did not leave us without hope. Under the inspiration of the Lord he gave us important keys for avoiding, individually and as a society, the fate of the Nephites, and he stressed to us that the Lord's blessing and help is available freely, and to all.

Surely the counsel of Helaman to his sons, Nephi and Lehi, was preserved on the golden plates because of its continuing relevance to our day: "My sons," said Helaman, "remember, remember that it is upon the rock of our Redeemer, who is Christ, the Son of God, that ye must build your foundation; that when the devil shall send forth his mighty winds, yea, his shafts in the whirlwind, yea, when all his hail and his mighty storm shall beat upon you, it shall have no power over you to drag you down to the gulf of misery and endless wo, because of the rock upon which ye are built, which is a sure foundation, a foundation whereon if men build they cannot fall." (Hel. 5:12.)

NOTES

1. Probably the best example of what we are discussing here is 4 Nephi 1:6. This verse has been greatly ridiculed by some critics of the Book of Mormon, but it is, in fact, an exceptionally good illustration of the annalist, Mormon, at work. Manifestly, he was summarizing other chronicles that he had before him. However, so little was happening in this period that even the conscientious Mormon began to omit annual accounts. It is apparently difficult even for inspired authors to make good and happy times live up to our taste for the sensational and the horrific. "May you live in interesting times!" is, in fact, an old Chinese curse. And Leo Tolstoy began his great novel *Anna Karenina* with the marvelous line: "Happy families are all alike; every unhappy family is unhappy in its own way." As a glance at the headlines of supermarket tabloids or five minutes listening to gossip will show, we fallen humans tend to find negative news much more interesting than positive.

2. This would, of course, be a time when the chief judge would be easily accessible to a would-be assassin. (One thinks of the similar murder of Saudi Arabia's King Faisal in 1975.) It would also make for a memorable public "statement," if such were the motive of Kishkumen's handlers.

3. The Assassins offer, in fact, a remarkably close parallel to the "secret combinations" of the Nephite and Jaredite traditions. Similar groups are also attested in ancient Mesoamerica. See, on the latter, John L. Sorenson, *An Ancient American Setting for the Book of Mormon* (Salt Lake City: Deseret

Book Company, and Provo, Utah: Foundation for Ancient Research and Mormon Studies, 1985), pp. 300-309.

4. On Amalickiah's rise to power and his subsequent career, see Alma 46-49, 51.

5. Hugh W. Nibley, *Since Cumorah* (Salt Lake City: Deseret Book Company, 1967), p. 367. Hitler's attack on the Soviet Union was likewise an initial triumph but foolish and disastrous in the long term — as Napoleon could have predicted from personal experience.

6. One cannot fail to be reminded of the takeover of an already-existing conspiratorial group in the Weimar Republic — the National Socialist German Workers' Party — by an ambitious young ex-corporal named Adolf Hitler. If anyone could be said to be "exceedingly expert in many words," it is he. Yet the pattern holds with remarkable consistency wherever such conspiracies arise: Lenin, Mussolini, and Castro also come to mind. All were leaders of revolutionary organizations; all were given to seemingly endless speeches.

7. This would not be anachronistic. We need only mention the *Ping-fa* ("The Art of War"), written about 400 B.C. by the Chinese military thinker, Sun-tzu. Its discussion of intelligence-gathering techniques shows that they are very ancient indeed.

8. On the Gadianton bands as guerrillas, see Ray C. Hillam, "The Gadianton Robbers and Protracted War," *Brigham Young University Studies* 15 (Winter 1975): 215-24. The present author is (sporadically) working on a lengthy study of the Gadianton organizations that will discuss this and several other aspects of their activities.

9. According to a model of Book of Mormon geography that is widely accepted among students of the subject, and which the present writer, too, finds plausible, this area may well have been the Valley of Mexico. See Sorenson, *Ancient American Setting*, pp. 266-67. It would seem, at any event, that the colonization of Teotihuacán occurred during the same period as the Nephite-Lamanite migrations to the north that are recorded in this and adjacent portions of the Book of Mormon. See David A. Palmer, *In Search of Cumorah* (Bountiful: Horizon Publishers, 1981), pp. 188-91. A variant of the Sorenson model (Palmer, *Cumorah*, p. 186) suggests the area of modern Veracruz as a possible site.

10. In conversation with Prof. John L. Sorenson on this point, he suggests that if the area is, in fact, to be identified with the Valley of Mexico, it is probably too far north to have actually been part of historic Jaredite territory. However, Nephite knowledge of northern geography beyond a certain point seems to have been vague at best. Certainly they *thought* this area to have been in formerly Jaredite country.

11. Mormon was to face the same mindset in his own day, and with even more calamitous results. See Mormon 4:8; 5:2, 6.

12. A challenging modern counterpart to this ancient principle may be found in the notable essay by President Spencer W. Kimball, entitled "The False Gods We Worship," in the *Ensign* for June 1976.

13. Nephi's spiritual sensitivity, with that of his brother, Lehi, probably owed much to the teaching of their father, Helaman. Hel. 5:6-7 speaks volumes of his desire to instill in them a sense of heritage and of the models they were to emulate. See also Hel. 5:8-12.

14. Mosiah's comments had been recalled a decade later by Amulek, speaking to the people of Ammonihah. (See Alma 10:19.) The similarity between the wording of this passage and that of Helaman 5:2 is striking.

15. For much of the remainder of the Book of Helaman, it is the Lamanites and not the Nephites who were the righteous followers of the Lord. This was, of course, the period of Samuel the Lamanite.

16. One recalls also the dissenters at Zarahemla. (See above, and Hel. 5:17.) This thought can be of comfort to parents who have watched their children reject their teachings and drift from or rebel against the Church. Gospel seeds once planted can bear fruit even many years later.

17. The principle underlying this situation is put in modern terms by the Nobel laureate economist Paul A. Samuelson, in his famous textbook, *Economics*, 8th ed. (New York: McGraw-Hill, 1970), p. 668: "There is essentially only one argument for free or freer trade, but it is an exceedingly powerful one, namely: *Unhampered trade promotes a mutually profitable international division of labor, greatly enhances the potential real national product of all countries, and makes possible higher standards of living all over the globe.*" (Emphasis in the original.) That the Book of Mormon so well depicts the operation of an economic law that was not generally recognized in Joseph Smith's time—and perhaps is not yet, even today—is a good illustration of its plausibility as authentic historiographical material.

10

GOD'S WAYS OR MAN'S: THE ULTIMATE CHOICE
(Helaman 7–12)

REX C. REEVE, JR.

The struggle between good and evil in the pre-earth life has continued on this earth since the days of Adam. Men and women in each generation have again been faced with the opportunity to choose good over evil. The Lord in his wisdom has provided a plan whereby each individual can be instructed sufficiently. Then all are free to choose according to the desires of their heart, either the path leading to eternal life or the path leading to eternal misery. They are not free, however, to choose the results. They must receive the consequences unalterably decreed of God that are attached to the path of their choice.

In the plan of the Lord, sufficient knowledge is revealed so that both paths, with their consequences, are clearly defined. Men and women are then invited to come unto Christ and partake of the rewards prepared for the righteous. The Book of Mormon is unequaled in all literature in outlining both paths and their consequences and then inviting and leading people to Christ if they desire to follow him. Joseph Smith said, "I told the brethren that the Book of Mormon was the most correct of any book on earth, and the keystone of our religion, and a man would get nearer to God by abiding by its precepts, than by any other book."[1] After someone has read and understood the Book of Mormon, he or she has been in-

---

Rex C. Reeve, Jr., is assistant professor of ancient scripture at Brigham Young University.

structed sufficiently to know good from evil. The final judgment, with reward or punishment, will hinge on the person's choices based on knowledge received from this book. The Book of Mormon is a book of contrasts: Nephi versus Laman, Jacob versus Sherem, Alma versus Korihor. As the Book of Mormon defines these contrasts, it shows clearly the rewards for good and the punishments for evil. The plan and the path leading in both directions with immediate and long-range consequences are clearly defined.

In abridging the records from the large plates of Nephi, Mormon included a classic example of the contrast between good and evil in Helaman 7-12. These chapters paint the picture of the wickedness of the Nephites contrasted with the righteousness of Nephi. On the one hand Mormon was moved to decry forcefully the terrible disobedience of the natural man. (Hel. 12.) On the other hand he included the great blessings and powers the Lord gave to Nephi because of his personal righteousness and his consistent obedience.

In Helaman 7-12 Mormon abridged the record of Nephi, the son of Helaman. The events of this portion of the Book of Mormon took place shortly before the birth of the Savior, between 23 B.C. and 7 B.C. The condition among the Nephites was one of wickedness. Gadianton robbers filled the judgment seats and were using the powers of government to further their purposes. They condemned the righteous because of their righteousness and let the wicked go unpunished because of their money. (Hel. 7:4-5.) This great iniquity was a cause of sorrow to Nephi; he wished that he could have lived in the days of father Lehi and Nephi when they first came out of Jerusalem. Then he could have had joy because of the righteousness of his brethren. Yet he realized that he was called to his own day and was destined to experience sorrow his whole life because of his people. (Hel. 7:6-9.)

The wicked would not soften their hearts even after Nephi's preaching, his miracles, and his prophecies about the murder of the chief judge. The leaders of his people were angry when he spoke plainly about their corruption, their secret works, and their impending destruction. In the hardness of their hearts they even rejected the testimony and doctrine of Christ that had been given by Abraham,

Moses, Zenos, Zenock, Ezias, Isaiah, Jeremiah, Lehi, and Nephi. (Hel. 8-9.)

About 20 B.C contention led to war among all the people of Nephi. The Gadianton robbers carried on their secret works, and it seemed that all the people would be destroyed. (Hel. 11:1-2.) In the second year of the war, Nephi pleaded with the Lord to send a famine to motivate the people to repentance rather than let them all die in war. (Hel. 11:4.)

According to Nephi's words, the Lord sent a famine; there was no rain and hence no yield of crops. The war ceased, but the death of thousands among the Nephites and the Lamanites continued because of the famine. (Hel. 11:4-5.) Faced with total destruction, the people began to remember the Lord and pleaded with Nephi to turn away God's wrath. (Hel. 11:7-8.) Seeing their repentance and their humility, Nephi asked the Lord to send rain and again bless the lands to be productive. Even though famine, pestilence, and death forced their repentance and humility, the Lord answered Nephi's prayers and sent rain. (Hel. 11:10-17.)

For some, the return to the Lord was permanent, and with thankfulness they remained faithful and steadfast. For others — a few at first, but the numbers steadily increased — repentance was short lived, and the memory of the goodness of the Lord was soon forgotten. Among those who dissented from their spiritual commitments, wickedness soon replaced righteousness. The secret plans of Gadianton were again sought out, and within a few years robbing, plundering, and murders returned and the people were again heading for destruction. (Hel. 11:24-37.)

The Unsteadiness of the Natural Man

The burden of abridging the records of this unstable and fickle period of Nephite history prompted Mormon to leave the history and make some general observations about humanity in this fallen state: "And thus we can behold how false, and also the unsteadiness of the hearts of the children of men." (Hel. 12:1.) "False" means being disloyal, unfaithful, or not being what one purports to be. "Unsteady"

109

refers to being changeable, inconsistent, erratic in habits, purpose, or behavior.

Mormon continued by noting: "Yea, we can see that the Lord in his great infinite goodness doth bless and prosper those who put their trust in him." (Hel. 12:1.) This was the original promise of the Lord to every group he brought to the promised land: If they would keep his commandments they would be blessed and prosper. (Ether 2:7-9; 1 Ne. 2:20.) Mormon then wrote: "Yea, and we may see at the very time when he doth prosper his people . . . yea, then is the time that they do harden their hearts, and do forget the Lord their God, and do trample under their feet the Holy One." (Hel. 12:2.) To trample God under their feet means to set aside his counsels and to be disobedient to his commands. (See 1 Ne. 19:7.)

Mormon's next observation is, "And thus we see that except the Lord doth chasten his people with many afflictions, yea, except he doth visit them with death and with terror, and with famine and with all manner of pestilence, they will not remember him." (Hel. 12:3) The experience of Nephi and his people with the famine provided ample evidence of the truth of Mormon's observation. Mormon continued by describing in plain terms the almost universal weaknesses in fallen humanity that are so offensive to the Lord.

Fallen men and women are (Hel. 12:4-6):

1. Foolish
2. Vain
3. Evil and devilish
4. Quick to do iniquity
5. Slow to do good
6. Quick to hearken to the words of the evil one
7. Quick to set their hearts on the vain things of the world
8. Quick to be lifted up in pride
9. Quick to boast
10. Slow to remember the Lord their God
11. Slow to give ear to God's counsels
12. Slow to walk in wisdom's paths
13. Not desirous that the Lord their God, who created them, should rule and reign over them

14. Eager to set aside God's counsel

15. Not desirous that God should be their guide

With the tendencies of fallen people to reject the Lord and not have him be their guide, Mormon declared that they are less than the dust of the earth. At least the dust obeys the voice of God when he commands it to move. At the voice of the Lord the hills and mountains quake and are broken up. By the power of his voice the whole earth shakes and the rocks tremble. In response to a divinely given command the earth actually stops in its rotation, thus lengthening the hours of the day. (Hel. 12:7-15.)[2] The elements gladly obey the voice of the Lord, but people willingly choose to disobey.

People have the freedom to disobey the Lord, but if they do, they must accept the consequences of disobedience. The Lord has the power to curse people or to cut them off from his presence forever because of their sins. Mormon lamented the fate of those who are accursed of the Lord, for they cannot be saved and shall be consigned to a state of endless misery or everlasting damnation. Though Mormon strongly decried the wicked and inconsistent tendencies of humanity, in a spirit of sweetness he reminded us that repentance has been provided that they may be saved. (Hel. 12:20-26.) In his mercy God has provided the opportunity for all to repent and change. (Hel. 12:22.) For those who will do so and obey the voice of the Lord, the fallen tendencies of disobedience and sin may be overcome. Mormon prayed that people would be brought to repentance and bring forth good works so they could receive the blessings of the Lord, because through the law of justice all will be "restored unto grace for grace, according to their works." (Hel. 12:24.)

The Spiritual Consistency of Nephi

In stark contrast to the wickedness and disobedience Mormon had been reporting, he chose to include in his record a few verses about Nephi. At a time when Nephi was "much cast down because of the wickedness of the people . . . a voice came unto him saying: Blessed art thou, Nephi, for those things which thou hast done." (Hel. 10:3-4.) Almost point for point Mormon showed how Nephi exhibited the exact opposite of the fallen tendencies of most others. By faithful obedience Nephi found favor with the Lord and was given power and great blessings.

The Lord's word continued: "For I have beheld how thou hast with unwearyingness declared the word, which I have given unto thee, unto this people." (Hel. 10:4.) The Lord had been watching, was aware of Nephi as an individual, and knew what he had done. How important it was for Nephi to know that his efforts were known and appreciated. Those lonely years when he quietly withstood temptation or when he stood firm against the tide of sin and wickedness among his people were not in vain. An effective tool of Satan in deceiving people is to make them think that they are alone and that no one knows or cares. For those who will listen, the Lord answers Satan's deceit simply by saying "I have beheld." The thing the Lord beheld that pleased him so was Nephi's consistency. The Lord used the word "unwearyingness" at least twice to describe how Nephi had declared the word. This is in contrast to the observation of Mormon about the unsteadiness of the hearts of others. A sign of spiritual maturity is the tendency to be consistent and steadfast in righteousness or in service.

The Lord continued to tell Nephi why he was pleased with him: "And thou hast not feared them, and hast not sought thine own life, but hast sought my will, and to keep my commandments." (Hel. 10:4.) Nephi did not fear those who opposed the will of the Lord; he did not yield to their demands that he join them; and he did not compromise his standards for fear of losing the favor of the world. This kind of spiritual courage, that displaces the fear of men, is another essential element in gaining favor with the Lord.

In contrast to Mormon's words that the natural man does not desire that God should be his guide or rule over him, Nephi was singled out for his willingness to do the will of the Lord, even ahead of his own will and desires. Putting God's will first in one's life is essential to pleasing the Lord. The first principle of the gospel is faith in the Lord Jesus Christ. Faith can be defined as coming to know the true Christ while never having seen him, or coming to know the true Christ well enough (not having seen him) that one desires to do things the Lord's way. The natural result of a successful effort to come to know Christ is the desire to do his will and keep his commandments. (See John 14:15, 23; 1 John 5:3.)

The Lord said to Nephi: "Because thou hast done this with such unwearyingness, behold, I will bless thee forever." (Hel. 10:5.) What does it mean to have the Lord say he will bless someone forever? Could there be a better promise given to anyone? From the Book of Mormon and from other modern revelations we know that eternal life — exaltation in the celestial kingdom — is the blessing the Lord provides forever (in the eternities) for his faithful children. From Mormon's account we learn that Nephi had done two basic things to bring such a treasured reward: First, he had not sought to do his own will, but rather the will of God. (Hel. 10:4.) Nephi brought his own will and desires into complete harmony with those of the Lord. Second, Nephi had unwearyingly labored to deliver the word of the Lord to the people. He had proven that he could be trusted to always fill his assignment, and he demonstrated a consistent concern for the welfare of his people.

In addition to the blessings of the eternities, Nephi was promised blessings and power in this life: "And I will make thee mighty in word and in deed, in faith and in works; yea, even that all things shall be done unto thee according to thy word, for thou shalt not ask that which is contrary to my will. . . . Ye shall have power over this people, and shall smite the earth with famine, and with pestilence." (Hel. 10:5-6.) Nephi was given power to have anything he desired: he could control the elements, he could have power over the people, and no one could stand against him. By diligent obedience he had gained the confidence of the Lord. God knew that Nephi could be trusted with this power and that he would not ask for anything contrary to the will of heaven.

The Lord continued by saying, "I give unto you power, that whatsoever ye shall seal on earth shall be sealed in heaven; and whatsoever ye shall loose on earth shall be loosed in heaven." (Hel. 10:7; cf. Matt. 16:16-19.) In addition to his other powers and blessings, Nephi was given power to perform acts in this life that would be valid and binding after death and recognized in heaven. For those of his people who would listen and respond, Nephi had the power to seal upon them the blessings of an eternal family and eternal increase.

Nephi continued to prove faithful to the trust and confidence of the Lord. He was instructed to declare to the people that the Lord God, who is almighty, was displeased with them and would destroy them if they did not repent. (Hel. 10:11.) The next verse recorded by Mormon seems to sum up the attitude and commitment of Nephi that was so appreciated by God. "When the Lord had spoken these words unto Nephi, he did stop and did not go unto his own house, but did return unto the multitudes who were scattered about upon the face of the land, and began to declare unto them the word of the Lord." (Hel. 10:12.) Even when faced with the difficult task of bringing his people to repentance, Nephi obeyed immediately. He demonstrated what it really means to have an eye single to the glory of God, to have one's own will swallowed up in the will of the Lord. It would have been natural to want to return to the comfort and security of his own home and family, but on this occasion Nephi did not return to his house until after he had accomplished with exactness the desires of the Lord.

Conclusion

Fallen humanity is an enemy to God. The natural man is quick to do wrong, and slow and unsteady in his obedience to the will of the Lord. The Lord, in order to reclaim his disobedient children, must chasten them with afflictions, suffering, and even natural disasters.

Each person is faced with the choice between good and evil as part of the plan of life. The Book of Mormon outlines the choices available and clearly defines the consequences. In these chapters Mormon gave examples of both extremes. The Nephite people were wicked, and only war, famine, and death could command their attention long enough to bring them to even a temporary state of repentance. Because of their choice to pursue their own desires and follow the wickedness of the world, they were in danger of being cursed forever. In contrast, Mormon included the account of Nephi, which shows that faithfulness is possible even when the majority of the people choose to disobey the Lord.

What Nephi did to gain such great favor and blessings from the Lord could be repeated by anyone in any generation. No insurmountable task is required to please the Lord; steady obedience brings the approval and blessings of heaven. The obedience and blessings of Nephi follow a pattern that is consistent throughout the Book of Mormon and that all true disciples of Christ must follow to gain the same blessings. Nephi, when faced with the choice between convenience and inconvenience, between good and evil, sought for and obtained the things of God. He rejected the allurements of his world and increased his effort to build his faith and be constant in his obedience to the Lord. He sought the welfare of his people and subjected his own desires to those of God.

Nephi was given the assurance that his efforts were pleasing to God and was thus given the right to use the Lord's power for the benefit of his people. He was given the sealing power of the priesthood, the power to bind and loose on earth and in heaven. Finally, he was given the assurance that his consistent obedience had prepared him for the blessings of the Lord throughout the eternities. He had successfully met the challenges of mortality and received the assurance that his salvation was secure. His soul was at rest. And his example is before us.

NOTES

1. Joseph Smith, *History of The Church of Jesus Christ of Latter-day Saints*, 2nd ed. rev., edited by B. H. Roberts (Salt Lake City: The Church of Jesus Christ of Latter-day Saints, 1932-51), 4:461.

2. Mormon explained that it is the earth that revolves around the sun, and not vice versa. (Hel. 12:14-15.)

11

SAMUEL THE LAMANITE
(Helaman 13–16)

MAE BLANCH

As the time of the Savior's birth approached, the Nephite people became increasingly wicked. Following a brief period of repentance after the Lord chastised the people with a famine, they rapidly fell back into their sinful ways. Mormon recorded, "In the eighty and second year they began again to forget the Lord their God. And in the eighty and third year they began to wax strong in iniquity. And in the eighty and fourth year they did not mend their ways. And it came to pass in the eighty and fifth year they did wax stronger and stronger in their pride, and in their wickedness; and thus they were ripening again for destruction." (Hel. 11:36-37.) But the Lord never destroys a people without giving them every chance to return to him. As he had done many times before, he sent a prophet to plead for their repentance and to warn them of the inevitable consequences if they refused to hear his message.

We know little about Samuel except that he was a Lamanite, that he came to Zarahemla to preach the word of God, that he was rejected and cast out by the people and was returning to his own country when he received revelation from the Lord that he should go back to the city and "prophesy unto the people whatsoever things should come into his heart." (Hel. 13:3.) Perhaps the fact that he was a Lamanite—from a people estranged from the Lord and the Nephites until some of them had been converted—would make his message from the Lord more impressive. But such was not the case. When he

---

Mae Blanch is professor of English literature at Brigham Young University.

returned to the city, the wicked Nephites would not let him enter, and he was forced to mount the wall surrounding Zarahemla to tell them what the Lord would have them know. Through Samuel's voice the Lord warned the Nephites of what would befall them unless they repented. Samuel recounted the ways in which they had offended the Lord, warned them of the immediate and long-range consequences of their sins, prophesied of the birth and death of the Lord Jesus whose mission made repentance possible, gave them an account of the faithful Lamanites as an example of true repentance, and made clear the choice the Lord was giving them. The account of Samuel closes with a brief description of the reaction of the people who heard him.

The Sins of the Nephites

The great sin of the people in Zarahemla was that they substituted love of riches for love of God. Samuel told them that they were "cursed because of [their] riches" and that the wealth itself was cursed because they had not heard and obeyed the commandments of God, who gave them the riches. Their materialism was summed up by Samuel: "Ye do not remember the Lord your God in the things with which he hath blessed you, but ye do always remember your riches." (Hel. 13:21-22.) And their materialism brought the usual train of sins: pride, boasting, ostentatious life-style ("great swelling"), envy, strife, malice, persecution, murder, and "all manner of iniquities." If we read current news accounts of crimes committed for the sake of riches, we recognize that, as Ecclesiastes says, there is nothing new under the sun. (Eccl. 1:9-10.)

With such sins on their conscience, the Nephites further offended God by rejecting his prophets. They not only cast them out of their cities, but they also mocked and stoned them, even killing them and doing "all manner of iniquity unto them, even as they did of old." (Hel. 13:24.) But they deceived themselves with the boast that had they lived in earlier days they would not have slain the prophets or cast them out. They maintained that their present action was justified since the prophets like Samuel whom they rejected were false prophets. Samuel pointed out their hypocrisy when he described those they accepted: "Behold, if a man shall come among you and shall say: Do this, and there is no iniquity; do that and ye shall not suffer; yea, he will say: Walk after the pride of your own hearts; yea, walk after the pride of your eyes, and do whatsoever your heart desireth — and if a man shall come among you and say this, ye will receive him, and say that he is a prophet." (Hel. 13:27.) The Nephites then were not willing to take the first step of repentance: to acknowledge their sins. Instead they quieted conscience with the soothing and false counsel of "foolish and blind guides." (Hel. 13:29.)

The Consequences of Unrepented Sin

As Samuel stood on the wall of the city, the Lord "put into his heart" many prophetic warnings of what would befall the wicked who failed to repent. The prophecies deal with immediate consequences and the long-range destruction that would wipe the Nephites from the earth. The first consequence of their sins, which evidently had taken place already, was the withdrawal of the Lord's Spirit. Since the people were unwilling to listen to Samuel, they gave evidence that they had already lost the Spirit of the Lord. Now the Lord warned them that he would "suffer them no longer." (Hel. 13:8.) Nevertheless, immediately after the warning that he would "visit them in [his] fierce anger," the Lord promised mercy to those who would repent. (Hel. 13:10-11.) That there were some righteous individuals in the city was the only thing that saved it from immediate destruction. But when the time came that they would cast out the faithful, the city would be destroyed. The curse placed on the land was an ironically appropriate punishment for the sins of the people. Since they worshipped riches rather than God, the Lord cursed the land so that "whoso shall hide up treasures in the earth shall find them again no more ... save he be a righteous man and shall hide it up unto the Lord." (Hel. 13:18.) The evil was not in the riches, but in the hearts of those who loved them more than they loved God. Therefore, they would lose the thing they had set their hearts on. Allied to this loss would be the loss of wealth and goods, which would become "slippery"; nothing could be kept safe. "Behold, we lay a tool here and on the morrow it is gone; and behold, our swords are taken from us in the day we have sought them for battle." (Hel. 13:34.) It is not surprising that in a society where wealth is more important than God, stealing should be raised to a fine art. Theft, fraud, deception, loss of treasure buried to keep it safe would bring the people to poverty—the loss of their false god.

It is interesting to note that the first warning from Samuel concerned the "heavy destruction" that would come upon the people when 400 years should pass. We know from the account in 3 Nephi that the wicked then alive would be entirely destroyed at the coming of the Savior, just a few short years away. But Samuel's warning seems to refer to the final battles of the Nephites, when they were destroyed by the Lamanites. We know that the Nephite people had been greatly blessed by the Lord throughout their history, that they had witnessed many miracles and had been taught the true gospel by many great prophets. Yet despite this evidence of God's love, they would fall into evil ways and bring destruction on themselves. Samuel must have seen that this pattern would be repeated until they would finally destroy their whole civilization.

Samuel Prophesies of Christ

Perhaps to give hope to those who may have been turned toward repentance, Samuel prophesied of the coming of the Savior in specific detail. He set an exact time: five years would pass and "then cometh the Son of God to redeem all those who shall believe on his name." (Hel. 14:2.) He told the people that there would be two days with no darkness, although they should see the rising and setting of the sun, but "the night shall not be darkened" on the night before the Savior would be born. There would also be a new star and other "signs and wonders in heaven." (Hel. 14:3-6.) How appropriate that the signs accompanying the birth of the "light of the world" should be wonders appearing in the light of heaven. The fulfillment of Samuel's prophecies is recorded in the first chapter of 3 Nephi. Samuel also told the Nephites the meaning of Christ's birth. "And it shall come to pass that whosoever shall believe on the Son of God, the same shall have everlasting life." (Hel. 14:8.)

Samuel spoke of the Savior's death, its meaning for mankind, and the signs that would accompany it. He taught that Christ "surely must die that salvation may come." (Hel. 14:15.) His death would be necessary to bring about the resurrection—overcoming physical death—which would bring man back into the presence of God. It would overcome the first spiritual death when Adam and Eve were cast out of God's presence for disobedience. Finally, "it bringeth to pass the condition of repentance, that whosoever repenteth" shall not be cast out of the presence of God a second time, thus suffering a second spiritual death, "cut off again as to things pertaining to righteousness." (Hel. 14:18.) Mortals will now have a choice: "He hath given unto you that ye might know good from evil, and he hath given unto you that ye might choose life or death; and ye can do good and be restored unto that which is good, or have that which is good restored unto you; or ye can do evil, and have that which is evil restored unto you." (Hel. 14:31.)[1] Thus the death of the Savior makes repentance and the resulting forgiveness possible; without Christ's sacrifice we would not have that choice.

Despite the necessity of Christ's death, Samuel warned the Nephites that it would be accompanied by terrifying signs. As light was the sign of his birth, so darkness would be the sign of his death: "In that day that he shall suffer death the sun shall be darkened and refuse to give his light unto you; and also the moon and the stars; and there shall be no light upon the face of this land, even from the time that he shall suffer death, for the space of three days, to the time that he shall rise again from the dead." (Hel. 14:20.) Light would be extinguished from the earth and the whole world of nature would be in turmoil. There would be tempests with thunder and lightnings, earthquakes so severe that mountains would become valleys and valleys mountains; many cities and highways would be destroyed. All of these violent signs would be given, said Samuel, "to the intent that there should be no cause for unbelief among the children of men." (Hel. 14:28.) The fulfillment of these prophecies about the death of Christ is found in 3 Nephi 8. If the people of Zarahemla had only accepted Christ and looked forward to his coming, they could have avoided the destruction of which Samuel had been sent to warn them.

The Lamanite Example of True Repentance

Perhaps in an effort to shame the Nephites into repenting, Samuel reminded them that "they have been a chosen people of the Lord; yea, the people of Nephi hath he loved, and also hath he chastened them; yea, in the days of their iniquities hath he chastened them because he loveth them." On the other hand, the Lamanites had been rejected for the evil committed "because of the iniquity of the tradition of their fathers." (Hel. 15:3-4.) But once they had been converted by righteous Nephites, they had proved more faithful than the Nephites. The example of the Lamanites follows the steps of repentance outlined by President Spencer W. Kimball:

1. Sorrow for sin.
2. Abandonment of sin.
3. Confession of sin.
4. Restitution for sin.
5. Doing the will of the Lord.[2]

Once converted, the Lamanites experienced such sorrow for their killing of the Nephites that their hearts were changed. They gave a clear sign of abandoning their sin by burying their weapons of war. Their fear that they might again be tempted to slay another human being is indicated by their willingness to "be trodden down and slain by their enemies" rather than "lift their swords against them, and this because of their faith in Christ." (Hel. 15:9.) Such action clearly confesses that their former action against those they considered enemies was sinful. They could not restore the lives they had taken, but they would give their own lives rather than commit further sin. Samuel further testified that the Lamanites were now doing the will of God: "The more part of them are in the path of their duty, and they do walk circumspectly before God, and they do observe to keep his commandments and his statutes and his judgments according to the law of Moses." (Hel. 15:5.) Not only did they follow the will of God in their daily lives, but they also sought "with unwearied diligence" and much success to convert the rest of the Lamanites. Samuel said, "There are many who do add to their numbers daily." (Hel. 15:6.) The prophet could rightfully point to the Lamanites as an example of true repentance for the Nephites, since they believed in "the holy scriptures, yea, the prophecies of the holy prophets, which are written, which leadeth them to faith on the Lord, and unto repentance, which faith and repentance bringeth a change of heart unto them." (Hel. 15:7.) Their contrast to the Nephites is reflected in Samuel's prophecy on their eventual fate. Unlike the Nephites, they would not be destroyed, but their days would be prolonged. They would suffer "afflictions," they would be "driven to and fro upon the face of the earth, and be hunted, and . . . smitten and scattered abroad, having no place for refuge," yet the Lord would show them mercy. (Hel. 15:12.) Yet their descendants would "be brought to the true knowledge . . . of their Redeemer, and . . . be numbered among his sheep." (Hel. 15:13.) Through Samuel, the Lord offered the same opportunity to the Nephites; if they would repent as the Lamanites had done, they too would be saved.

The Result of Samuel's Message

The great power of Samuel's sermon brought some of the Nephites to repentance. They sought out Nephi to confess their sins and be baptized. But most of the crowd attacked Samuel, throwing stones or shooting arrows at him in their anger at the truth. When Samuel was protected from their missiles by the Spirit of the Lord, many more of the Nephites recognized him as a prophet, believed his words, and also went to be baptized by Nephi. Nephi was likewise prophesying of the same things Samuel had foreseen, and thus those who believed Samuel were once again part of the Lord's people.

But the greater part of those who heard Samuel rejected his warning, rationalizing that the power that protected him from their attack was of the devil. When they called on their captains to seize him, Samuel "did cast himself down from the wall, and did flee out of their lands, yea, even unto his own country, and began to preach and to prophesy among his own people." (Hel. 16:7.) Samuel had followed the Lord's instructions, and some souls had been saved. The rest had assured their own destruction by rejecting God, who had lovingly sent Samuel in a last effort to reclaim them.

Their way of dealing with Samuel's prophecies when they began to be fulfilled is characteristic of those who have ears but will not hear. They "began to depend upon their own strength and upon their own wisdom, saying: Some things they may have guessed right, among so many; but behold, we know that all these great and marvelous works cannot come to pass." (Hel. 16:15-16.) They reasoned themselves into total disbelief, saying that if Christ should come, and if he were the Son of God, he would surely show himself to them as well as to those in Jerusalem, never realizing that had they believed, they would indeed have been privileged to see the Savior, that he would indeed visit his followers in their land.

To explain the courage and persistence of Samuel in bringing God's plea to their hostile ears, they "imagine[d] up in their hearts" a plot conceived by Samuel to keep them in ignorance by trying to convince them of "a wicked tradition," handed down by their fathers, of a "great and marvelous thing" which would happen in a distant land. They could have no firsthand knowledge of such a miracle, but those who maintained that it was so, did so to keep them in ignorance. Since the wicked Nephites would have to depend on the believers to teach them, they would be kept as servants to Samuel and those who taught what he taught. The lack of reason in such an explanation evidently did not trouble them, "for Satan did stir them up to do iniquity continually; yea, he did go about spreading rumors and contentions upon all the face of the land, that he might harden the hearts of the people against that which was good and against that which should come." (Hel. 16:22.)

Speaking the Word of the Lord

With our knowledge of the fulfillment of Samuel's prophecies, we might wonder how the people of Zarahemla could have been so blind to the truth. But Samuel's experience might be considered a typical one for the Lord's prophets. Elder Richard L. Evans once spoke of the general public reaction to the words of a prophet of God:

> We find ourselves often quoting the words of the prophets, and, lest there be some doubt as to what a prophet is, we submit that it is one who, under the appointment and inspiration of the Lord God, speaks truth as the spirit moves him,

regardless of what the world is thinking and regardless of what men would like to hear.

And, therefore, a prophet is seldom popular, and the cost of being a prophet is always great, for he may be called upon to say those things which are not pleasing, . . . and he may find himself fighting against a tide of mass-misconception, and, as history records, be stoned, crucified, banished, ridiculed, shunned, or rejected. For the truth is not pleasing unto all men, and time has proved that majorities are not always right. . . .

It is not important that a prophet should say those things with which you and I are in full accord. But it is important that you and I should bring ourselves into full accord with those things which a prophet speaks by virtue of his office and calling.[3]

Samuel fits this description. He spoke the word of the Lord to a people, the majority of whom were unwilling to hear him. But their unwillingness did not change the truth of his words or the fate that would fall upon them because they rejected him. The book of Helaman ends with his account, just one year before the birth of the Savior, which would mark the beginning of the fulfillment of all his prophecies.

NOTES

1. The principle of choice in salvation has been emphasized by many prophets. Moses so taught the children of Israel when they were wandering in the wilderness. (See Deuteronomy 30:15-20.) Lehi in his last sermon to his sons before his death made the same declaration. (See 2 Nephi 2:26-29.)

2. Spencer W. Kimball, "Be Ye Clean," *Brigham Young University Speeches of the Year* (Provo, 4 May 1954), pp. 8-9.

3. Richard L. Evans, *Improvement Era*, November 1939, p. 672.

12

A JUST AND A TRUE RECORD
(3 Nephi 1–5)

TERRENCE L. SZINK

Chapters one through five of 3 Nephi, covering twenty-five years of Nephite history, are primarily historical narrative, written by Mormon using the records he had at his disposal. Perhaps the most significant event in these chapters is the manifestation of the signs accompanying the birth of Christ, which Samuel the Lamanite had prophesied. In addition, there is a repetition of the cyclical pattern of righteousness-prosperity-pride-fall-repentance-righteousness, which seems to be a major theme of the Book of Mormon. In this cycle the Gadianton robbers play a major role, threatening the very existence of Nephite society. Finally, Mormon wrote directly to latter-day readers about his work as the compiler of the Book of Mormon and testified of that work.

The Fate of Nephi, the Son of Helaman

Third Nephi begins with an interesting statement about Nephi the son of Helaman. Mormon wrote that he "departed out of the land, and whither he went, no man knoweth" (3 Ne. 1:3) and that he "did not return to the land of Zarahemla, and could nowhere be found in all the land" (3 Ne. 2:9). This is reminiscent of a similar passage about Nephi's great-grandfather Alma the younger: "He departed out of the land of Zarahemla . . . and it came to pass that he was never heard of

---

Terrence L. Szink is a doctoral student in ancient Near Eastern studies at the University of California at Los Angeles.

more; as to his death or burial we know not of." (Alma 45:18.)[1] In Alma's day the church members speculated that he might have been "taken up" by the Lord as was Moses. Although there is no similar declaration in the Book of Mormon about Nephi the son of Helaman, he was certainly a candidate for translation considering the type of life he led and the power of God with which he was endowed.[2] Whatever his fate, he entrusted the records and the responsibilities that accompanied them to his son and namesake.

The First Christmas in the New World

In the Old World the events surrounding the birth of Christ were taking place. These would be recorded by the writers of the Gospels and come to be known as the Christmas story. This story has become, along with the accounts of Christ's death and resurrection, one of the best-known episodes in his life. No less dramatic were the happenings on the American continents.[3]

Several years had passed since Samuel the Lamanite had stood upon the walls of Zarahemla and foretold what would happen as the birth of the Savior drew near. Ironically, while the prophecies were "fulfilled more fully" the people began to doubt them even more. (3 Ne. 1:4-6.) Finally, in a way reminiscent of evil Haman's actions in the book of Esther, the wicked set a day for the death of the believers if the sign accompanying the birth of Jesus (a day, a night, and a day that should appear as one day) were not fulfilled. Nephi, sorrowed by the wickedness of the people, went before the Lord in behalf of his band of believers. We are told he prayed all day. As the evening approached, he heard the voice of the Lord: "Lift up your head and be of good cheer; for behold, the time is at hand, and on this night shall the sign be given, and on the morrow come I into the world, to show unto the world that I will fulfill all that which I have caused to be spoken by the mouth of my holy prophets." (3 Ne. 1:13.)

The mood here is similar to that of the angelic proclamation of "good tidings of great joy" to the shepherds in Judea, and rightly so, for those Nephites who had believed in the words of the prophets would be spared. That night the sign was given, and there was astonishment throughout all the land. The unbelievers saw that their plan to destroy the people of God had failed; now realizing that all which the prophets had said was true and seeing their own murderous nature, they began to fear. When the sun rose in the morning, Satan began trying to deceive the people, but so overwhelming was the power of this sign that for the time being "the more part of the people did believe, and were converted unto the Lord." (3 Ne. 1:22.) Though the conversion may have been genuine at that time, it did not last long. The passing of only three years found most of the people "hard in their hearts, and blind in their minds, and [they] began to disbelieve all which they had heard and seen." (3 Ne. 2:1.)

This slide toward general apostasy had been seen in a small group who believed that since Christ had been born it was no longer necessary to obey the law of Moses. They were most likely a sincere group of believers who had simply misunderstood the scriptures, for they "soon became converted, and were convinced of the error which they were in . . . and did confess their faults." (3 Ne. 1:25.) The law of Moses was indeed fulfilled in Christ, but not until after his death and resurrection.[4] When the resurrected Christ later appeared to the Nephites, he told them: "One jot nor one tittle hath not passed away from the law, but in me it hath all been fulfilled." (3 Ne. 12:18.) The old law would be fulfilled only when the higher law of the gospel was given in its place. (3 Ne. 12:19.)

During the first two years after the manifestation of the sign, many Nephites and Lamanites dissented and went into the wilderness to join the Gadianton robbers. These robbers hid in the mountains in caves and secret places; they were responsible for much violence among the Nephites.

The number of people who disbelieved the signs and the coming of Christ increased to such an extent that dissenters seemingly no longer felt the need to flee to the Gadianton robbers but remained with the Nephites and Lamanites. On the surface it is difficult to see how the people could fall so quickly after being converted.[5] As mentioned above, this conversion was the result of an outward sign and required no work on the part of the people. They had seen the sign but, for the most part, they did not sustain their faith. Thus Satan was able to blind their minds and harden their hearts until they "began to wax strong in wickedness and abominations." (3 Ne. 2:3.) It should also be recalled that before the sign of the night without darkness they had doubted the other signs even as they had begun to multiply. It is ironic, however, that although they did not believe the sign, "the Nephites began to reckon their time from this period when the sign was given, or from the coming of Christ." (3 Ne. 2:8.) They had previously marked time from when Lehi and his family had left Jerusalem and later from the start of the reign of the judges.[6] This is perhaps analogous to the situation in the western world where time is also calculated from the birth of Christ and yet a great number of people do not believe in Jesus as the Son of God.

The Gadianton Threat

No doubt strengthened by the number of dissenters that had joined them and encouraged by the weakening of society that usually attends any apostasy, the Gadianton robbers grew ever bolder.[7] They now began attacking entire cities successfully. To defend themselves against this threat, the converted Lamanites joined with the Nephites and were "numbered among" them. (3 Ne. 2:15-16.) This new combined army was able to achieve some success over the robbers, but this was short lived because of the general wickedness of the Nephites—for where there is corruption there is also weakness. The Lord's promise to Nephi about his descendants seems to apply in this case: "If it so be that they [the Nephites] rebel against me, they [the Lamanites, or in this case the Gadianton robbers] shall be a scourge unto thy seed, to stir them up in the ways of remembrance." (1 Ne. 2:24.)

The Nephite society was on the brink of annihilation, or as Mormon put it, "the sword of destruction did hang over them." (3 Ne. 2:19.)

At this point in the record, Mormon inserted a most unusual document—a letter written by Giddianhi, the leader of the Gadianton robbers, to Lachoneus, the governor of the Nephites. This text is interesting because it is one of the few places in the Book of Mormon that provides a glimpse of the so-called "traditions of the fathers" that characterized the groups that opposed the Nephite nation. Another example of the presentation of the alternative tradition is the letter of Ammoron, a Lamanite king, to captain Moroni, written forty-seven years earlier and recorded in Alma 54. A comparison between the two is informative. In both letters there is a request for the surrender of the Nephites (Alma 54:18; 3 Ne. 3:6-7), although in the case of Giddianhi, it is more an invitation to Lachoneus to turn the people over to him and join with him in oppressing them. Both opponents claim that they have been wronged and that they have been unjustly deprived of their "rights of government." (Alma 54:17-18; 3 Ne. 3:10.) Both letters contain a rejection of God (Alma 54:21-22; 3 Ne. 3:2); and finally, both threaten destruction (Alma 54:20; 3 Ne. 3:3-4).

The differences in the letters demonstrate that in the case of the Gadianton robbers, the Nephites were confronted with an enemy much more sophisticated and dangerous than any previous. Giddi-anhi's letter mentions oaths and describes his organization as a "secret society" whose works are of "ancient date." (3 Ne. 3:9.) Ancient indeed! Mormon explained that although the Gadianton robbers did not obtain their secret oaths from the twenty-four gold plates of the Jaredites, which had been discovered by an expedition sent by Limhi, they were the same oaths that secret societies have used since the foundation of the earth, for "they were put into the heart of Gadianton by that same being who did entice our first parents to partake of the forbidden fruit." (Hel. 6:26.) The oaths and plans that served as the foundation for this society were hidden up whenever the group was in danger of extinction due to the righteousness of the Nephite nation. (Hel. 11:25.) When the wickedness again allowed the robbers to operate effectively, the old plans and oaths were sought out and the Gadianton robbers returned. (Hel. 11:26.) The oaths were the glue that held the evil society together, the penalty for betrayal being death. This generated a devotion to corruption not found among any previous enemy of the Nephites. An example of this commitment is the fact that even after they were defeated by the Nephites and given a chance at freedom if they would promise to cease murdering, there were some who remained loyal to the Gadianton cause. (3 Ne. 5:5.)

Another difference in the letters is the sophisticated tone of Giddianhi's message. He continually complimented Lachoneus, referring to him as "most noble," praised his "firmness" and his "noble spirit in the field of battle." He claimed to be motivated by a feeling for the welfare of the Nephite leader. All this was intended to entice Lachoneus into selling his people out and joining with the robbers, and it is in striking contrast to the direct boldness of Ammoron's letter. Giddianhi was a "smooth operator," a man who, although apparently well educated, was entirely without conscience and not to be trusted under any circumstance.

A final difference is in the titles of the two leaders. Ammoron was the "king" of the Lamanites, while Giddianhi was the "governor of the secret society of Gadianton." We can in no way be sure that the term "governor" designated in this case an elected official of a democratic society. Yet it does serve to remind us that the Gadianton robbers began as a quasi-political organization (Hel. 2:1-5), and in the mind of its leader still was one. He claimed he was merely trying to recoup the rights of his people.

After examining Giddianhi's letter, it is clear why the Gadianton organization was so dangerous and, in fact, according to Mormon, ultimately "did prove the overthrow, yea, almost the entire destruction of the people of Nephi." (Hel. 2:13.) They were a sophisticated and murderous group who were after both political and economic power.[8] It is not difficult to see parallels to the Gadianton robbers in our day. Perhaps the most obvious examples are the rich and powerful drug trafficking organizations that threaten to destroy our society. They use many of the same tactics and have the same goals as the Gadianton robbers.[9]

As captain Moroni had done before him, Lachoneus showed true courage in his response to Giddianhi's letter. Realizing that his people were in grave danger, he sent a proclamation to all the people and told them to build strong fortifications and gather themselves together with all their animals and provisions. Furthermore, he understood that military preparations were not enough, warning his people: "As the Lord liveth, except ye repent of all your iniquities, and cry unto the Lord, ye will in nowise be delivered out of the hands of those Gadianton robbers." (3 Ne. 3:15.)

As part of the preparations, a "great prophet" who "had the spirit of revelation" named Gidgiddoni was appointed chief captain over the Nephite armies. (3 Ne. 3:19.)[10] Although the people had faith in Gidgiddoni as a prophet, they misunderstood his role in leading them. They assumed he could lead them in a successful offensive battle against the Gadianton robbers; however, he explained that the Lord would not help them launch a first-strike attack against their enemies but would only help them defend themselves.[11]

By the end of the seventeenth year (from the time of the sign of the birth of Christ), the defensive preparations were near completion. Not only had the people gathered themselves together, but perhaps more importantly "they did repent of all their sins; and they did put up their prayers unto the Lord their God, that he would deliver them in the time that their enemies should come down against them to battle." (3 Ne. 3:25.)

Almost a year passed before the armies of robbers descended from the mountains to attack the Nephites and dispossess them of their lands and property. They must have been greatly surprised to find that the Nephites had assembled in a strong defensive position and that the land had been stripped of everything. The weakness of the Gadianton robbers was now exposed: "There was no way that they could subsist save it were to plunder and rob and murder." (3 Ne. 4:5.) They were literally a parasite whose host was no longer providing food.

Giddianhi decided to attack the Nephites despite their great numbers and strong position. The description Mormon gave of the robbers as they approached is unusually detailed and graphic: "They were girded about after the manner of robbers; and they had a lamb-skin about their loins, and they were dyed in blood, and their heads were shorn, and they had headplates upon them; and great and terrible was the appearance of the armies of Giddianhi, because of their armor, and because of their being dyed in blood." (3 Ne. 4:7.)

As this army of robbers advanced, the Nephites fell to the earth in prayer, which caused the robbers to assume incorrectly that they had fallen because of fear. What followed was a horrific battle in which more life was lost than at any time since Lehi had left Jerusalem. (3 Ne. 4:11.) The robbers were beaten and Giddianhi was killed.

At least two and a half years passed before the robbers, led by a man named Zemnarihah, appeared again. This time instead of a direct attack, they tried to lay siege, but the Nephites had stored enough food to last seven years (3 Ne. 4:4) while the robbers had to rely on game hunted in the wilderness. Soon the robbers were "about to perish with hunger" and were losing large numbers of men to the Nephites who were "continually marching out by day and by night, and falling upon their armies." (3 Ne. 4:20-21.)

Zemnarihah saw that continuing the siege was useless and decided to withdraw and take his people north. Gidgiddoni knew of the robber's plan and did not want them to escape, perhaps fearing that they would only wait until they had regained strength and return. He also knew of their weakness because of lack of food and sent his troops out at night to cut off all ways of retreat and surround the robbers. Seeing their predicament, many of the robbers surrendered; those who did not were killed by the Nephites. The fate of the leader Zemnarihah is interesting: "Their leader, Zemnarihah, was taken and hanged upon a tree, yea, even upon the top thereof until he was dead. And when they had hanged him until he was dead they did fell the tree to the earth, and did cry with a loud voice, saying: May the Lord preserve his people in righteousness and in holiness of heart, that they may cause to be felled to the earth all who shall seek to slay them because of power and secret combinations, even as this man hath been felled to the earth." (3 Ne. 4:28-29.)

This ritual is similar in underlying thought to Egyptian oaths called execration texts. In such texts, the Egyptians of the Middle Kingdom ritually cursed their enemies by writing their names on bowls or figures of clay and then smashing them. As they broke the bowls or figures they believed they were destroying the power of those whose names were inscribed thereon. The following is an example of a text written on such a bowl: "All men, all people, all folk, all males, all eunuchs, all women, and all officials, who may rebel, who may plot, who may fight, who may talk of fighting, or who may talk of rebelling, and every rebel who talks of rebelling—in this entire land."[12]

Note that there is a subtle difference in the two rituals—the Egyptians directly cursed the enemy, while in the Book of Mormon the people asked that they might be strengthened through their righteousness in order that they may destroy the enemy.

The victory over the Gadianton robbers was celebrated joyously. The people praised God for their deliverance, for they realized that he had been the one who had saved them: "'Their hearts were swollen with joy, unto the gushing out of many tears, because of the great goodness of God in delivering them out of the hands of their enemies; and they knew it was because of their repentance and their humility that they had been delivered from an everlasting destruction." (3 Ne. 4:33.)

This passage contains the principle Lachoneus was trying to teach his people and the message Mormon wanted to convey to us when he wrote this section of the Book of Mormon: The only way to combat the kind of wickedness the Gadianton robbers represented is with the strength obtained through personal and collective righteousness. To overcome the evil power of secret oaths we must make sacred covenants with God and abide by them. For example, above I mentioned my belief that traffickers in illegal drugs represent a modern-day example of the Gadianton robbers. The *demand* for these drugs must be cut off just as the Nephites cut off the food supply of the army of the robbers. This can be done through obedience to the word of God.

The triumph over the robbers was complete; not one escaped. All who were not killed were cast into prison, where the word of God was taught to them. Some converted and covenanted to cease murdering; however, as noted above, some chose to remain loyal to the Gadianton philosophy. These were punished according to the law.

Significantly, Mormon wrote that at this time "there was not a living soul among all the people of the Nephites who did doubt in the least the words of all the holy prophets who had spoken; for they knew that it must needs be that they must be fulfilled." (3 Ne. 5:1.)

This statement implied that any dissenters subsequent to this period would be in willful rebellion against God. The people of the

Nephite nation remained together for another three years after the victory over the Gadianton robbers. Apparently they lived off the provisions they had stored.[13] This small period of time must have been a golden era, for the people had forsaken their sins and "did serve God with all diligence day and night." (3 Ne. 5:3.)

Mormon and His Book

At this point Mormon interrupted the narrative and inserted an explanation about the sources he was working with and a testimony of his work. These few verses are fascinating because in them Mormon stepped back from his role as editor and discussed that role with the reader. Evidently the three years following the defeat of the Gadianton robbers was a period of great literary activity. With no wars to fight and a large supply of food, the people had time to write about the experiences through which they had just passed. Perhaps these experiences, which Mormon described as "great and marvelous" (3 Ne. 5:8), included the "many signs which had been given" (3 Ne. 5:2) both preceding the birth of Christ (3 Ne. 1:4) and since that time. At any rate, Mormon wrote that his book does not contain "even a hundredth part" of all that happened. He did indicate that "there are records which do contain all the proceedings of this people." (3 Ne. 5:8-9.) He also mentioned a "shorter but true account" written by Nephi. Mormon was here referring to Nephi the son of Nephi, since at this point his remarks seem to be confined to the twenty-five years following the manifestation of the sign of the birth of Christ. This "shorter but true account" given by Nephi the son of Nephi was recorded on the large plates of Nephi and served as the basis for the Book of Mormon's version of what happened during the twenty-five years. (3 Ne. 5:9-11.)

The discussion about his sources led Mormon to testify about his record; this testimony can be best understood when compared to Nephi's statement at the beginning of the small plates. The two have many points in common: the writer or editor (a) declared that he made the plates with his own hand (1 Ne. 1:3; 3 Ne. 5:11), (b) gave a short autobiographical statement (1 Ne. 1:1; 3 Ne. 5:12-13), (c) briefly stated the source of his information—Nephi wrote "I make it according to my knowledge" (1 Ne. 1:3), while Mormon wrote: "Therefore I do make my record from the accounts which have been given by those who were before me, until the commencement of my day; and then I do make a record of the things which I have seen with mine own eyes" (3 Ne. 5:16-17), (d) testified of his record—Nephi wrote, "I know that the record which I make is true" (1 Ne. 1:3); Mormon testified in almost the same language "I know the record which I make to be a just and a true record" (3 Ne. 5:18), and (e) mentioned his language (1 Ne. 1:2; 3 Ne. 5:18).[14] So many similarities cannot be attributed to mere chance; I believe that these two prophets employed what was a specific Nephite formula for giving testimony. It is difficult to say whether the formula was a literary device or had formed part of the Nephite legal system.

It is interesting that this was the first time in the Book of Mormon, as Mormon compiled it, that he identified himself by name, for though his name appears in the Words of Mormon, that book was written on the small plates of Nephi.[15] One might have expected Mormon to introduce himself and testify at the beginning of the record, as did Nephi in the small plates of Nephi; perhaps such an introduction and testimony were found in the first part of the book of Lehi, which constituted the 116 pages of manuscript lost by Martin Harris.

Mormon finished his small personal insertion into the text with a short prophecy regarding Israel. He began by declaring that he was a "pure descendant of Lehi" (3 Ne. 5:20), implying that careful genealogy was kept among the Nephites. Third Nephi 5:21 is a statement of what the Lord had done for Israel in the past. This verse is a wonderful example of parallelism, a poetic device used often in the Old Testament.[16] The following arrangement illustrates the poetic structure:

| Surely he hath blessed | the house | of Jacob |
| and hath been merciful unto | the seed | of Joseph. |

Notice how each unit in the first half of the verse is balanced by a similar unit in the second half. The opening statement is followed by an elaboration and the prophecy concerning each group. The seed of Joseph, a subgroup of the house of Jacob, will again be brought "to the knowledge of the Lord their God." (3 Ne. 5:23.) This must have been especially meaningful for Mormon because the seed of Joseph included the descendants of Lehi. The last three verses of 3 Nephi 5 pertain to the house of Jacob as a whole. Its members will again be made aware of the covenant they have made and will come to a knowledge of Jesus Christ. Then they shall be "gathered in from the four quarters of the earth unto their own lands." (3 Ne. 5:26.)

Conclusion

These five chapters demonstrate how splendidly complex the Book of Mormon is. They contain history, prophecy, poetry, drama, and a touch of mystery (what happened to Nephi?). More importantly, their editor, Mormon, constructed them as he did the Book of Mormon as a whole, so that they teach us valuable lessons. We can learn about the significance of the Spirit's help in gaining a strong testimony, the dangers of evil organizations, and, most importantly, the power of righteousness over evil.

Notes

I would like to thank Todd Compton, Dale Baldwin, and Dick Walker for their valuable assistance in the preparation of this chapter.

1. Nephi and Alma in fact led very similar lives. Among other things both were judges (Nephi—Helaman 3:37; Alma—Mosiah 29:42-44), both gave up their judgeship to devote more time to service in the church (Nephi—Helaman 5:1-4; Alma—Alma 4:20), both were thrown into prison because of their preachings but were miraculously delivered (Nephi—Helaman 5:21-44; Alma—Alma 14:22-28), both were granted great power (Nephi—Helaman 10:5-10; Alma—Alma 8:31), and, finally, weary with the wickedness of their people, both wished for something different than the circumstances in which they found themselves: Nephi wanted to live in the days when Lehi and his family left Jerusalem (Helaman 7:7), and Alma wanted to speak with the voice of an angel (Alma 29:1-3).

2. Other Book of Mormon commentators have also suggested that Nephi may have been translated. See Joseph Fielding Smith, *Doctrines of*

Salvation, 3 vols., compiled by Bruce R. McConkie (Salt Lake City: Bookcraft, 1954-56), 2:107, 110; Sidney B. Sperry, *The Book of Mormon Testifies,* 3rd ed. (Salt Lake City: Bookcraft, 1952), p. 285; Brian Best, "Nephi, Lehi, and Samuel the Lamanite," *Ensign* (December 1977), p. 51. Daniel Ludlow notes the similarities between Nephi and Alma but does not speculate regarding the fate of Nephi. (*A Companion to Your Study of the Book of Mormon* (Salt Lake City: Deseret Book Company, 1976), pp. 252-53.

    3. Sidney Sperry included verses 4-21 of the first chapter of 3 Nephi in what he entitled "the American Gospel," maintaining that it serves as a prologue to Christ's teachings in the Nephite record in the same way the story of the birth of the Savior is an introduction to the New Testament Gospels. (*The Book of Mormon Testifies,* p. 286.)

    4. See Ludlow, *A Companion to Your Study of the Book of Mormon,* pp. 253-54.

    5. See Sperry, *The Book of Mormon Testifies,* p. 286.

    6. For an interesting discussion of the Nephite reckoning of time see John L. Sorenson, *An Ancient American Setting for the Book of Mormon* (Salt Lake City: Deseret Book Company, and Provo, Utah: Foundation for Ancient Research and Mormon Studies, 1985), pp. 270-76.

    7. Hugh Nibley has written insightfully on the problem of the Gadianton robbers. For an interesting evaluation of this society see "The Way of the Wicked," *An Approach to the Book of Mormon,* 2nd ed. (Salt Lake City: Deseret Book Company, 1978), pp. 317-36; "Good People and Bad People," *Since Cumorah* (Salt Lake City: Deseret Book Company, 1967), pp. 373-409.

    8. Sorenson sees control of trade as both a primary motive and fundamental tactic of the Gadianton robbers; *An Ancient American Setting for the Book of Mormon,* pp. 300-309.

    9. Recent articles in *Time* (March 14, 1988) document the seriousness of the problems caused by drug traffickers. According to the article, among other things "70% of all local crimes (in Detroit) are drug related" (p. 21), and 67% of a rising number of murders in Washington, D.C., are due to local drug wars (p. 22). According to Ed Koch, mayor of New York, "the political aim of the drug traffickers is to make addicts of all of us." (P. 20.) Attorney General Edwin Meese said about the efforts by some countries in helping the U.S. stop the supply of drugs, "They are less than fully successful because of intimidation, bribery and corruption." (P. 18.) And finally, Sterling Johnson, a special narcotics prosecutor in New York City, suggests, "Every American better just pray each night that we don't lose [the war on drugs]." (P. 20.)

10. See J. Lindblom, *Prophecy in Ancient Israel* (Philadelphia: Fortress, 1962), p. 75, for a discussion of Old Testament prophets involved in military activities.

11. See Ludlow, *A Companion to Your Study of the Book of Mormon*, pp. 254-56, for an explanation of the Lord's counsel regarding the waging of offensive war.

12. John A. Wilson, "Egyptian Rituals and Incantations," in *Ancient Near Eastern Texts Relating to the Old Testament*, ed. James B. Pritchard, 3rd ed. (Princeton: Princeton University Press, 1969), p. 329.

13. Not only had the provisions lasted seven years (year 18 to year 25) just as Mormon had said (3 Ne. 4:4), but there were some left over (3 Ne. 6:2).

14. D. Kelly Ogden has also noted some of these characteristics in "Answering the Lord's Call," *Studies in Scripture, Vol. 7: 1 Nephi to Alma 29*, ed. Kent P. Jackson (Salt Lake City: Deseret Book Company, 1987), pp. 17-18.

15. See Sperry, *The Book of Mormon Testifies*, pp. 166-67; Victor L. Ludlow, "Scribes and Scriptures," *Studies in Scripture, Vol. 7: 1 Nephi to Alma 29*, p. 202.

16. For a brief examination of parallelism in the Bible see N.K. Gottwald, "Parallelism," *Interpreters Dictionary of the Bible* (Nashville: Abingdon, 1962), pp. 830-34.

13

THE DOWNFALL OF THE NEPHITE NATION: LESSONS FOR OUR TIME
(3 Nephi 6–10)

GARY LEE WALKER

During the twenty-five years that passed after the birth of Jesus Christ in Bethlehem, both the Nephites and the Lamanites were greatly troubled by the Gadianton robbers. By A.D. 13, this band of thieves and murderers "had become so numerous, and did slay so many of the people, and did lay waste so many cities, and did spread so much death and carnage throughout the land, that it became expedient that all the people, both the Nephites and the Lamanites, should take up arms against them." (3 Ne. 2:11.) Amid this great crisis, "the converted Lamanites" joined the Nephite nation.

The next eight years were times of wars and great trials for the Nephites. Lachoneus, the righteous governor of the land, gathered his people into the central areas of Zarahemla and Bountiful and appointed Gidgiddoni, a great military and spiritual leader, to guide the Nephite army. (3 Ne. 3:13-19.) Hearkening to the counsel of their inspired leaders, the Nephite people repented "of all their sins; and they did put up their prayers unto the Lord their God, that he would deliver them in the time that their enemies should come down against them to battle." (3 Ne. 3:25.)

The faith of the righteous was rewarded, for all the Gadianton robbers were either captured or slain by the Nephite armies. (3 Ne. 5:4-6.) Thus, the Nephites "put an end to all those wicked, and secret,

---

Gary Lee Walker is a doctoral student in history at Brigham Young University.

and abominable combinations, in the which there was so much wickedness, and so many murders committed." (3 Ne. 5:6.)

The years between A.D. 26 and A.D. 29 saw the Nephites prosper and again become an industrious people. Demonstrating that they were true Saints, the Nephites preached the word of God to the incarcerated robbers and gave them the opportunity to "repent of their sins and enter into a covenant that they would murder no more." (3 Ne. 5:4.) The repentant prisoners were mercifully allowed to work on their own lands so that they might provide for themselves and live peacefully with the Nephites. (3 Ne. 6:3.) Law and order was established because "they had formed their laws according to equity and justice." (3 Ne. 6:4.) Building programs ensued that included the establishment of new cities and the repair of many old ones. (3 Ne. 6:7.) Transportation improved by way of new roads and highways that were "cast up" (3 Ne. 6:8), suggesting that the latter were major construction projects that provided significant routes to important centers throughout the land.

Pride: A Tool of Satan

Within three short years, however, the great wealth and prosperity enjoyed by the people became a burden with which they could not cope, and pride began to enter into the hearts of the rich and the powerful. (3 Ne. 6:10-11.) Many years before, the prophet Jacob had warned: "Wo unto the rich, who are rich as to the things of the world. For because they are rich they despise the poor, and they persecute the meek, and their hearts are upon their treasures; wherefore, their treasure is their god. And behold, their treasure shall perish with them also." (2 Ne. 9:30, 42.) The words of Jacob would find part of their fulfillment in the punishments that were soon to be meted out to the proud and boastful Nephites.

The record states that class distinctions developed and that learning became more important to the rich than humility. (3 Ne. 6:12-13.) The resulting feelings of inequality caused not only class distinctions but an emergence of church factions, "insomuch that the church began to be broken up" (3 Ne. 6:14) in A.D. 30. With the exception of a small group of faithful, steadfast Lamanites (3 Ne.

6:14), a general apostasy from the church resulted from the insidious pride of the people. This self-exaltation blinded the multitude from the truth as taught by the Lord's servants and provided the key for Satan to again have "great power, unto the stirring up of the people to do all manner of iniquity, and to the puffing them up with pride, tempting them to seek for power, and authority, and riches, and the vain things of the world." (3 Ne. 6:15.) With this power, the Evil One was given unlimited license to lead the Nephites to "a state of awful wickedness." (3 Ne. 6:17.)

More condemnation was brought upon the heads of the Nephites because they rejected the teachings of the brass plates and the servants of the Lord. "Now they did not sin ignorantly, for they knew the will of God concerning them, for it had been taught unto them; therefore they did wilfully rebel against God." (3 Ne. 6:18.) The high and mighty of the land joined in numerous conspiracies and had the inspired prophets murdered, which was not only an offense against God but also against the laws of the land. (3 Ne. 6:21-24.) These servants of the Lord had both warned the people of their sins and testified of the death and resurrection of Jesus Christ, which was shortly to take place. (3 Ne. 6:20.) Pride and wealth had closed the eyes and ears of the haughty Nephites and had opened the gate for Satan to seduce them into doing his bidding. Secret combinations were formed again, and covenants were made to destroy the people of God and the established government of the land. (3 Ne. 6:27-30.)

The Fruits of Rejecting God's Servants

As the wickedness of the people increased and those who had made covenants in the secret orders gained more power, the government collapsed and the chief judge was murdered. The resulting chaos brought the Nephite society into disorganization. (3 Ne. 7:1-2.) With no centralized government, the people turned to a tribal organization. Mormon recorded that they separated "one from another into tribes, every man according to his family and his kindred and friends; ... and every tribe did appoint a chief or a leader over them; and thus they became tribes and leaders of tribes." (3 Ne. 7:2-3.)[1] Although a greater stability would be restored after the appearance of the resurrected Lord, it is interesting to note that this "tribal" organization would again prevail after the final collapse of the government around A.D. 400. One thousand years later, when the Americas were "discovered" by the Europeans, a tribal organization would still exist among the descendants of these people.

The secret combinations, now in full power, managed to elevate a leader called Jacob to the position of king. He is described by Mormon as "one of the chiefest who had given his voice against the prophets who testified of Jesus." (3 Ne. 7:10.) Although a disjointed social structure now existed in the land (3 Ne. 7:14), the various groups were united against the secret combination that terrorized them (3 Ne. 7:11). This is not to say that these tribal units were righteous, for we are told that "their hearts were turned from the Lord their God, and they did stone the prophets and did cast them out from among them." (3 Ne. 7:14.)

This period in Nephite history was a time of terror, anarchy, and bloodshed. Into this maelstrom came one of the greatest prophets of all time. Nephi, son of Nephi and grandson of Helaman (3 Ne. 1:2-3), had been given custodianship of the records by his father in A.D. 1. Greatly blessed and endowed with many spiritual gifts, this great Nephite prophet bore a final witness to the wicked of his generation. His ministrations and preachings were attended by great miracles that he performed in the name of the Lord. (3 Ne. 7:15-26.) The wicked recognized the power and authority of this great prophet, but, as is tragically true in all generations, the truth only made the wicked angry. Thus, they rejected the word of the Lord from his authorized servant. (3 Ne. 7:18, 20.) Nephi labored for three years among his people, crying repentance and baptizing those who would heed his words. By A.D. 33, he apparently experienced some success, for he ordained "men unto this ministry, that all such as should come unto them should be baptized with water." (3 Ne. 7:23-25.) The number of converts would have been relatively small, however, when one considers the destruction that would shortly befall this wicked generation.

Hundreds of years earlier, Nephi, son of Lehi, was given a vision of the great calamities that would befall the Nephite nation in A.D.

34. (1 Ne. 12:2-5.) Forty years before the crucifixion of the Messiah, Samuel the Lamanite enumerated in glorious prophecy the exact nature of the events that would accompany the voluntary death of the Savior on the cross at Golgotha, outside Jerusalem. (Hel. 14:20-28.) As A.D. 34 dawned, the people were now ripe in iniquity for the judgments of God.

On the other side of the world, at the appointed hour, the Master hung on the cross and voluntarily gave up his life with the words: "Father, into thy hands I commend my spirit." (Luke 23:46.) As the veil of the temple was torn asunder by a great earthquake, the American continent also experienced great calamities — storms, tempests, earthquakes, thunders, and lightnings "as never had been known in all the land." (3 Ne. 8:5-7.) The severity of these natural calamities cannot be overemphasized. Mormon wrote that they continued for three hours (3 Ne. 8:19), an incredible span of time when one considers the damage done to many great cities by earthquakes lasting only a few seconds.[2]

Through the violence and destructive powers of these elements, controlled and used by the Lord to fulfill His purposes,[3] "the face of the whole earth became deformed." (3 Ne. 8:17.) The destruction was devastating: great cities were destroyed by fire or covered by the sea or with earth; plain areas, once level and smooth, were rippled and disfigured and covered with rocks and boulders thrown up from the bowels of the earth; great chasms swallowed entire towns and their populations; buildings were leveled; people were carried away in great whirlwinds, never to be seen again. (3 Ne. 8:8-18.) Jacobugath, the center of government of king Jacob and the secret combinations, was burned with fire "because of their sins and their wickedness, which was above all the wickedness of the whole earth, because of their secret murders and combinations; for it was they that did destroy the peace of [the] people and the government of the land." (3 Ne. 9:9.)

After the three hours of destruction had passed, a thick darkness fell over the land, "insomuch that the inhabitants thereof who had not fallen could feel the vapor of darkness." (3 Ne. 8:20.) As terrible as the natural calamities had been, the ensuing darkness must have been equally horrifying if not more so, for it lasted for three days. (3 Ne. 8:23.) During this time, the darkness was so oppressive that no light shone from the sky and no fire could be kindled. (3 Ne. 8:21-22.) Recognizing their sins and the evils that they had allowed to consume their lives, the survivors howled and lamented. (3 Ne. 8:23-25.) We are not told how many of the Nephites perished, but the number must have been great when one considers the magnitude of the natural disasters unleashed by the Lord. Mormon wrote: "It was the more righteous part of the people who were saved, and it was they who received the prophets and stoned them not; and it was they who had not shed the blood of the saints, who were spared." (3 Ne. 10:12.)

The Voice of the Lord to a Stricken People

As the remaining Nephites lamented their tragic state in the oppressive darkness, the voice of the Lord was heard throughout the land, dispelling the spiritual darkness that had so long engulfed the nation. (3 Ne. 9:1.) The extent of the destruction was revealed to the survivors. The Messiah stated that he had caused the deaths of the wicked. His purpose, he said, was "to hide their wickedness and abominations from before my face, that the blood of the prophets and the saints should not come up any more unto me against them." (3 Ne. 9:8.) After promising eternal life to all who would repent and follow him, Jesus declared his divinity and announced that the preparatory law of Moses was now "fulfilled." (3 Ne. 9:14-17; 15:5.) The new requirement of a broken heart and a contrite spirit was declared. (3 Ne. 9:20.) After Jesus attested to his resurrection, silence fell over the land. (3 Ne. 9:22; 10:1.)

The words of the Master had a tremendous impact on the multitude, for "they did cease lamenting and howling for the loss of their kindred which had been slain." (3 Ne. 10:2.) Although there would be more tears and lamentation (3 Ne. 10:8), hope was surely beginning to return to the stricken people. Later, the voice of the Lord again spoke to the Nephites, telling them how many times he had warned them and had tried to save them from the calamities, if only they would have heeded his words spoken by his servants. (3 Ne.

10:4-7; compare D&C 43:24-25.) During this period, there were great noises because the earth was in constant commotion. (3 Ne. 10:9.) As the elements and the earth returned to normal, the people found joy in their survival and in the words spoken by the Lord. (3 Ne. 10:10.)

Mormon concludes his words by testifying that the events of the past three days had been foretold by many prophets, including Zenos and Zenock, whose records are still lost to us. (3 Ne. 10:15-17.) He revealed that the Nephites and Lamanites were descendants of the ancient Israelite prophets, which may help account for the extensive quoting of their words in the Book of Mormon.[4] He ended his account by announcing the greatest event recorded in the Book of Mormon: the appearance of Jesus Christ to the righteous remnants of the Nephites and the Lamanites.

Lessons for Our Time

President Ezra Taft Benson has stated that the Book of Mormon "was written for our day."[5] He has counseled us to ask ourselves while studying these scriptures: "Why did the Lord inspire Mormon (or Moroni or Alma) to include that in his record?"[6] Asking this question can bring great insight as one reads the Nephite history recorded in 3 Nephi 6-10. Although there are many lessons to be learned by carefully studying these chapters, the striking parallels between the ancient Nephite nation and our generation are significant.

The period of Nephite history under consideration took place just a few short years before the death and resurrection of the Lord Jesus Christ. Our present generation is living in the twilight years before his glorious second coming. The condition of our time is very similar to that of the Nephite nation prior to A.D. 34. They were greatly blessed with learning, and many acquired great wealth and position. Paul, speaking of our time, said that people would be "ever learning, and never able to come to the knowledge of the truth" (2 Tim. 3:7), referring to the gospel plan. These words equally apply to the Nephites before A.D. 34. Their pride and self-aggrandizement blinded them to the teachings of the servants of the Lord. Their achievements in learning caused them to forsake righteousness. How strikingly poignant are the words of Mormon as he described the sorry state of his people who "had turned from their righteousness, like the dog to his vomit, or like the sow to her wallowing in the mire." (3 Ne. 7:8.)

The pride and self-exaltation of the Nephites created an atmosphere of contention that resulted in class distinctions and church factions. Satan was given power to control the minds and actions of the wicked Nephites. Today, he again is exhibiting great strength in disrupting societies and world peace. The earth abounds with false religions, false philosophies, and church factions. Moroni, in speaking of our time, said it would be "a day when the power of God shall be denied, and churches become defiled and be lifted up in the pride of their hearts; yea, even in a day when leaders of churches and teachers shall rise in the pride of their hearts, even to the envying of them who belong to their churches." (Morm. 8:28.) He continued on to prophesy that there would be "churches built up that shall say: Come unto me, and for your money you shall be forgiven of your sins." (Morm. 8:32.) The Nephites allowed wickedness to corrupt and destroy their churches and society. Can we not learn from their bad example and avoid disputations and controversies that might cause contention in our churches, communities, and families?

As the apostasy in the land rapidly increased, the Nephites again entered into forbidden covenants and secret combinations. Prophets and authorized ministers were killed, and Satan ruled supreme. Again, the parallels to our day are obvious. Speaking of our time, the Lord said that "iniquity shall abound" (JS–M 1:30) and that "the whole earth shall be in commotion" (D&C 45:26). Our day witnesses political unrest, terrorist activities, destruction of life and property, wars and riots, and political movements that are committed to the overthrow of righteous institutions. Does not this sound like Nephi's description of his day (compare 3 Ne. 6-7)? As we contemplate these tragic occurrences of our time, we need only to study 3 Nephi 8-9 to ascertain the fate that awaits the wicked of our generation if they continue on their present course.

Moroni, by the gift of prophecy, foresaw our day and wrote in vivid detail about the conditions that would prevail in it. (See Morm. 8:26-40.) In vision, he saw our time plagued by the very problems mentioned in the preceding paragraph. The Doctrine and Covenants explicitly describes the events of the last days and the signs and wonders that will be displayed and recognized by the righteous prior to the Second Coming. The Nephites also had been given prophecy and signs that told of the death and resurrection of the Lord. (3 Ne. 8:3-4.) If the signs had been heeded instead of doubted, many thousands more of the Nephites would have been saved from the destructions and calamities that accompanied the death of the Savior on the cross.

Elder Bruce R. McConkie, in speaking about the details of the events recorded in 3 Nephi 8-10, wrote: "No single historical event in the whole Book of Mormon account is recorded in so great detail or at such extended length as the fulfillment of the signs signifying that Jesus had been lifted up upon the cross and had voluntarily laid down his life for the world."[7]

The Lord desired that these events be testified of in our generation; this is one of the purposes of the coming forth of the Book of Mormon in our time. We can benefit from the careful reading of the tragic events that befell the major portion of the Nephite nation. Surely these things are a pattern of what is yet to come at the Second Coming. The Lord has preserved these accounts for our generation to learn from and to serve as a warning to the wicked of the world. In the Lord's preface to the Doctrine and Covenants, he said: "The voice of the Lord is unto all men, and there is none to escape; and there is no eye that shall not see, neither ear that shall not hear, neither heart that shall not be penetrated. . . . And the voice of warning shall be unto all people." (D&C 1:2, 4.)

The voice of the Lord can be found within the pages of the Book of Mormon. It is for our day. The catastrophic events that befell the wicked Nephites at the time of the death and resurrection of Jesus Christ are a pattern of occurrences yet to come. Our goal is to prayerfully search the Book of Mormon and study the lessons contained therein, that we may be warned and prepared.

NOTES

1. See Daniel H. Ludlow, *A Companion to Your Study of the Book of Mormon* (Salt Lake City: Deseret Book Company, 1976), p. 258.

2. See *Book of Mormon (Religion 121-122) Student Manual*, 2nd ed. (Salt Lake City: The Church of Jesus Christ of Latter-day Saints, 1979), pp. 390-91 for some interesting facts about the destructive force of modern-day earthquakes.

3. Bruce R. McConkie, *Mormon Doctrine*, 2nd ed. (Salt Lake City: Book-craft, 1966), pp. 211-12. Also see *Conference Report*, April 1977, pp. 4-5 for President Spencer W. Kimball's remarks on the Lord's use of the weather to discipline his people.

4. Ludlow, *Companion*, pp. 244, 260.

5. *Ensign*, Nov. 1986, p. 6.

6. Ibid.

7. Bruce R. McConkie, *The Promised Messiah: The First Coming of Christ* (Salt Lake City: Deseret Book Company, 1978), p. 542.

14

THE APPEARANCE OF CHRIST TO THE PEOPLE OF NEPHI
(3 Nephi 11–14)

S. BRENT FARLEY

"I am the light and the life of the world." (3 Ne. 9:18.) The apex of the Book of Mormon is revealed in the personal appearance of Jesus Christ to the more righteous part of Lehi's descendants, who had witnessed the sweet and the bitter in the years preceding this grand event. A night with no darkness had heralded the day of the Savior's birth. Numerous conversions were countered by rampant apostasy. Civil war raged as the Gadianton robbers threatened destruction. Murderous villians took the lives of prophets, while others like Nephi stood with such power that none could disbelieve their words. Finally, God himself rained destruction upon rampant wickedness as city after city was destroyed in the Americas. As the devil laughed in his darkened kingdom, the Savior revealed his word and his will to those who remained upon the earth, saved from destruction by their righteousness.

Soon after the holocaust, a great multitude of people was gathered, marveling about the great changes that had occurred in the earth's surface. Significantly, they were gathered near the temple in Bountiful, a land whose name signifies a plenteous bestowal of gifts. As they were discussing the mission of Christ, "they heard a voice as if it came out of heaven," a small or quiet voice that "did pierce them to the very soul, and did cause their hearts to burn." (3 Ne. 11:3.)

S. Brent Farley is an instructor at the LDS Institute of Religion at Utah State University.

A solemn awe overshadowed them as they cast their eyes around, not understanding the communication. A second time the voice came. A second time they did not understand. As they attuned themselves in deep concentration, they were prepared by the Father for the introduction of his Son. When the voice came the third time, they listened with more than their physical ears, for they were able to decipher the sound as they gazed intently toward heaven, whence the voice came. "Behold my Beloved Son, in whom I am well pleased, in whom I have glorified my name—hear ye him." (3 Ne. 11:7.)

The very reading of such a glorious account brings peace to the heart; but how much more so when we read that "they saw a Man descending out of heaven; and he was clothed in a white robe; and he came down and stood in the midst of them." (3 Ne. 11:8.) None dared to speak; eyes were fixed upon this being they thought to be an angel. But what a glorious thrill must have surged through their souls as they heard the words, "Behold, I am Jesus Christ, whom the prophets testified shall come into the world." (3 Ne. 11:10.) Before them stood a God; a premortal brother; a perfect man now clothed with a resurrected, immortal body of flesh and bone. He had paid the awful price of the sins of all humanity in the garden of Gethsemane and upon the cross. He was, under the Father, the very creator of the earth upon which he now stood. He was, in the sight of the gathered multitude, the one being in all eternity who could open to them the gates of heaven if they so believed.

Who could possibly comprehend the emotions of those who gazed at their Savior? But imagine further their feelings at his invitation: "Arise and come forth unto me, that ye may thrust your hands into my side, and also that ye may feel the prints of the nails in my hands and in my feet, that ye may know that I am the God of Israel, and the God of the whole earth, and have been slain for the sins of the world." (3 Ne. 11:14.) Obediently and with solemn reverence they went forth "and thrust their hands into his side, and did feel the prints of the nails in his hands and in his feet; and this they did do, going forth *one by one* until they had *all* gone forth, and did see with their eyes and did feel with their hands, and did know of a surety and did bear record, that it was he, of whom it was written by the prophets, that should come." (3 Ne. 11:15, emphasis added.) The prints of the nails in his hands and his feet! Little children had felt; the aged touched; the sick and the lame reached out to his hands; not one soul was left out. All had come to Christ, one at a time, and gained the sure witness of his divinity. In unity they cried out: "Hosanna! Blessed be the name of the Most High God!" (3 Ne. 11:17.) Then they fell again to their knees in worship.

Authority and Ordinances

What would the Lord do next? How long would he stay? Would he have any more to say to his people? If so, what would have greatest priority? He called Nephi from the congregation. Nephi was the prophet, the mouthpiece of the Lord; he would stand as the representative of Christ upon that continent when Jesus again ascended into heaven. He would speak to the church, as directed by the Lord. Then the Twelve were called forth. As with the old world, so with the new: The Church of Jesus Christ would be directed by a prophet at the head of the church and a quorum of twelve other leaders. (3 Ne. 11:18-22.)

Primary emphasis was placed upon baptism. In just twenty-two verses containing the opening remarks of the Savior, the word *baptism* (or one of its forms) occurs nineteen times. (3 Ne. 11:22–12:2.) Without valid baptism by one having authority from the Lord, we could not return to dwell with the Father and the Son in heaven. Baptism is, in the literal and eternal sense, a unifying ordinance between God and his people. Hence, the principle of unity as exemplified in the Godhead was connected with the instructions regarding baptism: "After this manner shall ye baptize in my name; for behold, verily I say unto you, that the Father, and the Son, and the Holy Ghost are one." (3 Ne. 11:27.) Given the new church organization (no longer under the law of Moses), all were to be baptized as an entrance into the Lord's newly formed church.[1]

In the beginning of chapter 12, the Twelve were commissioned and presented to the multitude "to be your servants" (verse 1); they were given power and authority from God to unify his children in harmony with gospel principles and ordinances. If the people accepted the Lord's representatives as ministers of the gospel and complied with their preaching, God himself would baptize them "with fire and with the Holy Ghost." (3 Ne. 12:1.) Believing God's servants was tantamount to believing God.

The Beatitudes

The resurrected Christ next gave to the disciples the unifying course of instruction that he had given to his disciples in Judea, now known as the Sermon on the Mount. This beautiful discourse provides a pattern by which one can follow the example of the Savior and strive for perfection. The prelude is referred to as the Beatitudes.

1. "Blessed are the poor in spirit who come unto me, for theirs is the kingdom of heaven." (3 Ne. 12:3.) In one sense, to be "poor in spirit" is to realize that we are nothing in mortality without a Savior. Without an atoning sacrifice, none could leave mortality to return to the presence of God. In fact, all would die only to become angels to the devil, to remain in misery forever. (2 Ne. 9:8-9.) How destitute and poor indeed!

Being "poor in spirit" is not to feel continuous hopelessness because of our fallen state; it is to feel continuous dependence upon the Savior. We realize the difference between God and his mortal children, appreciate the condescending love of the Savior, and humbly seek to unify ourselves with God. We never attribute greatness to ourselves but seek to emulate the example of the Atoning One to the best of our mortal ability, ever aware of the need to overcome weakness and resist temptation.

2. "Blessed are all they that mourn." (3 Ne. 12:4.) Who would not mourn at the hopeless prospect of our fallen state? But they shall be comforted. Our lost and fallen state may be overcome. A Savior was provided whereby all will be resurrected and all may be saved in the kingdom of God. What great comfort! A Savior atoned for the sins of all who would accept him. Thus all may become blessed and happy if they so choose.

When the humble Saints mourn over trial and difficulty, they are promised comfort. They are given the peace that comes from Christ, wherein their hearts are not to be troubled or afraid. (John 14:27.)

They are given "the Comforter, which is the Holy Ghost" to teach them and guide them. (John 14:26.) When death, trial, or tragedy strikes, their hearts are softened and comforted by the Spirit of Truth, which whispers peace and opens the perspective of eternal joy. If one sins, the mourning is a godly sorrow that brings repentance, forgiveness, and the comfort of restored peace. (2 Cor. 7:10; Mosiah 4:3.)

3. "And blessed are the meek, for they shall inherit the earth." (3 Ne. 12:5.) Elder Bruce R. McConkie explained: "In the scriptural sense the meek are the God-fearing and the righteous. . . . [They] are those who keep the commandments and are fit persons to associate with Him in whom meekness was perfected."[2] To be meek is to be mild and gentle. It does not imply weakness, for the prime example of meekness calmed the angry waves, cast out devils, and performed mighty miracles. To be meek is to be humble. It is a characteristic of strength.

4. "And blessed are all they who do hunger and thirst after righteousness, for they shall be filled with the Holy Ghost." (3 Ne. 12:6.) The closer we grow to God, the greater is our desire to improve. This desire is like thirsting for water or hungering for food. It is a critical longing for nourishment and health: it is the longing for the health of the spirit. Those who sup at the table of the Lord become as dependent upon his words for their spirits as they are upon food for their bodies. The satisfaction of that desire for righteousness is fed by the constant companionship of the Holy Ghost. Losing that closeness is akin to the threat of starvation.

5. "And blessed are the merciful, for they shall obtain mercy." (3 Ne. 12:7.) The merciful are those who are "compassionate; tender; unwilling to give pain; not cruel."[3] Such shall receive the blessing of mercy, which "tempers justice, and induces . . . [forgiveness of] trespasses and injuries, and to forbear punishment, or inflict less than law or justice will warrant. In this sense, there is perhaps no word in our language precisely synonymous with *mercy*. That which comes nearest to it is grace."[4]

6. "And blessed are all the pure in heart, for they shall see God." (3 Ne. 12:8.) To be pure is to be free from the taint of unrepented

sins. This, of course, is only possible through the gospel of Jesus Christ. Though none are perfect in this life (except for the Savior), those who are striving to the best of their abilities qualify for the ongoing and renewable quality of purity of heart. Such may obtain closeness to God and see him. This may be symbolic in the sense of recognizing the hand of God in all things and feeling his influence in life, but its apex is literal. This promise has the seal of God, who testified: "It shall come to pass that every soul who forsaketh his sins and cometh unto me, and calleth on my name, and obeyeth my voice, and keepeth my commandments, shall see my face and know that I am." (D&C 93:1.) Elder Bruce R. McConkie testified: "We have the power—and it is our privilege—so to live, that becoming pure in heart, we shall see the face of God while we yet dwell as mortals."[5] It is not a requirement that we see God in this life in order to be saved; it is a possible blessing. However, it is a guaranteed right of all who are pure in heart to see God, whether in this life or the next, or in both.

There follow two more beatitudes (peacemaking and enduring persecution); but what could be a more transcending point than to qualify to do what the Nephite/Lamanite culture was now doing—to see the face of the Lord?

The Higher Plane of the Gospel

Those who follow the path marked by the beatitudes are accounted as "salt" and "light"! (3 Ne. 12:13-16.) Salt has a distinctive property (or savor) that enhances the flavor of foods. Its addition tends to bring out the best of that to which it is added. So would the Saints become the enhancers of those who accept the gospel. The commission to do this had a warning, however. If the savor was lost, then "wherewith shall the earth be salted? The salt shall be thenceforth good for nothing, but to be cast out and to be trodden under foot of men." (3 Ne. 12:13.) Salt does not lose its savor by age, but rather by mixture and contamination. Correspondingly, the gospel does not lose its savor by age, but rather when it is mixed with the philosophies of men and devils. Salt is also a preservative. The gospel was intended to be preserved in purity. Its effects were to preserve the Saints in righteousness that they might attain their celestial destiny. How appropriate was the Lord's analogy!

The Saints, the "salt of the earth," were to be the lights to which people in a darkened world could seek. In the book of Revelation, the church organizations were compared to candlesticks, and the servants in those organizations were compared to stars. (See Rev. 1:20.) Jesus himself had "his countenance . . . as the sun shining in his strength." (JST, Rev. 1:16.) What was the light that would emanate from the mortal servants? It was not the light of their own development, but rather the light of the master they served. "Behold I am the light which ye shall hold up—that which ye have seen me do." (3 Ne. 18:24.) The commission to be a light to the world had two aspects: (1) a missionary charge to guide others to Christ, and (2) a charge to remain faithful and constantly progress until perfect.

The symbolism of light and salt were appropriately placed together in the sacred text. Old Testament sacrificial rituals used salt as a token of gospel covenants. (See Lev. 2:13 and Num. 18:19.) The Lord explained to Joseph Smith: "I have sent mine everlasting *covenant* into the world, to be a *light* to the world, and to be a standard for my people, and for the Gentiles to seek to it, and to be a messenger before my face to prepare the way before me." (D&C 45:9; emphasis added.) Thus salt represents the gospel covenant, which is a light to the world.

The higher plane of Christianity for which the law of Moses served as a schoolmaster was now contrasted with the letter of the Mosiac law. It was well known that killing was condemned and carried an awful penalty; but short of this heinous sin, anger also carried a condemnation that could bring the punishment of hell. Even the manifestation of contempt ("Raca") or belittlement ("thou fool") toward a fellow being carried a punishment so terrible as to merit a sentence in hell. (3 Ne. 12:22.) To come to God required one's best efforts to live in unity with one's brothers and sisters. (3 Ne. 12:23-26.)

Next to murder in seriousness was adultery, expressly forbidden by God. Jesus also noted the seriousness of lust: "Whosoever looketh on a woman, to lust after her, hath committed adultery already in his heart." (3 Ne. 12:28.) The thoughts precede the actions: "For as he thinketh in his heart, so is he." (Prov. 23:7.) Jesus was teaching accountability for thoughts as well as actions; either of these could cost one's salvation. Controlling the mind and impulses could obliterate the outward commission of serious sin. Knowing that Satan often clothes temptations in attractive apparel, Jesus commanded denial; therein would one take up his cross (3 Ne. 12:29-30), for it would be a battle and a trial to learn to resist the influence of Satan.

What was the ultimate goal the Lord had in mind for those who controlled their thoughts and actions? It was perfection. "Therefore I would that ye should be perfect even as I, or your Father who is in heaven is perfect." (3 Ne. 12:48.) The gospel is a ladder of progression whose top rung sits in eternity, but whose legs are planted firmly upon the earth. The Savior was teaching how to take the steps on this side of the veil. In so doing, his followers would be building a Zion society. They would be striving to be "of one heart and one mind, and [to dwell] in righteousness." (Moses 7:18.)

Attached to that definition of Zion was the injunction that there be "no poor among them." The Savior expressed his will that "ye should do alms unto the poor." (3 Ne. 13:1.) The giving of alms is most often associated with money; the Greek origin, however, suggests "kindness" and "kind acts."[6] Monetary support is only a portion of almsgiving. The Saints were to help the unfortunate; but they were not to do it to build their own reputations. They were to do it to build up the poor and help establish Zion. "Take heed that ye do not your alms before men to be seen of them; otherwise ye have no reward of your Father who is in heaven." (3 Ne. 13:1.)

The Lord's Prayer

As with the giving of alms, so with the offering of personal prayers. The hypocrites prayed in public for public reward, and that was what they received. The Saints were to pray in secret to their Eternal Father, who, hearing in secret, would reward them openly. Vain (or fruitless) repetitions were unnecessary and unhelpful; lengthy prayers (for the sake of expounding) were not approved. (3 Ne. 13:5-8.) The Lord repeated to his American Saints the concise model referred to as "the Lord's prayer." The total prayer could easily be read in less than thirty seconds. The intent was not to encourage short prayers but to make a valid contrast with the "much speaking" and the "vain repetitions" of the hypocrites, who prayed for show. In doing so, the Lord left a basic pattern to guide the secret prayers of the children of his kingdom.

"Our Father who art in heaven, hallowed be thy name." (3 Ne. 13:9.) All prayers were to be directed to the Father of our spirits, the Heavenly Parent from whose presence we came at birth. It was to be a Father/son or Father/daughter relationship between him and his offspring; that attitude and that goal should temper our prayers.

"Thy will be done on earth as it is in heaven." (3 Ne. 13:10.) (The phrase "thy kingdom come" was dropped, the establishment of the church possibly fulfilling that plea). We typically give thanks early in our prayers for the blessings we have received. We then typically (and rightfully) ask for the Lord's help in our daily concerns. Whatever the plea, whether for self or family, for sacred purpose or secular, the guiding principle is that it should all be in harmony with God's will. That is a guiding principle of prayer.

"And forgive us our debts, as we forgive our debtors." (3 Ne. 13:11.) Since "all have sinned, and come short of the glory of God" (Rom. 3:23), then all need the redemptive power gained through repentance and forgiveness. The debts we would most want to be relieved of are our debts to justice when we have sinned. Such relief is available through repentance. And, as we are seeking mercy, we are required as a prerequisite to extend mercy to others. "I, the Lord, will forgive whom I will forgive, but of you it is required to forgive all." (D&C 64:10.) This relieves the one offended of the destructive burden that resentment and anger can cause.[7]

"And lead us not into temptation, but deliver us from evil." (3 Ne. 13:12.) Or, as the Joseph Smith Translation of Matthew 6:14 clarifies, "And suffer us not to be led into temptation." A basic and regular element of our prayers should be a plea for help in avoiding the pitfalls and snares laid by Satan. He is a major adversary to God, and thus to God's children. Temptation is a constant threat, and the devil a constant foe; it is necessary and wise in our prayers to seek guidance to follow the path of the Lord and avoid the crossroads offered by Perdition. Our plea is that in the end we will be delivered from evil forever to dwell with God in his kingdom of glory.

"For thine is the kingdom, and the power, and the glory, forever." (3 Ne. 13:13.) We acknowledge that God's plan is perfect and that his kingdom is the greatest reward for the human race. His is the glory forever, which he is willing to share with those who humbly and diligently seek to do his will on earth. As thoughts precede actions, so do prayers precede progress.

Building upon the Rock of Christ

When harmony exists between prayers and actions, mortal endeavors build eternal rewards "where neither moth nor rust doth corrupt, and where thieves do not break through nor steal." (3 Ne. 13:13.) But it requires the commitment of the heart; if the heart is set on earthly treasures, then the reward will be that of the hypocrites: an earthly reward. When the heart is set upon the things of heaven, then the light of heaven is borne in upon that soul until the fullness of light is attained. No compromise is possible between light and darkness. "Ye cannot serve God and Mammon." (3 Ne. 13:24.) "Mammon" refers to riches. The problem is not that a good person cannot be rich and righteous; the problem is that if the person serves riches, he or she has crowded out the true God for a false one of worldly origin. (3 Ne. 13:19-24.) How many souls have been purchased by Satan through wealth!

After giving special instructions to the Twelve (3 Ne. 13:25-34), Jesus addressed the topic of judgment. In the familiar words of the biblical account, he said, "Judge not, that ye be not judged." (3 Ne. 14:1; Matt. 7:1.) The Joseph Smith Translation adds an important qualification: "Judge not unrighteously, that ye be not judged: but judge righteous judgment." (JST, Matt. 7:1-2.) Life is a series of judgments, but caution is especially needed when we judge our fellow beings. Misjudgment is common because we know not the hearts, minds, and intents of those around us. Jesus asked: "Why beholdest thou the mote that is in thy brother's eye, but considerest not the beam that is in thine own eye?" (3 Ne. 13:3.) The mote referred to a speck or chip, whereas the beam referred to a large wooden beam used in constructing buildings. Before we can judge another and offer help, we must be rid of the impairments to our own vision, which may consist of false information, hypocrisy, sin, or any number of things. Being in tune with the Spirit is the only safe basis for judgment: "He that is spiritual judgeth all things." (1 Cor. 2:15.) Some priesthood leaders (such as bishops and stake presidents) are given a special commission of judgment; they are to judge under the inspired direction of their Master, to whom all judgment is given. (John 5:22.)

The Savior promised that to those who asked would be given; to those who knocked, the door would be opened. (3 Ne. 14:7-8.) What were the qualifications for worthy asking and receiving? The golden rule (3 Ne. 14:12) and the keeping of the commandments (referred to as a strait or narrow gate and a narrow way—verses 13-14). Those who entered therein and remained upon the path of obedience would obtain. Those who led in other directions were "false prophets, who come to you in sheep's clothing, but inwardly they are ravening wolves." (3 Ne. 14:15.)

Their fruits would give them away (3 Ne. 14:16-23), for many of their hearts would be set on mammon, whether of money, of public acclaim, or of Satanic obedience. Their homes would be upon sandy foundations and would fall when the storms came. (3 Ne. 14:26-27.)

Those who brought forth good fruit would be solidly anchored, for they followed the teachings of the Savior. They listened and applied; they progressed along the narrow way as explained in the Sermon on the Mount; they judged righteous judgment and were humble. They sought from the Lord and obtained from his hand. They were the ones who heard the Lord's sayings and did them. They were likened "unto a wise man, who built his house upon a rock." (3 Ne. 14:24-25.) The rock upon which they built was Christ. The Christ now stood before them, teaching eternal truths with eternal rewards. God himself translated heavenly concepts into language appropriate to the understanding of his listeners. His truth was consistent and constant. It was intended for all: for those who were listening firsthand, and for those millions who would later read the account. The scripture produced came directly from the lips of the Savior of the world; he knew whereof he spake. And so do those who follow his teachings, for the Spirit of Truth enters their hearts just as readily as in the days of the Nephite and Lamanite congregation there, in his presence.[8]

NOTES

1. Joseph Fielding Smith, *Answers to Gospel Questions*, (Salt Lake City: Deseret Book Company, 1960), vol 3, pp. 205-6.

2. Bruce R. McConkie, *The Millennial Messiah* (Salt Lake City: Deseret Book Company, 1982), p. 698.

3. Noah Webster, *1828 American Dictionary Of The English Language* (San Francisco: Foundation For American Christian Education, 1985), "merciful."

4. Ibid., "mercy."

5. Bruce R. McConkie, *Conference Report*, Oct. 1977, p. 52.

6. Robert Young, *Young's Analytical Concordance to the Bible* (Grand Rapids: Wm. B. Eerdmans Publishing Companion, 1970), p. 28.

7. Marion D. Hanks, *Conference Report*, Oct. 1973, pp. 15-16.

8. For further information on the Sermon on the Mount, see Robert A. Cloward, "The Sermon on the Mount in the JST and the Book of Mormon," pp. 163-200 in *The Joseph Smith Translation: The Restoration of Plain and Precious Things*, ed. M. S. Nyman and R. L. Millet (Provo, Utah: Religious Studies Center, Brigham Young University, 1985); Catherine Thomas, "The Sermon on the Mount: The Sacrifice of the Human Heart," pp. 236-50 in *Studies in Scripture, Vol. 5: The Gospels*, ed. Kent P. Jackson and Robert L. Millet (Salt Lake City: Deseret Book Company, 1986).

15

CHRIST'S AUTHORITY, HIS OTHER SHEEP, AND THE REDEMPTION OF ISRAEL
(3 Nephi 15-16)

ROBERT J. MATTHEWS

Jesus was speaking to about twenty-five hundred assembled Nephites on his first visit to them after his resurrection. (3 Ne. 17:25.) He had just shown them his glorified body and told them he was the promised Messiah whom the prophets had testified would come. They had examined the marks of the crucifixion in his hands, feet, and side. He selected twelve special disciples and testified to the multitude of their divine calling. (3 Ne. 12.) These twelve were, in fact, apostles, although the record does not specifically so designate them. (See Moroni 2:1-3.)[1]

Jesus then gave the Nephite twelve and multitude instructions similar to the Sermon on the Mount, with some important variations due to the different setting and circumstances of this sermon compared to the one in Palestine. (Compare Matt. 5-7 with 3 Ne. 12-14.)

The Authority of Jesus

That portion of the Savior's instruction that parallels the Sermon on the Mount seems to have a natural ending at the close of 3 Nephi 14, concluding with the parable of the houses built on sand and on rock. However, readers of the New Testament will remember that Matthew 7:28-29 adds a comment that Jesus' hearers in Palestine

Robert J. Matthews is professor of ancient scripture at Brigham Young University.

were "astonished at his doctrine: for he taught them as one having authority, and not as the scribes." The JST records this as: "He taught them as one having authority from God, and not as having authority from the Scribes." (JST Matt. 7:37.) At first glance it appears that this item concerning Jesus' authority is missing in the 3 Nephi account. Its parallel however, is in fact found in the subsequent chapter, in 3 Nephi 15:1-10. The two-verse, one-sentence observation of 28 words in Matthew is in 3 Nephi a ten-verse, thirteen-sentence, 364-word declaration by Jesus. The 3 Nephi expression includes several concepts dealing with Jesus' authority. First Jesus affirmed that the instruction he had just given them contained "the things which I taught [in the Holy Land] before I ascended to my Father" (v. 1). He then explained: "I am he who gave the law" to Moses, and "the law in me is fulfilled" (vv. 3-8). He further established his identity, and thus his authority, by saying that he, Jesus, was the God who covenanted with Israel (v. 5). Earlier, at the beginning of this visit, he had declared to the multitude that he was "the God of Israel, and the God of the whole earth," and had "been slain for the sins of the world." (3 Ne. 11:14.)

Jesus further attested to his authority by saying, "I am the law, and the light. Look unto me . . . and ye shall live," and he promised that unto those who obey him to the end, he would "give eternal life." (3 Ne. 15:9.) The authority theme is continued with Jesus saying: "*I* have given unto you the commandments; therefore keep *my* commandments. And this is the law and the prophets, for they truly testified of *me*" (v. 10, emphasis added).

It would be difficult to miss the point that Jesus in these verses was giving an unqualified statement of his authority and primal position (under the Father) both on earth and in heaven. As noted, this is a much stronger statement than the brief comment by Matthew at the close of the Sermon on the Mount, yet it is parallel to it in its placement at the end of the Sermon.

Other Sheep

The remaining fourteen verses of chapter 15 deal chiefly with a detailed explanation that the Nephites and the Lamanites are the "other sheep" once spoken of by Jesus to the Jews in Palestine, as recorded in John 10:16. Most readers of the Book of Mormon are aware that Jesus visited these "other sheep" in America. However, the Savior was so definitive on this point that it deserves particular attention. The passage in John 10:16 was cited by Jesus in 3 Nephi 15:16-17 as follows: "This much did the Father command me, that I should tell unto them: That other sheep I have which are not of this fold; them also I must bring, and they shall hear my voice; and there shall be one fold, and one shepherd."

Jesus said that the Father had commanded him to teach the Jews about the "other sheep," but when he did so (as explained in this verse), the Jews failed to understand the meaning. It appears that it was not only the multitude of the Jews but even the brethren in the Jewish Church who missed the meaning. This failure came from "stiffneckedness and unbelief." Therefore Jesus was "commanded to say no more of the Father" to the Jews about the subject. (3 Ne. 15:18.)

The Jews thought that the "other sheep" were the Gentiles. (3 Ne. 15:22.) This is suggested also in John 7:35, when the unbelieving Jews said, "Will he go unto the dispersed among the Gentiles, and teach the Gentiles?" This misconception has been a popular interpretation by modern biblical scholars also.[2]

It is at this point in Jesus' explanation that the doctrine becomes extremely valuable to our understanding of Jesus' worldwide mission, and also as an aid to the intepretation of scripture. Jesus' words to the Nephites are as follows:

> Verily I say unto you, that ye are they of whom I said: Other sheep I have which are not of this fold; them also I must bring, and they shall hear my voice; and there shall be one fold, and one shepherd. And they [the Jews] understood me not, for they supposed it had been the Gentiles; for they understood not that the Gentiles should be converted through their preaching. And they understood me not that I said they shall hear my voice; and they understood me not that the Gentiles should not at any time hear my voice — that I should not manifest myself unto them save it were by the Holy Ghost. But behold, ye have both heard my voice, and seen me, and

ye are my sheep, and ye are numbered among those whom
the Father hath given me. (3 Ne. 15:21-24.)

The crux of the statement is that Jesus will not at any time manifest
himself personally nor by his audible voice to a Gentile nation. Such
an event is declared to be a blessing reserved for those who are of
the house of Israel. The Gentiles are to be converted through the
preaching of those who are of Israel, and Jesus will manifest himself
to the believing Gentiles through the Holy Ghost. This same concept
is referred to in 1 Nephi 10:11, wherein Lehi said that Jesus would
"make himself manifest, by the Holy Ghost, unto the Gentiles." This
procedure is a provision of, and is in harmony with, the covenant to
Abraham, as stated in Abraham 2:9-10, that Abraham's descendants
have the responsibility of the ministry and will carry the priesthood
and the gospel unto all nations.

Emphasis on the covenant of Abraham, which places a responsibility for the ministry on his literal seed, does not mean that a
faithful Gentile has less access to the blessings of heaven than do
those of Abraham's seed. Once a Gentile has the gospel and obeys
it, all the blessings of eternal life are offered to that person. But in
the timetable and economy of the Lord, in the meridian of time and
even before, those of literal Israelite lineage had the first opportunity
to receive the gospel, and also the responsibility to carry it to the
other nations. It is a priority of opportunity, not only in the time of
Jesus, but ever since the time of Abraham himself.

The Sheep of Yet Another Fold to Be Visited

In addition to clearly establishing the identity of the Book of
Mormon peoples as the "other sheep" of John 10:16, the Savior told
of yet other "sheep" of Israel whom he would visit. He had already
alluded to this third group in 3 Nephi 15:20 with the words: "The
other tribes hath the Father separated from them [the Jews]; and it
is because of their [the Jews'] iniquity that they [the Jews] know not
of them." In other words, because of their own unbelief the Jews did
not know of the Nephites or of the other tribes.

The Savior then told the Nephites about the third group, the so-
called "lost tribes," by saying precisely these things about them: (1)

"I have other sheep, which are not of this land [America], neither of the land of Jerusalem, neither in any parts of that land round about whither I have been to minister." (3 Ne. 16:1.) (2) These other sheep had never been visited personally by the Savior, but (3) they were about to receive such a visit. This would probably be similar to his visit to the Nephites. We read: "They of whom I speak are they who have not as yet *heard my voice*; neither have I at any time manifested myself unto them. But I have received a commandment of the Father that I shall go unto them, and that they shall *hear my voice*, and shall be numbered among my sheep, that there may be one fold and one shepherd; therefore I go to *show* myself unto them." (3 Ne. 16:2-3; emphasis added.)

General information concerning the "lost tribes" need not be a mystery. They were captured and led away from the land of Palestine about 735-721 B.C. by the Assyrians. (2 Kgs. 15-17.) They consist primarily of all the tribes of Israel except Judah and Benjamin, which are the Jews. Nephi makes reference to them in his own day, about 130-150 years after the tribes had departed from Palestine: "It appears that the house of Israel, sooner or later, will be scattered upon all the face of the earth, and also among all nations. And behold, there are many who are already lost from the knowledge of those who are at Jerusalem. Yea, the more part of all the tribes have been led away; and they are scattered to and fro upon the isles of the sea; and whither they are none of us knoweth, save that we know that they have been led away." (1 Ne. 22:3-4.)

And Jacob added: "The Lord God has led away from time to time from the house of Israel, according to his will and pleasure. And now behold, the Lord remembereth all them who have been broken off." (2 Ne. 10:22.)

Later Nephi quoted the Lord as saying:

> I shall speak unto the Jews and they shall write it; and I shall also speak unto the Nephites and they shall write it; and I shall also speak unto the other tribes of the house of Israel, which I have led away, and they shall write it; and I shall also speak unto all nations of the earth and they shall write it.
>
> And it shall come to pass that the Jews shall have the words of the Nephites, and the Nephites shall have the words

of the Jews; and the Nephites and the Jews shall have the words of the lost tribes of Israel; and the lost tribes of Israel shall have the words of the Nephites and the Jews. (2 Ne. 29:12-13.)

In 3 Nephi 17:4 Jesus told the Nephites he was ready to visit the "lost tribes of Israel" and to "show" himself unto them, "for they are not lost unto the Father, for he knoweth whither he hath taken them." The Tenth Article of Faith speaks also of the restoration of the ten lost tribes. Furthermore, the keys for gathering them were given to the Prophet Joseph Smith in the Kirtland Temple on April 3, 1836. (D&C 110:11.)

It seems natural to conclude that when we receive the record of the lost tribes, it will contain an account of Jesus' visit, showing his body to them with the same unmistakable evidence as he did to the Nephites, whereby they saw him, touched him, heard him, and knew for a certainty that he is the God of Israel and was slain for the sins of the world and raised from the grave as a resurrected personage.

Ask and Ye Shall Receive

It is very clear in the material we have covered that the Savior revealed much more to the Nephites (and thus to all who read the Book of Mormon) than he did to the Jews, and he was desirous that a record should be kept of this visit. Therefore Jesus commanded the Nephites to write an account of it. A major concept at work in this whole episode is that one must seek for spiritual knowledge. The rule, as given in 3 Nephi 14:7-8, and in many other places, is that knowledge is given to those who ask, seek, and knock. If we do not ask for gospel knowledge, we probably will not receive it. Hence the Lord's instructions were as follows:

> I command you that ye shall write these sayings after I am gone, that if it so be that my people at Jerusalem, they who have seen me and been with me in my ministry, do not ask the Father in my name, that they may receive a knowledge of you by the Holy Ghost, and also of the other tribes whom they know not of, that these sayings which ye shall write shall be kept and shall be manifested unto the Gentiles, that through

> the fulness of the Gentiles, the remnant of their seed, who shall be scattered forth upon the face of the earth because of their unbelief, may be brought in, or may be brought to a knowledge of me, their Redeemer. (3 Ne. 16:4.)

The Lord wanted the various groups of scattered Israel to be known, especially in the last days, and if the Jewish New Testament apostles didn't ask, and therefore didn't learn of these groups (and consequently would not include it in the New Testament), the world could, in the last days, receive an awareness of these groups from the Book of Mormon.

Since the New Testament contains only the one brief mention in John 10:16, and since no explanation or further identification is given, then in light of the Savior's instruction in 3 Nephi 16:4 (cited above), we conclude that the New Testament people did not ask and did not receive the information. We are therefore doubly indebted to the Book of Mormon for its singular ability to enlarge our comprehension of the Savior's worldwide mission and personal visits to the various groups of Israel—the Jews, the Nephites, and the lost tribes.

Pattern Prophecies of Isaiah

The Lord continued his instruction by saying that since those peoples who are on a national basis primarily descendants of Israel (the Jews, Lehi's descendants, the other tribes, etc.) will have rejected the gospel, in the "latter day" the truth shall come first to the Gentiles and from them to the house of Israel. (3 Ne. 16:7.) This is a reversal of the order in earlier days.

However (the Lord continued), if the Gentiles do not honor the gospel after having so great a blessing offered to them, and after having scattered the remnants of Israel (the Lamanites) in the Americas, the Lord will then remember the covenants he made with the forebears of present-day Israel (that is, the covenants with Abraham, Isaac, Jacob, Joseph, Moses, Lehi, Nephi, Jacob, Enos, Mormon, etc.) and will put judgments upon the Gentiles and take the fullness of the gospel away from them. He will bring forth his people Israel out of obscurity, out of oppression, and Israel will be gathered and restored to the true Church and fold of God. Israel will then be blessed with the same knowledge and the same promises of salvation that were given to their righteous fathers. (3 Ne. 16:8-16.)

Jesus informed his hearers that at the time of gathering and restoration of Israel, these words of Isaiah would be fulfilled: "Thy watchmen shall lift up the voice; with the voice together shall they sing, for they shall see eye to eye when the Lord shall bring again Zion. Break forth into joy, sing together, ye waste places of Jerusalem; for the Lord hath comforted his people, he hath redeemed Jerusalem. The Lord hath made bare his holy arm in the eyes of all the nations; and all the ends of the earth shall see the salvation of God." (3 Ne. 16:18-20; Isa. 52:8-10.)

There is a lesson to be observed here. Blessings once offered become cursings if they are rejected. The Gentiles will be given great opportunity, but if they "sin against" the gospel and treat it lightly, they will lose it and have to bear the consequences.

The events spoken of in this chapter dealing with the Gentiles and the reclamation and restoration of Israel, whether it be the Jews, the Nephites and Lamanites, or the lost tribes, is a pattern that will be repeated wherever there are Gentiles who do not believe and Israelites who do believe. In the foregoing passage, Isaiah speaks of "Jerusalem," yet Jesus used these verses with reference to the Nephites. Much of Isaiah's prophesying can be termed what I call "pattern prophecies." They can and will be fulfilled at different times and in different places, among the various groups of Israel. Therefore, Nephi wrote, "Hear ye the words of the prophet [Isaiah] . . . and liken them unto yourselves." (1 Ne. 19:23-24; 2 Ne. 11:8.)

"Gentiles" in the Book of Mormon

The Book of Mormon speaks of the Gentiles on the American continent, in contrast to the Nephites and Lamanites, who are Israelites. It is the Gentile who will bring the gospel to the Lamanites. The Book of Mormon will come forth "by way of the Gentile." (See 1 Nephi 15:17; also title page.) The early settlers of North America of European heritage are spoken of as Gentiles. (1 Ne. 13:13-19.) Yet, Latter-day Saints of European descent hold that they are of Israel, particularly descended through Joseph and Ephraim. They learn this through their patriarchal blessings. This merits additional discussion.

Two terms frequently appearing in the scriptures are *Israel* and *Gentile*. These were originally used to designate distinct peoples. Israel meant the literal descendants of Jacob and the twelve sons of Jacob, or house of Israel. The Gentiles, as the word literally means, were "the other people." The word "Gentile" first appears in Genesis 10:4-5 with reference to the descendants of Japheth. Eventually both of these words were enlarged in their scope to include land designations — the land where the Israelites lived, and the land where the Gentiles lived. Still a third meaning eventually developed, so that "Israel" designated those who by covenant accept the true religion, and "Gentiles" meant those who did not. This is evident in Paul's statement, "They are not all Israel, which are of Israel." (Rom. 9:6.) That is, Paul says there is believing Israel and there is blood Israel, and sometimes these two conditions are not found in the same people. Thus a Gentile, one not genealogically of the blood of Israel, may become an Israelite by adoption through his or her belief, baptism, and the action of the Holy Ghost.[3]

America, as is the case with Europe, has been peopled by those who have been without the fullness of the gospel for many centuries, yet they have much of the blood of Israel in their veins. They are not easily identified or recognized as Israelites and therefore are spoken of as Gentiles, in contrast to those of more recognizable Israelite identity such as the Jews and the Lamanites. Hence, the great American nation is spoken of in the Book of Mormon as a Gentile nation, even though we, as Church members, know we have the blood of Israel in us. This condition is described by the Prophet Joseph Smith in D&C 109:58, 60, saying we are "the sons of Jacob" but are "identified with the Gentiles."

It is actually a fact that the membership of the Church is largely of the literal seed of Abraham through Joseph, by blood descent. This is the message of D&C 86:9-10: "Ye are lawful heirs, according to the flesh, . . . and the priesthood . . . must needs remain through you and your lineage." The same concept is continued in D&C 90:10; 96:7; 98:32; 113:8; 132:30-31.[4]

The Lord is using the descendants of Joseph, through Ephraim and Mannasseh, being drawn out of Gentile society, to bring the gospel to the world in the last days. As Joseph fed his brothers with bread in ancient times and thus was a blessing to them—although for a long time they did not know or recognize him—so in the last days the seed of Joseph, ordained and clothed with the gospel of salvation, has the "bread of life" to nourish the inhabitants of the earth who are in an impoverished spiritual condition.

As it was anciently, so is it now. The recipients have hardly recognized or sensed that their benefactors are the literal descendants of Joseph, fulfilling their responsibility under the covenant of Abraham. That Joseph's seed should have such a mission is the message of an informative textual restoration found in JST Genesis 48:8-11, with Jacob speaking to his son Joseph:

> O my son, [God] hath blessed me in raising thee up to be a servant unto me, in saving my house from death; in delivering my people, thy brethren, from famine which was sore in the land; wherefore the God of thy fathers shall bless thee, and the fruit of thy loins, that they shall be blessed above thy brethren, and above thy father's house; for thou hast prevailed, and thy father's house hath bowed down unto thee, even as it was shown unto thee, before thou wast sold into Egypt by the hands of thy brethren; wherefore thy brethren shall bow down unto thee, from generation to generation, unto the fruit of thy loins for ever; for thou shalt be a light unto my people, to deliver them in the days of their captivity, from bondage; and to bring salvation unto them, when they are altogether bowed down under sin. (JST Gen. 48:8-11.)

The "bondage" spoken of in verse 11 must not be confused with the bondage of Israel in Egypt, for it was Moses (of the tribe of Levi) and not Joseph's seed who led Israel out of that. It is a spiritual bondage of the last days, a universal apostasy, from which Joseph's seed rescues his brothers and sisters in the fullness of times. A careful reading of the passage makes this clear, as does the subsequent chapter of Genesis wherein Joseph, speaking to his brethren, prophesies first of Moses and of Aaron, and then of a latter-day seer named Joseph as found in JST Genesis 50:24-38. This prophecy, which was in the plates of brass, is the basis of Lehi's words in 2 Nephi 3:6-18, and is also restored to us through the Joseph Smith Translation of Genesis by the Prophet Joseph Smith.

NOTES

1. See also the chapter heading to Moroni 2, and Joseph Smith, the "Wentworth Letter," *History of The Church of Jesus Christ of Latter-day Saints*, 2nd ed. rev., edited by B. H. Roberts (Salt Lake City: The Church of Jesus Christ of Latter-day Saints, 1932-51), 4:538.

2. For example, the noted and respected F. F. Bruce approvingly quotes R. A. Knox as saying of John 10:16, "Our Lord evidently refers to the Gentiles who would believe him." (F. F. Bruce, *The Books and the Parchments* [London: Revell Company, 1955], p. 199.) The Reverend J. R. Dummelow in his *Commentary on the Holy Bible* (New York: MacMillan, 1960, p. 792) also interprets the "other sheep" of John 10:16 as the Gentiles and writes, "The Gentiles are also God's children. The gospel is for them also, and Jew and Gentile shall form one Church under one shepherd."

3. Joseph Smith, *Teachings of the Prophet Joseph Smith*, selected by Joseph Fielding Smith (Salt Lake City: Deseret Book Company, 1938), pp. 149-50.

4. Further reading on this subject can be found in Joseph Fielding Smith, "Who are the Gentiles?" *Answers to Gospel Questions*, 5 vols., compiled by Joseph Fielding Smith, Jr. (Salt Lake City: Deseret Book Company, 1957-66), 1:138-41; Bruce R. McConkie, "Gentiles," *Mormon Doctrine*, 2nd ed. (Salt Lake City: Bookcraft, 1966); and Bruce R. McConkie, *A New Witness for the Articles of Faith* (Salt Lake City: Deseret Book Company, 1985), pp. 518, 529-30.

16

THEOPHANY
(3 Nephi 17–19)

CATHERINE THOMAS

Only after 1830 could one who sought God turn to a book to read about the true nature and post-resurrection ministry of the living, corporeal, resurrected Son of God. But when Joseph Smith entered the grove in 1820, the world had lain more than 1,600 years in ignorance of the nature of God. About A.D. 180 Irenaeus, Bishop of Lyons, France, wrote: "The Father of all is at a vast distance from those affections and passions which operate among men. He is a simple, uncompounded Being, without diverse members, and altogether like, and equal to Himself, since He is wholly understanding, and wholly spirit, and wholly thought, and wholly intelligence, and wholly reason, and wholly hearing, and wholly seeing, and wholly light, and the whole source of all that is good."[1]

A few years after Irenaeus, Origen (ca. A.D. 230), a church scholar, described the Father and the Son: "Setting aside all thought of a material body, we say that [Christ] was begotten of the invisible and incorporeal God apart from any bodily feeling, like an act of will proceeding from the mind."[2] Much of the Christian world today repeats creeds that describe a passionless, bodiless God.

The Prophet Joseph had seen more truth in a short interview with the Father and the Son than centuries of theological sophistry could discover. Further truths concerning the nature of God poured into our dark world through the pages of 3 Nephi. Joseph Smith

---

Catherine Thomas is a doctoral student in ancient history at Brigham Young University.

remarked near the end of his life: "If men do not comprehend the character of God, they do not comprehend themselves."[3] We will examine here several insights from 3 Nephi 17-19 that pertain to the divine nature and its implications for man.

The First Day: God Revealed As a Man

One of the first doctrines to disappear when apostasy conceives in the hearts of mortals is the fact that God is a glorified man. When people repress that doctrine, they forget who they really are and what they may become (cf. the Zoramites, Alma 31:15). One of the first things Joseph Smith learned as the Lord undertook to educate him was that he was created in the literal image of the Father and the Son. Many express outrage at this doctrine, believing that it diminishes God and at the same time presumptuously exalts man. But Joseph Smith did not invent the idea. The Bible plainly speaks of man's creation in the image of God (Gen. 1:26-27); Jacob saw God face to face (Gen. 32:30); God has feet (Ex. 24:10); he has a finger (Ex. 31:18); Moses saw his face (Ex. 33:11) and his back parts (Ex. 33:23) and spoke to God mouth to mouth (Num. 12:8). The "eyes of the Lord" and the "ears of the Lord" occur frequently in the Prophets and in Psalms. In Genesis God walks about in the garden. (Genesis 3:8.)

As apostasy progressed in the intertestamental period, as well as in the post–New Testament period, many theologians found the idea that God has a body and emotions to be an embarrassment.[4] In spite of the fact that both the Old and New Testaments abound in expressions of God's love, joy, sadness, pity, and compassion, theologians of the third and fourth centuries A.D. preferred to envision God as impassible. R.M. Grant writes: "From the writings of early Christians after New Testament times we can discover relatively few references to God's love, though a few writers provide exceptions. In general the themes which were first developed were those related to God's transcendence and his relation to the cosmos."[5] Hilary of Poitiers (ca. A.D. 350) declared that Christ felt the *assault* of suffering but not the *pain* of suffering; it was as if a weapon were to pierce water or fire or air. He allowed that Christ did display thirst and sorrow and hunger, but only for the sake of others, not to satisfy his own needs.[6] Origen and other fathers avoided the themes of Christ's physical suffering in Gethsemane and of the atonement. The writings of even the Apostolic Fathers (second century A.D.) showed a marked weakening of the atonement idea, giving a minor place to the atoning value of his death.[7] These themes of the nebulous and unfeeling nature of God sufficiently distanced God from mortals that they could occupy themselves with irrelevant spiritual debates. Settling for less in God, they could require less of themselves. But in Joseph Smith's day a new generation had come to the earth, and it was ripe for restoration of true doctrine.

With the sweet refreshment of simple truth, 3 Nephi described the appearance of the resurrected Christ: From heaven a Man descended clothed in a white robe. He declared he was the Christ and invited the people to confirm that by coming forward and thrusting their hands into his side and feeling the prints of the nails. (3 Ne. 11:14.) Twenty-five hundred people (3 Ne. 17:25), one by one, saw with their eyes, felt with their hands, and bore record that it was indeed Christ (3 Ne. 11:15).[8] Each person saw and felt the tangible body of the resurrected Christ. The Apostle John declared: "Every spirit that confesseth that Jesus Christ is come in the flesh is of God: and every spirit that confesseth not that Jesus Christ is come in the flesh is not of God: and this is that spirit of antichrist." (1 Jn. 4:2-3.)

God's Response to Man's Desire

As it grew late in the first day of the Savior's visit, and he had finished the teaching tasks of that day, he looked round on the people and declared: "Behold, my time is at hand." (3 Ne. 17:1.) "Go ye unto your homes, and ponder upon the things which I have said, and ask of the Father, in my name, that ye may understand, and prepare your minds[9] for the morrow, and I come unto you again. But now I go unto the Father and . . . unto the lost tribes of Israel." (3 Ne. 17:4.) Emotionally and physically spent, the people were overwhelmed. Yet their eyes held his.

Earlier the Lord taught them: "Blessed are all they who do hunger and thirst after righteousness, for they shall be filled with the Holy

Ghost." (3 Ne. 12:6.) They were not satisfied; they were hungry. They yearned for him. His intent was to go to the bosom of his Father and to visit the Lost Tribes, but the Nephites' desire prevailed with him. He invited them to bring their sick. As many as could crowd near him kissed his feet and bathed them with their tears. (3 Ne. 17:10.) He was compelled by their longing for him. They brought all their children. Then Jesus commanded the multitude to kneel. Groaning "within himself," he prayed; he was standing: "Father, I am troubled because of the wickedness of the people of the house of Israel." (3 Ne. 17:14.) Kneeling, he continued his prayer, uttering things that could not be written; but those of the multitude who heard him bore record (3 Ne. 17:15): "The eye hath never seen, neither hath the ear heard, before, so great and marvelous things as we saw and heard Jesus speak unto the Father; and no tongue can speak, neither can there be written by any man, neither can the hearts of men conceive so great and marvelous things as we both saw and heard Jesus speak; and no one can conceive of the joy which filled our souls at the time we heard him pray for us unto the Father." (3 Ne. 17:16-17.) Jesus arose to find the multitude overcome with joy. His joy was full in theirs. (3 Ne. 17:20.) Weeping, he took the children one by one,[10] blessed them, and prayed to the Father for them. Then he wept again (3 Ne. 17:22): "Behold your little ones." The heavens opened, and angels descended in a fiery element that encircled the children; the angels ministered to them.[11]

Rendering comfort, relief, and healing knowledge belong to eternity. The whole host of heaven serves the cause of the healing and exaltation of God's children. Such simple virtues will continue into the eternities. Whatever Christ models for us is designed to endure in us. Whatever he teaches us he himself practices. Jesus, even though master of all, is servant of all. (Matt. 20:27.)

Bread of Life and the Mind of Christ

The Savior's next act was to institute the sacrament. (3 Ne. 18.) The Nephites ascended in their divine experience. They had witnessed outward manifestations of the Holy Ghost; now Jesus showed them how they could realize the promise of being inwardly filled in their hunger for the divine presence. He blessed bread and wine and instructed them to eat.

The Lord uses the image of "eating," whether fruit or bread or fish or living water, to provide a tangible symbol of obtaining a higher spiritual life, as though one could "eat" to replace one's old self with new cells of more dynamic and gifted life. Adam and Eve ate a new way of life (Gen. 3); the ancient Israelites ate the elements of the Passover and were delivered from spiritual and physical death (Ex. 12); they lived by the manna from heaven in the wilderness (Ex. 16); Lehi ate the fruit of the tree of Christ's love (1 Ne. 8); Jeremiah, Ezekiel, and John ate the words of Christ (Jer. 15:16; Ezek. 3:1; Rev. 10:10); Jesus bade the squeamish Jews to live by eating his flesh and blood (John 6:48-58). In each case, the people "ingested" the Holy Ghost, or obtained access to blessings through Christ. (1 Cor. 2:16.) The scripture records that the disciples and multitude were filled. (3 Ne. 18:4-5.) They were not only physically satisfied from an abundance of food, but also with what bread and wine represent: the spirit and body of Christ through the atonement. (3 Ne. 18:7.) Their physical satisfaction served as a device to teach spiritual satisfaction. In the sacrament covenant we promise to keep the commandments in exchange for the power to keep the commandments. We eat the emblems of the atonement to receive the spirit, the power, and the mind of Christ. The sacrament is not optional; it is the ordinance that unlocks the flow of the Holy Ghost and provides progression along the path of light and fulness.

True Prayer

True prayer is characterized by the presence of the Holy Ghost; that is, the Holy Ghost shows us what we may ask for and what we may obtain power to do: "Wherefore . . . feast upon the words of Christ; for behold, the words of Christ will tell you all things what ye should do. . . . It [the Holy Ghost] will show unto you all things what ye should do." (2 Ne. 32:3, 5.) The words of Christ come not only from the scripture, but through the Holy Ghost as well.

Now that the multitude had eaten the sacrament, they were prepared to receive the mind of Christ through prayer. He is the light;

he has set the example in prayer. (3 Ne. 18:16.) If we do not pray, we are in danger, because without the influence of Christ, we will absorb the influence of Satan. (3 Ne. 18:15, 18.) The Lord taught specifics:

1. (V. 19.) We pray to the Father of our spirits in the name of Christ, who is the Father of our spiritual rebirth. Our first Father holds the power of exaltation (Matt. 20:23; 3 Ne. 27:14-16); our second Father, Christ, holds the power of our spiritual rebirth on the path to our exaltation.

2. (V. 20.) (a) Ask aright, (b) believe, (c) receive: Prayer is *labor* in the spirit. Casually done, it has no power. We strain upward in spirit to grasp the answers we seek. We live for the Holy Ghost so that when we pray, we know what to ask for. Having power in the Holy Ghost, we have assurance that what we pray for will be granted. We believe, that is, we envision the realized blessing and actively receive it. "Believing," as it is used in the scriptures, signifies powerful confidence born of personal righteousness. (Hel. 14:13.)

3. (Vv. 21-23.) We learn that we may draw down the blessings of heaven on our loved ones, on the community of Saints, and on those who come to investigate. Prayer is not optional. We simply cannot move forward on the path of light without the Holy Ghost to illuminate the way.

The light that we must hold up, that must not be veiled in bushels of sin, fear, or pride, is the spirit of Christ that springs in us: "Behold I am the light which ye shall hold up — that which ye have seen me do." (3 Ne. 18:24.) We hold up, not the darkness of our own wills, but the light and love of God as Jesus demonstrated. He calls us to his works — not only sacrament, baptism, and so on, but also mighty miracles.

The image of holding up a light suggests that we hold up Christ's light in a dark world so those who are lost may come and have refuge in Jesus. Christ has given all in total consecration to the cause of saving God's children. We are to do the same in giving ourselves physically ("that ye might feel and see" [3 Ne. 18:25]) as well as spiritually, standing always behind his will rather than trotting ours out to the fore, being blind guides. (D&C 19:38-41.) For us to give less than all is by definition temptation and sin. (3 Ne. 18:25.) In fact, the implication is that if we do not actively and with full purpose of heart pursue the dissemination of Christ's light, we will find ourselves at cross purposes with God's will. Consecration saves us from ourselves.

Though we pray for and nurture those who live at the fringes of gospel commitment, the sacrament is reserved only for those in full fellowship. An unworthy person who takes the sacrament enters into spiritual chaos. If dangerous to the flock, the person shall not be numbered among them; that is, he or she may not be kept on the records of the church. But our responsibility to *minister* to the person continues as long as he or she will be ministered to. We never give up on someone lest Christ should "heal" the person and we be the means of bringing salvation to him or her. (3 Ne. 18:32.)

"And now I go unto the Father, because it is expedient that I should go unto the Father for your sakes." (3 Ne. 18:35.) The Lord made a similar statement to his apostles in Jerusalem: "It is expedient for you that I go away: for if I go not away, the Comforter will not come unto you; but if I depart, I will send him unto you." (John 16:7.) Christ had unveiled his glory to these Nephites. Spiritual realities were visually present with him. But we are here to live by faith, not by sight (2 Cor. 5:7), even though we lived by sight in our premortal home. It is not helpful for us at this stage of our progression to live with external visual heavenly manifestations. That fact underlies our separation from our premortal home. The reason is that *inner* perceptors of truth may not develop in the presence of manifestations. Now that we live on earth, we have even greater need for contact with our Heavenly Father. The Holy Ghost is sent to provide this contact by developing these inner perceptors. When those spiritual senses are developed, then we may reenter the presence of heavenly beings. The Second Comforter, or the physical presence of Christ and the Father, can come when we have developed our inner spiritual senses through the Holy Ghost.

The Savior's last act on this first day was to give his twelve disciples power to bestow the indispensable gift of the Holy Ghost (3 Ne.

18:36-37), that unseen link with the spiritual world. A heavenly cloud veiled his ascension into heaven.

The Second Day: Transfiguration

Through the night the people made known widely the fact that Jesus would return the next day. At the appointed time, Nephi and the rest of the Twelve divided the multitude into twelve groups; each disciple commenced teaching. After prayer, they accurately repeated the very words that Jesus had spoken the day before. (3 Ne. 19:8.) They prayed as Jesus had taught them, which was to pray for the Holy Ghost. Then Nephi baptized the rest of the Twelve, who received the Holy Ghost[12] and the baptism of fire; angels returned to minister again. Jesus appeared in the midst of this heavenly fire, and at his command his disciples began to pray to him, calling him their Lord and God. (3 Ne. 19:18.) Jesus explained in 3 Nephi 19:22 that they prayed to him rather than the Father because Jesus was with them. But the instruction under all other circumstances was to pray to the Father in the name of Jesus Christ. (3 Ne. 19:7.) We want to ask what they prayed to him. We cannot answer fully until we have experienced this kind of prayer ourselves, because the experience is grasped in one's spirit. But one thing we observe is that Jesus — even after his resurrection — continued to set the example in prayer.

Jesus thanked the Father for the giving of the Holy Ghost and prayed that all who heard the words of his disciples would believe them. The Lord encircled them with his love and righteousness, and they entered together into at-one-ment as Jesus prayed for that state of oneness. (3 Ne. 19:23.) It was a joyful fruition of his recent painful atonement.

It is the possession of the fullness that brings people into oneness with each other. As the Father has granted fullness to the Son, so a portion had been granted through the Holy Ghost to the disciples.

Jesus returned from prayer to find the disciples still praying: "It was given unto them what they should pray, and they were filled with desire. And it came pass that Jesus blessed them as they did pray unto him; and his countenance did smile upon them, and the light of his countenance did shine upon them, and behold they were as white as the countenance and also the garments of Jesus; and behold the whiteness thereof did exceed all the whiteness, yea, even there could be nothing upon earth so white as the whiteness thereof. And Jesus said unto them: Pray on; nevertheless they did not cease to pray." (3 Ne. 19:24-26.)

The Holy Ghost performs two of his functions in these passages: he fills those praying with catalytic desire, and he burns out impurities and cleanses them. In this process the disciples were transfigured, being empowered to endure the presence of heavenly elements and beings without being wholly consumed. (D&C 76:118.)

"Father, I thank thee that thou hast purified those whom I have chosen, because of their faith, and I pray for them, and also for them who shall believe on their words, that they may be purified in me, through faith on their words, even as they are purified in me." (3 Ne. 19:28.) We grasp here the meaning of the promise to those disciples who believe the words of the Lord's apostles and prophets. We too can experience this increasing purification and glory of the Lord. The Holy Ghost performs this purification for our entrance into the Lord's presence. We cannot cleanse ourselves. This process is initiated by our desire and effort, but it is consummated by the power of the Lord. (D&C 88:74.)

"Father, I pray not for the world, but for those whom thou hast given me out of the world, because of their faith, that they may be purified in me, that I may be in them as thou, Father, art in me, that we may be one, that I may be glorified in them." (3 Ne. 19:29.) Jesus spoke of being *glorified*. As we understand from D&C 93, *glory* is a manifestation related to light, truth, and intelligence; that is, to fullness. The reception of the fullness causes one to be glorified.

"When Jesus had spoken these words he came again unto his disciples; and behold they did pray steadfastly, without ceasing, unto him; and he did smile upon them again; and behold they were white, even as Jesus." (3 Ne. 19:30.) What does the shining, smiling face of God signify? The smile reflects the joy in God's nature and his giving of that joy to his receptive children. Elder Melvin J. Ballard experienced that divine smile:

> As I entered the door, I saw, seated on a raised platform,

the most glorious Being my eyes have ever beheld or that I ever conceived existed in all the eternal worlds. As I approached to be introduced, he arose and stepped towards me with extended arms, and he smiled as he softly spoke my name. If I shall live to be a million years old, I shall never forget that smile. He took me into his arms and kissed me, pressed me to his bosom, and blessed me, until the marrow of my bones seemed to melt! When he had finished, I knelt at his feet, and, as I bathed them with my tears and kisses, I saw the prints of the nails in the feet of the Redeemer of the world. The feeling that I had in the presence of him who hath all things in his hands, to have his love, his affection, and his blessing was such that if I ever can receive that of which I had but a foretaste, I would give all that I am, all that I ever hope to be, to feel what I then felt.[13]

"The multitude did hear and do bear record; and their hearts were open and they did understand in their hearts the words which he prayed . . . [which] cannot be written, neither can they be uttered by man." (3 Ne. 19:33.) God has granted to many the right and power to communicate to others important things pertaining to the mysteries of the kingdom (although even this information is understood by the Holy Ghost). But there is reserved by God that knowledge which is communicated only by God directly to the one whose heart is prepared. This knowledge cannot be communicated to others. Joseph Smith wrote as he viewed the mysteries and works of God: "Which [works and mysteries of God] he commanded us we should not write while we were yet in the Spirit, and are not lawful for man to utter; neither is man capable to make them known, for they are only to be seen and understood by the power of the Holy Spirit, which God bestows on those who love him, and purify themselves before him; to whom he grants this privilege of seeing and knowing for themselves; that through the power and manifestation of the Spirit, while in the flesh, they may be able to bear his presence in the world of glory." (D&C 76:115-118.)

Conclusion

In these chapters we observe how like God man is, how he is organized on the same principles that God is, and how it is man's destiny to develop into a Godly being. Through Christ, we learn that God is a man, that he has a tangible body; we see that he is deeply sensitive, patient, loving, and responsive to the pure desires of his children. He teaches us to study him and be as he is. We observe that coming to the sacrament table hungry in spirit will prepare us to receive the Holy Ghost and the mind of Christ. We begin to understand how intimate a relationship he offers us. We learn that he stands ready to share his fullness as fast as we can put aside the veil of fear and sin. We sense that a stronger envisioning of the spiritual realities around us might draw us closer to a face-to-face view.

NOTES

1. "Adversus Haereses," 10.3. *The Ante-Nicene Fathers* (Grand Rapids: Eerdmans, 1885).

2. "De Principiis," 4.4.1, in G.W. Butterworth, ed., *Origen: On First Principles* (New York: Harper & Row, 1966), pp. 313-14.

3. King Follett Discourse (Willard Richards's account) in *The Words of Joseph Smith*, Andrew F. Ehat and Lyndon W. Cook eds. (Provo, Utah: Religious Studies Center, 1981), p. 340.

4. Edwin Hatch, *The Influence of Greek Ideas and Usages upon the Christian Church* (London: Williams and Norgate, 1914), p. 69; for anthropomorphisms in the Old Testament, see Cecil Roth, "Anthropomorphism," *Encyclopaedia Judaica*, vol. 3 (Jerusalem: Keter Publishing House, 1972), p. 53.

5. Robert M. Grant, *The Early Christian Doctrine of God* (Charlottesville: Univ. Press of Virginia, 1966), pp. 4-5.

6. *De Trinitas*, 10-23.

7. J.N.D. Kelly, *Early Christian Doctrines*, rev. ed. (San Franciso: Harper & Row, 1978), p. 165.

8. The image of 2,500 people going forth one by one arrests our attention. Even if each person had only ten seconds to touch the Lord's body, that adds up to nearly seven hours that he stood patiently and graciously allowed this examination.

9. The Lord reminded us of the place our agency has in our receiving spiritual growth and blessing. We may understand spiritual experience too

passively, *waiting* for something to happen to us. Perhaps we wait too patiently for the arrival of the spiritual blessings we need. We may not realize that many blessings require, initially, acts of will on our part, a labor in the spirit, a setting aside of time: cleansing of selfish purpose from the heart, submission, envisioning the blessing, thanks in anticipation of receiving the blessing. God gave us agency, and it may have more power than we have used.

10. This is the second use of "one by one" and reassures us of the Lord's individual attention to each of his children. Again we calculate how much time the blessing of many hundreds of children individually must have taken. He illustrated what he says later: "I know my sheep, and they are numbered." (3 Ne. 18:31.)

11. Cf. Matt 20:28: "The Son of man came not to be ministered unto, but to minister." *The New Bible Dictionary* notes that the Hebrew term *mesaret* (LXX *leitourgos*) and its correlates normally refer to temple service, or else to the ministration of angels. It refers to service in general, has the special connotation of lowly service, often of a subordinate. In Luke 22:27 Christ appears among the disciples as *ho diakonon*, "one who serves." (J. D. Douglas, ed. *New Bible Dictionary*, 2nd ed. [Wheaton, Illinois: Tyndale House Publishers, 1982].) Ministering suggests the giving of spiritual gifts for relief and comfort.

12. These Nephites had baptism all along, but with the establishment of a new organization of the Church, they all underwent baptism and confirmation for admission into the new order.

13. Bryant S. Hinckley, *Sermons and Missionary Service of Melvin J. Ballard* (Salt Lake City: Deseret Book Company, 1949), pp. 155-56.

17

THE FINAL GATHERING TO CHRIST
(3 Nephi 20–22)

JOSEPH F. MCCONKIE

The instruction given by Christ to the Nephites included a prophetic description of the most singular events of the last days. In teaching of such things, the Savior affirmed that the Father had not forgotten the covenant he had made with his people—the house of Israel—and that his word would be fulfilled, every jot and tittle. Briefly stated, that promise was that they would be gathered in from "the east and from the west, and from the south and from the north," and that they would "be brought to the knowledge of the Lord their God, who hath redeemed them." (3 Ne. 20:13.) This latter-day gathering, Christ testified, would be first spiritual and then temporal. Israel, he said, must return first to their covenants and then to their covenant lands.

The Sword of God's Justice

Christ commanded the Nephites to record the things he said to them. He prophesied that what was written would eventually come forth through the Gentiles [Joseph Smith and the tribe of Ephraim] to the remnant of Israel who had been scattered throughout the earth for faithless rejection of the Messiah. Christ affirmed that in the last days they would be gathered on condition of faithful acceptance of him. That is, through the testimony of the Nephite record they would

---

Joseph F. McConkie is professor of ancient scripture at Brigham Young University.

obtain a knowledge of their Redeemer and "then" be gathered in, that Christ might fulfill the covenant he had made with "all the people of the house of Israel." (3 Ne. 16:4-5.)

Christ gave the Nephites a prophetic description of the restoration of the fullness of the gospel in the last days, announcing that it would come through the Gentiles. The word *Gentile* is used in this context to emphasize that it would not be the nation of Israel — that nation formed by God — who would bring forth the word of life, but rather those possessing believing blood who had been scattered among Gentile nations. Thus *Gentiles* as used in the Book of Mormon includes faithful descendants of Abraham, Isaac, and Jacob who are not of the tribe of Judah or who are not transplanted Jewish nationals; that is, citizens of the Southern Kingdom. This time of restoration is known to us as the "times of the Gentiles." When the time comes that the Gentiles partake of that same dark spirit known to the tribe of Judah in the meridian of time, they too, the Savior said, would come to know the chastening hand of the Lord and know it in the same measure. Of that day and time the resurrected Christ said, "Then will I remember my covenant which I have made unto my people, O house of Israel, and I will bring my gospel unto them." (See 3 Ne. 16:11, 6-14.) Thus the Savior explained that in the final dispensation the gospel would go first to the Gentiles; after they had rejected it, it would be taken to the Jews.

We learn from the Joseph Smith Translation that Christ foretold these same events to the inner circle of faithful Saints in the Old World. In a private explanation of the parable of the householder, he said that the kingdom of God would be taken from the Jews in the meridian day and given to the Gentiles. He said that in the last days, he would "let again his vineyard unto other husbandmen," also Gentiles, who would "render him the fruits in their seasons." Nevertheless, wicked Gentiles would also be destroyed, he prophesied, "when the Lord should descend out of heaven to reign in his vineyard, which is the earth and the inhabitants thereof." (JST, Matt. 21:47-56.)

This day of vengeance is millennial; it refers to the Second Coming. Christ used the words of Micah to describe it: "The remnant of Jacob shall be among the Gentiles in the midst of many people as a lion among the beasts of the forest, as a young lion among the flocks of sheep: who, if he go through, both treadeth down, and teareth in pieces, and none can deliver." (Micah 5:8; 3 Ne. 20:16; 21:12.) The prophecy has no reference to the Lamanites or any other remnant of Israel waging war against Gentile oppressors. Such is not the Lord's system. At his coming, the wicked will be destroyed and the righteous preserved; those who have rejected his prophets "shall be cut off." Elder Bruce R. McConkie explained: "It shall be with power, as though a young lion went forth rending and tearing in pieces a helpless flock of sheep. And so, if the Gentiles do not repent and believe in Christ after the gospel is restored among them, then, when the Lord comes, they will be destroyed and the triumph of Israel—because they kept the commandments and did receive the gospel—that triumph will be complete."[1]

Christ further emphasized that this final gathering was to be his doing and not that of mortals—a matter of making bare his arm in contrast to the arm of flesh. He said, "I will gather my people together as a man gathereth his sheaves into the floor." He then added to the imagery of the ferocious lion that of a goring bull. Again the prophetic promise is given in the words of Micah: "I will make thine horn iron, and I will make thy hoofs brass: and thou shalt beat in pieces many people: and I will consecrate their gain unto the Lord, and their substance unto the Lord of the whole earth."[2] (Micah 4:13.) Christ's commentary was simple and direct: "And behold, I am he who doeth it." The sword of God's justice, he declared, shall hang over all the nations of the Gentiles, and unless they repent it shall fall upon them. As for the house of Israel—it would be for God to establish his own people. (3 Ne. 20:19-21.)

The New Jerusalem

As to the establishment of his people, the Savior told the Nephites that their land would be the place of a New Jerusalem. The Americas— apparently the whole land—had been promised to the seed of Joseph, for such was the covenant Christ made with Joseph's father, Jacob. Jacob had prophesied that Joseph's branches (Ephraim and

Manasseh) would cross the waters to inherit "the utmost bound of the everlasting hills." (Gen. 49:22, 26; see also Deut. 33:15.) Yet long before that day, Enoch had written of a time when the Lord would gather his elect from the four quarters of the earth, to a place he would prepare, a holy city, wherein his people would ready themselves for his coming, and wherein would be found his tabernacle (the temple). This place was to be "called Zion, a New Jerusalem." (Moses 7:62.) At that time, and again this is clearly millennial, Christ said, "The powers of heaven shall be in the midst of this people; yea, even I will be in the midst of you." (3 Ne. 20:22.)

A little later in this same discourse, Christ again quoted Micah relative to the ravishing lion and the destruction of the unrepentant Gentiles. Again he announced that the rebellious were to be cut off from the house of Israel, while promising that the righteous would be numbered among his church. "And they shall come in unto the covenant and be numbered among this the remnant of Jacob, unto whom I have given this land for their inheritance," he said. (3 Ne. 21:12-22; Micah 5:8-15.) Thus the believing and obedient will be called on to build the New Jerusalem. "And they shall assist my people, the remnant of Jacob, and also as many of the house of Israel as shall come, that they may build a city, which shall be called the New Jerusalem." (3 Ne. 21:23.) All such labors, we learn from the Doctrine and Covenants, are to be accomplished by the authority of the priesthood and under the direction of those holding its keys. (D&C 42:8-9, 30-42; 45:66-71; 52:2, 42-43; 57:1-5; 58:7, 44-58; 84:2-5.) "And then shall they [those who have embraced the restored covenant through baptism] assist my people that they may be gathered in, who are scattered upon all the face of the land, in unto the New Jerusalem." As we shall yet see, the greater part of the gathering will take place after the building of the New Jerusalem, for only then "shall the power of heaven come down among them" and Christ reign personally upon the earth. (See 3 Ne. 21:20-25.)

Thus, this New Jerusalem shall become "a land of peace, a city of refuge, a place of safety for the saints of the Most High God; and the glory of the Lord shall be there, and the terror of the Lord also shall be there, insomuch that the wicked will not come unto it, and it shall be called Zion. And it shall come to pass among the wicked, that every man that will not take his sword against his neighbor must needs flee unto Zion for safety. And there shall be gathered unto it out of every nation under heaven; and it shall be the only people that shall not be at war one with another. And it shall be said among the wicked: Let us not go up to battle against Zion, for the inhabitants of Zion are terrible; wherefore we cannot stand. And it shall come to pass that the righteous shall be gathered out from among all nations, and shall come to Zion, singing with songs of everlasting joy." (D&C 45:66-71.)

All of Israel's Prophets Testified of Christ

Surely the reader of Christ's discourse on the gathering will not overlook how closely he tied the Nephites to their ancient forebears in the Old World. Though they would have their own Zion, their own Jerusalem, their own prophets, and their own scripture, they were to be united with the faithful of all nations and all ages. There is but one Shepherd and one fold—one Christ and one message of salvation. All prophets speak with the same voice. "I am he of whom Moses spake," Christ declared, and thus it follows that to profess Moses is to profess Christ. "Verily I say unto you, yea, and all the prophets from Samuel [the first prophet of the nation of Israel] and those that follow after [and this is everlastingly so], as many as have spoken, have testified of me." (3 Ne. 20:23-24.) We have no greater evidence of the taking of the "plain" and the "precious" from the records of the Old Testament than the expunging of the testimony of its prophets relative to Christ.

Blessings of the Covenant

Joseph Smith's translation of the Abraham papyrus opens to us a flood of knowledge about the covenant God made with our ancient father—knowledge now lost to those whose understanding is limited to the Bible. From the record we learn that Abraham was promised that his seed—his literal descendants—were to hold the priesthood and carry the message of salvation, even the blessings of eternal life, to all nations. (Abr. 2:9, 11.) This right has not been given to those of any other lineage. In our present text, Christ reminds the Nephites that they are the children of the prophets and thus inheritors of the promises made to Abraham. It was because of that covenant that Christ had come to them and sought to turn them from their iniquities. (3 Ne. 20:25-26.)

Amplifying the Abrahamic covenant over that preserved for us in the Bible, the Savior said that he had promised Abraham that through his posterity all the families of the earth would be blessed by the "pouring out of the Holy Ghost," which blessing would make the Gentiles "mighty above all, unto the scattering of . . . [the] house of Israel." The Gentiles, he said, would be a "scourge unto the people of this land," meaning Lehi's descendants in the last days. Nevertheless, after the fullness of the gospel had gone forth among the Gentiles, if they hardened their hearts and returned to their iniquities all these evils would return to them. (3 Ne. 20:27-28.)

The Day of Jewish Conversion

When the day of the Gentile has been fulfilled, that is, when the gospel will be taken from them because of their iniquities, the Savior will remember the covenant he made with those of Judah to return them to their ancient covenant land. Of this yet future day, he said, "The fulness of my gospel shall be preached unto them; and they shall believe in me, that I am Jesus Christ, the Son of God, and shall pray unto the Father in my name." After their conversion to Christ, after that time when their "watchmen" come to see "eye to eye" with their Savior, "then will the Father gather them together again, and give unto them Jerusalem for the land of their inheritance." (3 Ne. 20:29-33.)

Of this matter Elder Bruce R. McConkie wrote: "As all the world knows, many Jews are now gathering to Palestine, where they have their own nation and way of worship, all without reference to a belief in Christ or an acceptance of the laws and ordinances of his everlasting gospel. Is this the latter-day gathering of the Jews of which the scriptures speak? No! It is not; let there be no misunderstanding in any discerning mind on this point. This gathering of the Jews to their homeland, and their organization into a nation and a kingdom, is not the gathering promised by the prophets. It does not fulfill the ancient promises. Those who have thus assembled have not gathered into the true Church and fold of their ancient Messiah. They have not received again the saving truths of that very gospel which blessed Moses their lawgiver, and Elijah their prophet, and Peter, James, and John, whom their fathers rejected."[3]

It will be in this future setting, the Savior explained, that the prophecies of Isaiah relative to Zion putting on her strength (the authority of the priesthood), and loosing herself from the bands of her neck (returning to the Lord and receiving revelation) shall be fulfilled. (See Isaiah 52:1-2; D&C 113:7-10.) This is to be a day in which "my people shall know my name; yea, in that day they shall know that I am he that doth speak." In that day they will rejoice in those who have brought the message of salvation to them and invited them to depart a wicked world to once more worship their God with pure hearts and clean hands and to clothe themselves in white garments, having been washed in the blood of the Lamb. (See 3 Ne. 20:39-42; 2 Ne. 25:16; Ether 13:10-12.)

The Great Prophet of the Restoration

To this point Christ was describing the restoration of the gospel, Israel being clothed again with the priesthood, and the coming of the revelations of heaven, all of which are requisite to the gathering of Israel in the last days. It is natural at this point that some reference be made to the servant-prophet who would represent the Lord in accomplishing such a marvelous work and wonder. This is precisely what Christ did, though he went about it in an unusual way. He quoted four verses from Isaiah that are obviously Messianic—verses descriptive of his mortal ministry, which was now complete. (See 3 Ne. 20:42-45; Isa. 52:12-15.) The context in which Christ used these verses and the manner in which he returned to phrases from them a little later in this discourse make it obvious that he was applying them to the great prophet of the Restoration, who, like himself, was to be a suffering servant. Obviously these verses, like many others—

and this is particularly so in the writings of Isaiah—were intended by the spirit of revelation to embrace multiple fulfillment.[4]

Concluding his prophetic description of the return of those of Judah to their ancient land, Christ testified: "All these things shall surely come, even as the Father hath commanded me. Then shall this covenant which the Father hath covenanted with his people be fulfilled; and then shall Jerusalem be inhabited again with my people, and it shall be the land of their inheritance." (3 Ne. 20:46.)

Jesus then gave his Nephite congregation a sign so they would know when these things—specifically the gathering of Israel and the establishment of Zion—"shall be about to take place." The sign embraced a series of events including the establishment of a free people in the United States of America; the restoration of the gospel; the taking of the gospel to the Lamanites; and the martyrdom of the prophet-servant of the Restoration and his eternal triumph in the kingdom of God. Commenting on this prophecy, Moroni later wrote: "When ye shall receive this record [the Book of Mormon] ye may know that the work of the Father has commenced upon all the face of the land." (3 Ne. 21:1-10; Ether 4:17.)

At this point in the Savior's remarks it becomes evident why he quoted Isaiah's prophecies about a suffering servant to identify the great prophet who would stand at the head of the latter-day gathering of Israel. The prophet was to be "hurt" or "marred," even as the Savior had been "hurt" and "marred" in his mortal ministry by the enemies of truth. How perfect the parallel between Joseph Smith and Jesus Christ—both were hounded and rejected by the religious leaders of their day; both were scorned and accused of being possessed by a devil; indeed, both were accused of blasphemy; and of course both sealed their testimony with their blood as martyrs, having given offense to none but the legions of darkness.

The Magnitude of the Gathering

The greatness of Israel's gathering must match the greatness of its scattering. For thousands of years the children of Abraham have been sifted among the nations of the earth. Even today the scattering of the chosen seed continues. Israel has been scattered for rebellion against their God; for rejecting his prophets; for breaking their covenants; indeed, for crucifying their Messiah. The gathering, which comes in answer to the scattering, must be equally extensive. It must reach to the ends of the earth, center in obedience to the God of heaven, call forth living prophets, and demand acceptance of Jesus as the Christ.

By what voice is scattered Israel to be called back to the covenants and lands of their fathers? Should it not be by the voice of their fathers? A voice from the dust? A voice bearing the testimony common to all the holy prophets since the world began? Ought it not to center in the testimony of Christ? Such was the promise of the Savior — a book to come forth — a book containing the testimony of Christ and the true points of doctrine, a book bringing those of the latter days to the knowledge of their forebears, a book containing the knowledge of the covenants of salvation. Such was the promise of the Savior, a promise with a warning that all who reject the book and its witness "shall be cut off from among the people who are of the covenant." (3 Ne. 21:11.)

"But if they will repent and hearken unto my words," the Savior declared, "and harden not their hearts, I will establish my church among them, and they shall come in unto the covenant and be numbered among this the remnant of Jacob" — having reference to Lehi's seed; for they and as many as shall come to the covenant shall help build the New Jerusalem. "Then shall the power of heaven come down among them" and the Savior be in their midst. (3 Ne. 21:22-25.)

The text then declares that at this time — and it is clearly millennial — the work of the Father shall "commence" in gathering the dispersed of Israel — the tribes that have been lost — back to the land of their inheritance. There is no mistaking the intended meaning. Four times in three verses the Lord said that the labor of gathering Israel will "commence" at this time. (See 3 Ne. 21:26-28.) Having so declared, Jesus then sustained his point by quoting Isaiah 54, with the announcement that this is also the time of its fulfillment. This chapter tells the story of returning Israel using the metaphor of the marriage covenant. "More are the children of the desolate than the children of the married wife, saith the Lord." That is, greater are the numbers of Israel born outside of the covenant than those born within it. "Enlarge the place of thy tent, and let them stretch forth the curtains of thy habitations; spare not, lengthen thy cords and strengthen thy stakes." Make ready for the great numbers who will be gathered, that is, join the Church, during the millennium—so great, in fact, that the number of those who joined before is not even a beginning in comparison. "For thou shalt break forth on the right hand and on the left, and thy seed shall inherit the Gentiles and make the desolate cities to be inhabited." (3 Ne. 22:1-3; Isa. 54:1-3.)

"And all thy children shall be taught of the Lord; and great shall be the peace of thy children.... No weapon that is formed against thee shall prosper; and every tongue that shall revile against thee in judgment thou shalt condemn. This is the heritage of the servants of the Lord, and their righteousness is of me, saith the Lord." (3 Ne. 22:13, 17; Isa. 54:13, 17.)

Conclusion

We have no more authoritative or informative source on the latter-day gathering of Israel than the words of Christ recorded in 3 Nephi 20-22. The discourse has not received its proper due among those who have taught and written on the subject. In fact, it has often been the source of doctrinal mischief. As is so often the case where faulty interpretations are concerned, those claiming these teachings of the Savior as their source practice what could be termed theological kidnapping—taking a passage out of context and holding it hostage to sustain some speculative view. Perhaps the greatest error in the interpretation of the Savior's words has been the failure to read them as a unit.

These comments of the Savior certainly affirm that neither he nor his Father has forgotten the covenants made to our ancient progenitors. The promises God made to the posterity of Abraham, Isaac, and Jacob are real! The Abrahamic covenant is not an allegory; it is not a Bible story that is to be spiritualized away. The gathering of Israel will be literal, and it is literal Israel that is to be gathered. The promises given to the seed of Abraham are as real as the dirt and dust upon which he set his feet of flesh and blood, they are as real as the brick and mortar with which the New Jerusalem is to be built, as real as the sweat and tears with which the Jerusalem of old is to be rebuilt.

Yet, as is always the case, a spiritual gathering must precede the physical gathering—a gathering that centers in the restoration of the "fulness of the gospel," the "pouring out of the Holy Ghost," the reestablishing of the "true points" of Christ's doctrine, the believing in his words, the repentance of sin and coming unto the "Beloved Son." "I will establish my church among them," Christ declared, "and they shall come in unto the covenant."

The heart of the gathering is the testimony of Jesus. Those who reject that testimony particularly and specifically as it comes forth in the record of the Nephites and at the hands of the Prophet Joseph Smith are to be cut off from among the Lord's people. One can hardly overstate the importance of the Book of Mormon in this epic drama of Israel's gathering. "What, then, is the power of the Book of Mormon?" Elder McConkie asked. "It will build the New Jerusalem; it will prepare a people for the Second Coming; it will usher in the Millennium—at least it will play such an important part in all of these that its value and power can scarcely be overstated."[5]

NOTES

1. Bruce R. McConkie, *The Mortal Messiah*, 4 vols. (Salt Lake City: Deseret Book Company, 1979-81), 4:334-35. See also *The Millennial Messiah* (Salt Lake City: Deseret Book Company, 1982), pp. 244-48.

2. We are told in the Doctrine and Covenants that returning Israel will bring "their rich treasures" with them. (D&C 133:30.) Traditionally it has been supposed that this means scriptural records. It is, however, quite possible that the text means what it says—that returning Israel will in fact bring rich treasures. When Abraham and Sarah returned after their trial in Egypt to that sacred land promised them, they went "rich in cattle, in silver, and in gold," returning first to Bethel—the house of God—and its altar that they might call upon the name of the Lord. (Gen. 13:2-4.) Similarly, before the children of Israel left Egypt to return to the promised land to rebuild

their temple and call upon God, they were directed to obtain from the Egyptians their "jewels of silver, and jewels of gold." (Ex. 11:2.) When the Jews were freed from their captivity in Babylon to return to Palestine to rebuild the Holy City and its temple, the treasure houses of that great nation were opened to them, and they returned laden with silver and gold. (Ezra 7:15-21.) Thus, when Israel returns to claim the blessings of the temple in the last days, should they not return with their rich treasures as their forebears did before them?

3. *The Millennial Messiah*, p. 229.

4. See Joseph Fielding McConkie and Robert L. Millet, *Doctrinal Commentary on the Book of Mormon* (Salt Lake City: Bookcraft, 1987), 1:157.

5. *The Millennial Messiah*, p. 171.

18

TEACHING FROM THE WORDS OF THE PROPHETS
(3 Nephi 23–26)

KENT P. JACKSON

The greatest instructional session recorded in history took place while the resurrected Jesus taught his disciples in the Americas. The Lord God Almighty—who had revealed covenants, laws, and ordinances to his children since the beginning—stood among mortals who had purified themselves and had been found worthy to be in his presence. In this setting Jesus was with individuals who were saints, "holy ones," whose faith had enabled them to escape the cleansing destruction preceding his coming and to enjoy his subsequent visit among them. Thus Jesus could teach them his gospel in its fullness and purity, unconstrained by the presence of the unfaithful.

It is instructive in this context to observe how Jesus taught his disciples.[1] In his sermons he drew freely from the words he had inspired his earlier messengers to write, much more so than he had done in his mortal ministry in Palestine as far as we can tell from the New Testament. He frequently cited passages from the Hebrew scriptures and gave divine commentary to them. He also quoted entire chapters. (3 Ne. 22 = Isa. 54; 3 Ne. 24-25 = Mal. 3-4.)

Great Are the Words

After having quoted the 54th chapter of Isaiah (3 Ne. 22), Jesus gave Isaiah an unprecedented endorsement, calling his words "great"

Kent P. Jackson is associate professor of ancient scripture at Brigham Young University.

and commanding his disciples to search them. (3 Ne. 23:1.)[2] Isaiah's words are great because they touch on "all things" concerning the house of Israel, thus also being of importance to the Gentiles. (3 Ne. 23:2.) Jesus reminded his listeners of the eternal value of such scripture: those who hearken to the Lord's revealed word, repent, and are baptized will be saved. (3 Ne. 23:5.)

As the word of God revealed to prophets is precious, it is important that it be recorded properly, along with the fulfillment of things that God makes known. Jesus, noting the absence of some important information in the Nephite record, commanded that it be included. (3 Ne. 23:6-13.)

The Savior taught from the scriptures, setting the example for all gospel teachers to follow. As Mormon reported, he "expounded all the scriptures in one." (3 Ne. 23:14; see also 24:1; 26:1-2.) To "expound all scriptures in one" perhaps means to bring all the revealed word of God to one focal point, laying stress on that toward which all scripture points — the mission of Jesus Christ.[3] Having done this, Jesus commanded his disciples that they teach to others what he had taught them, thus building a chain of pure doctrinal understanding that would continue into subsequent generations.

As Jesus expounded the scriptures to his American saints, he quoted to them the revelations that now comprise Malachi 3 and 4 in the Old Testament. These chapters contain significant doctrinal material that reveals much concerning the Lord's coming. Perhaps that is why the Lord directed that they be written in the Nephite record, and perhaps it is why Mormon was inspired to include them in his Book of Mormon abridgment for us.

Because of the fragmented nature of the material in Malachi 3 and 4, in which a diverse variety of topics is discussed in short (sometimes unconnected) segments, this section appears to be a collection of utterances — a quote book — and not a continuous prophecy. Perhaps some of the brief quotations may not even be those of Malachi himself. Elder Bruce R. McConkie suggested that Malachi was quoting (specifically in Mal. 4:1-2) from the words of the ancient prophet Zenos, whose writings were contained on the plates of brass but are not found in the Bible as it stands today. (See 1 Ne. 22:15, 24.)[4]

The Day of Christ's Coming

The revelation in 3 Nephi 24:1-2 (Mal. 3:1-2) prophesies of the Lord's messenger who would be sent to prepare the way before His coming in glory. The terminology in this passage seems to refer clearly to the Second Coming, yet the same words are used in the New Testament to describe John the Baptist, the messenger sent to prepare the way before the Lord's coming in mortality. (See Matt. 11:10; Mark 1:2.) The passage was rightly applied to John, who prepared the way for the Lord's first coming, but the ultimate fulfillment of the prophecy will be in the latter days. It tells of the appearance of the Lord "suddenly" in his temple, asking rhetorically who will be able to endure his coming and the cleansing that will accompany it.

The scriptures do not identify the messenger to whom Malachi referred. Many messengers have in fact been involved in preparing the way for Christ, participating in the restoration of the gospel before his coming. Some of these messengers have been mortal and some angelic. Among the heavenly messengers of the Restoration the following could be listed: John the Baptist and Peter, James, and John, who restored priesthood power to Joseph Smith; Elijah, the bearer of priesthood keys, whose coming is the subject of discussion in Malachi's next chapter; and Moroni, the heavenly messenger who set the latter-day work into motion.[5] Perhaps what Malachi envisioned was not an individual but the *collective ministry* of all the messengers who restored doctrine and keys in the last days, each in turn preparing the way for Christ.

The Prophet Joseph Smith was also a great messenger sent to prepare the way for the Lord. As John was sent anciently, Joseph Smith was sent into the world in modern times to establish the Lord's work prior to the Second Coming.[6]

Perhaps an even broader interpretation may be of value. The Lord revealed: "I have sent mine everlasting covenant into the world, to be a light to the world, and to be a standard for my people, and for the Gentiles to seek to it, and to be a messenger before my face to prepare the way before me." (D&C 45:9.) Thus the gospel—restored in the latter days to make the world ready for the Lord—is a messenger sent before him.

As Malachi foretold, when Christ comes he will "purify the sons of Levi," so they will "offer unto the Lord an offering in righteousness." (3 Ne. 24:3.) The descendants of Levi, who still exist among the Jews throughout the world, are rightful heirs to the Priesthood of Aaron. Yet they are now outside of the covenants of the gospel, which are found only in The Church of Jesus Christ of Latter-day Saints, and thus are unable to fill the role to which their family had been chosen by revelation and set apart in ancient times. As part of the restoration of all things, the tribe of Levi once again will fill a priesthood function in the Lord's kingdom—after they become converted, are purified at the Lord's coming, join the Church of Jesus Christ, and are born again of the Spirit. Joseph Smith taught:

> All the ordinances and duties that ever have been required by the priesthood under the direction and commandments of the Almighty, in any of the dispensations, shall all be had in the last dispensation. Therefore all things had under the authority of the priesthood at any former period shall be had again—bringing to pass the restoration spoken of by the mouth of all the holy prophets. Then shall the sons of Levi offer an acceptable sacrifice to the Lord. . . .
>
> We frequently have mention made of the offering of sacrifice by the servants of the Most High in ancient days prior to the Law of Moses, which ordinances will be continued when the priesthood is restored with all its authority, power, and blessings. . . . These sacrifices as well as every ordinance belonging to the priesthood will, when the temple of the Lord shall be built and the sons [of] Levi be purified, be fully restored and attended to—then all their powers, ramifications, and blessings. This ever was and will exist when the powers of the Melchizedek Priesthood are sufficiently manifest. Else how can the restitution of all things spoken of by all the holy prophets be brought to pass? It is not to be understood that the Law of Moses will be established again with all its rites and variety of ceremonies; this had never been spoken of by

the prophets. But those things which existed prior [to] Moses'
day, namely sacrifice, will be continued.[7]

From this passage it appears that the Levites will offer animal
sacrifice in the Millennium, in restoration of the offerings that were
in force before the Law of Moses. From our available information on
the subject, it cannot be said whether this will be a lasting, ongoing
ordinance or a short-term event to complete this cycle of the restoration of all things and signal that the Levites are again in the
covenant and have assumed their rightful priesthood function in the
house of Israel.[8] In any case, as Joseph Smith taught, "The Lord will
purify the sons of Levi, good or bad, for it is through them that
blessings flow to Israel. . . . And then, and not till then, 'shall the offering of Judah and Jerusalem be pleasant unto the Lord, as in days
of old and as in former years' [3 Ne. 24:4]."[9]

In verses 5-7, the Lord directed his anger against individuals
and societies who are guilty of sins against God and fellow beings.
(3 Ne. 24:5.) "Return unto me," he pleaded, "and I will return unto
you." (3 Ne. 24:7.) One matter of concern specified by the Lord is
tithing. That Malachi's great passage regarding the payment of tithes
(3 Ne. 24:8-12; Mal. 3:8-12) was quoted by the Savior on this occasion
highlights its importance. Latter-day Saints who have put the Lord to
the test, as he invited (verse 10), can testify to the fulfillment of
God's promises. It is not unlikely that the law of tithing was an
important part of the Lord's plan for the Nephites, as it is for us today.

Malachi's revelation drew a stark contrast between those who
are humble and receptive to the Lord's will and those who are not.
Some speak against God, find no value in doing his will, and even
question his justice. (3 Ne. 24:13-15.) But those who revere the Lord
can rejoice that their righteousness is recorded in God's "book of
remembrance." (3 Ne. 24:16.) Their reward is sure: "They shall be
mine, saith the Lord of Hosts, in that day when I make up my jewels."
(3 Ne. 24:17.) The relevance of this section of Malachi to Jesus'
audience seems clear. Those who did not trust the prophetic an-
nouncements of his coming—and thus did not prepare—were cut
off. Yet those who were faithful enjoyed the Savior's presence, even

then. Later Jesus rejoiced that they would not be lost. (3 Ne. 27:30-31.)

With Healing in His Wings

The setting for the fulfillment of 3 Nephi 25:1 (Mal. 4:1) is the destruction of the wicked that will be part of the earth's cleansing preparatory to the Lord's return in glory. When Jesus returns, the earth must be purified. Whether by repentance or by destruction, wickedness of all forms must be removed before Christ will dwell here, for only those who are worthy will be privileged to live in his presence.[10]

Verses 2 and 3 continue the theme of the cleansing that will attend the Second Coming. The Lord foretold the condition of those who "fear [his] name." For them, "the Son of Righteousness [shall] arise with healing in his wings." In the Bible the term "Sun" is used, whereas here in the Book of Mormon the record uses "Son." The translators of the King James Bible correctly recognized the term "Sun of righteousness" as an allusion to the Lord, noting this understanding by the use of the capital letter in the word "Sun." Their interpretation is borne out by the Book of Mormon, where the phrase is personified completely—"Son of Righteousness." (3 Ne. 25:2.)[11] Verse 3 speaks of the righteous treading on the wicked in that day of the Lord's justice. This should be interpreted in the context of the overall destruction of evil and the ultimate victory of good over bad.[12]

The setting in which Jesus quoted this passage helps us understand its relevance to the situation of his listeners. The Savior's visit to the Americas provides a pattern that will be followed on a worldwide scale at his second coming. As Malachi foretold, the day of the Lord's coming is one of destruction for the wicked, while for the righteous it will be a day of unimaginable blessings. (3 Ne. 25:1-2.) What could better describe what the Nephites had gone through and were then experiencing? The "Son of Righteousness" had arisen in their midst, "with healing in his wings."

Verse 4, on face value, appears to be a reminder to observe the Law of Moses, which was in force in Malachi's day but was fulfilled in Christ. Perhaps we can suggest that Malachi's statement makes reference to something else. Joseph Smith, in commenting on this verse, taught: "[The] law revealed to Moses in Horeb *never was revealed to the children of Israel*,"[13] apparently referring to the *higher law* revealed to Moses that Israel did not receive because of rebellion. (See JST Ex. 34:1-2; D&C 84:23-25.) It may be that Malachi's intent, and Jesus' in quoting the verse, was to draw attention to the higher law that Moses obtained but that Israel was unworthy to receive. In that case, the reference to the law received by Moses would not be out of place with the discussion in the following verses concerning Elijah's coming. Jesus' listeners on this occasion were worthy and able to receive the higher law, priesthood, ordinances, and blessings that God revealed to Moses on the mountain but that their Israelite ancestors had forfeited.

The Coming of Elijah

When Moroni appeared to the Prophet Joseph Smith during the night of September 21-22, 1823, he quoted Malachi 4:5-6 (3 Ne. 25:5-6) quite differently than it is recorded in either the Bible or the Book of Mormon: "Behold, I will reveal unto you the Priesthood, by the hand of Elijah the prophet, before the coming of the great and dreadful day of the Lord. And he shall plant in the hearts of the children the promises made to the fathers, and the hearts of the children shall turn to their fathers. If it were not so, the whole earth would be utterly wasted at his coming." (JS–H 1:38-39; see also D&C 2.) This passage, in either version, is one of the most important scriptures of the Restoration, since it foretells the creation of the links of priesthood power that bind and seal both ordinances and generations on earth and in heaven.[14] The prophecy of Elijah's coming was fulfilled on April 3, 1836, as the ancient prophet who held the keys of sealing power appeared to the founding prophet of the last dispensation to restore those keys to the earth. (D&C 110:13-16.)[15]

In the recorded teachings and writings of Joseph Smith, the Prophet taught on the subject of Malachi 4:5-6 more than on any other passage of scripture. Among other things, he taught: "Elijah was the last prophet that held the keys of this priesthood, and who will, before the last dispensation, restore the authority and deliver the keys of this priesthood in order that all the ordinances may be attended to in righteousness. . . . Why send Elijah? Because he holds the keys of the authority to administer in all the ordinances of the priesthood, and without the authority the ordinances could not be administered in righteousness."[16] The priesthood keys restored by Elijah provide the sealing power for all ordinances of the priesthood, making those performed on earth valid in the heavens and enabling worthy couples and families to be sealed together for the eternities. On another occasion the Prophet taught:

> Now the word "turn" here should be translated "bind" or "seal." But what is the object of this important mission, or how is it to be fulfilled? The keys are to be delivered, the spirit of Elijah is to come, the gospel to be established, the Saints of God gathered, Zion built up, and the Saints to come up as saviors on Mount Zion. But how are they to become saviors on Mount Zion? By building their temples, erecting their baptismal fonts, and going forth and receiving all the ordinances, baptisms, confirmations, washings, anointings, ordinations, and sealing powers upon our heads in behalf of all our progenitors who are dead, and redeem them that they may come forth in the first resurrection and be exalted to thrones of glory with us. And herein is the chain that binds the hearts of the fathers to the children, and the children to the fathers, which fulfills the mission of Elijah.[17]

Since ordinances performed on earth are valid in the eternities, it follows, in the Lord's plan, that ordinances can be performed by this power on earth in behalf of those who are already in the spirit world. Thus Elijah's coming makes temple work for the dead possible and provides the welding link between generations.

It is not unlikely that the Savior's visit to the Nephites initiated an era of intense temple activity among them. It is also not unreasonable that he used Malachi's prophecy as a means to stress eternal marriage and the other blessings of Elijah's sealing mission. (See 4 Ne. 1:11.) How appropriate, then, was his quoting of this important passage for their benefit and for the blessing of those in the future who would read their record.

Greater Things

Using the revelations of Malachi as his starting point, Jesus taught his disciples of the future of the world, the earth's regeneration, his coming in glory, and the judgment that all will face, "according to the mercy, and the justice, and the holiness which is in Christ." (3 Ne. 26:5.) Concerning this transcendent instructional session, Mormon wrote: "There cannot be written in this book even a hundredth part of the things which Jesus did truly teach unto the people." (3 Ne. 26:6.)

Mormon included in his account some important information concerning the writing of his record, and in doing so he taught an important gospel principle. He mentioned that a fuller account of Jesus' teaching was contained on the plates of Nephi, from which he had abridged the record that we have in 3 Nephi. (3 Ne. 26:7.) Concerning the latter-day readers of his account, he wrote: "When they shall have received this, which is expedient that they should have first, to try their faith, and if it shall so be that they shall believe these things then shall the greater things be made manifest unto them." (3 Ne. 26:9.) The "greater things" will be made known to us, in the Lord's due time, in accordance with the faith with which we receive what has already been revealed. The corollary is also true: "If it so be that they will not believe these things, then shall the greater things be withheld from them, unto their condemnation." (3 Ne. 26:10.) This principle was taught eloquently by Alma: "He that will harden his heart, the same receiveth the lesser portion of the word; and he that will not harden his heart, to him is given the greater portion of the word until it is given unto him to know the mysteries of God until he know them in full. And they that will harden their hearts, to them is given the lesser portion of the word, until they know nothing concerning his mysteries; and then they are taken captive by the devil, and led by his will down to destruction." (Alma 12:10-11.)

The importance of this principle should not be overlooked by anyone. In the Lord's mercy, he has revealed to us what in his wisdom he knows that we need. (Alma 29:8.) If we feast on—and believe in—what has been revealed already, more will be revealed to us, either through the inspiration of the Holy Spirit or through the revelation of more scripture at a later time. If we do not learn—and thus do not gain faith in—what the Lord has made known to the world already, we are closing the door on wonderful opportunities. It is no wonder, then, that modern prophets have counseled us repeatedly to make scripture study an important part of our lives.[18]

Mormon's account preserves examples of the principle described in the preceding paragraphs. As he was about to write more concerning the Savior's teachings, the Lord forbade him, saying, "I will try the faith of my people." (3 Ne. 26:11.) In the remainder of 3 Nephi 26, prohibitions against writing more are expressed in two other places (verses 16, 18).

Jesus taught his Nephite saints for three days, after which he appeared to them frequently. On these occasions one of the most remarkable occurrences in all of human history took place. As the Savior taught and ministered to the young children of the assembled believers, he so filled them with the Spirit that they said "great and marvelous things" to their parents, even greater than Christ himself had revealed to them! So great were the "marvelous things" the children taught their parents that it was forbidden that anyone should write them. (3 Ne. 26:14, 16.)

Jesus' ministry healed physical as well as spiritual infirmities. He restored the sick to health and cured the lame, the blind, and the deaf; he even raised a man from the dead. (3 Ne. 26:15.) As the Master had set his priesthood organization into operation earlier in his visit, those whom he had chosen administered the blessings of the gospel to others, teaching and baptizing. Those who received baptism "were filled with the Holy Ghost. And many of them saw and heard unspeakable things, which are not lawful to be written." (3 Ne. 26:17-18.)

Mormon summarized the results of Jesus' visit on the lives of the people: they ministered one to another, "they had all things common . . . every man dealing justly, one with another" and doing "all things even as Jesus had commanded them." (3 Ne. 26:19-20.)

A Pattern for the Last Days

One reason why the Book of Mormon is so important for our time is that it provides a pattern for the events of the last days. Thus, we would do well to observe what it teaches us. Just as in ancient America, the period preceding Christ's second coming will be characterized by wickedness, wars, and social chaos. (3 Ne. 2-7; JS—M 1:29-30.) At the same time that the Saints will be strengthening Zion in anticipation of the Lord's return (3 Ne. 7:15-26; Moses 7:62), Satan's work will be spreading in the earth (3 Ne. 2-7; JS—M 1:22). Destruction of wickedness will cleanse the earth (3 Ne. 8-10; D&C 29:14-21), and those to whom the Savior will appear will be among "the more righteous" (3 Ne. 10:12; D&C 45:56-57). Members of the Church, who enjoy gospel blessings prior to his coming, will teach the gospel to everyone else, and the whole world will soon be converted. (4 Ne. 1:1-2; Jer. 31:34.) The Lord will be with his people and teach them (3 Ne. 11-27; D&C 101:32-34), and a glorious period of peace and righteousness will follow (4 Ne. 1:1-18; Isa. 11:6-9).

NOTES

1. See the discussions in chapters 14-19 in this book.

2. For a discussion of Isaiah in the Book of Mormon, see Kent P. Jackson, "Nephi and Isaiah," in *Studies in Scripture, Vol. 7: 1 Nephi to Alma 29*, ed. Kent P. Jackson (Salt Lake City: Deseret Book Company, 1987), pp. 131-45.

3. See Bruce R. McConkie, *The Mortal Messiah: From Bethlehem to Calvary*, 4 vols. (Salt Lake City: Deseret Book Company, 1979-81), 4:365-68.

4. Bruce R. McConkie, "The Doctrinal Restoration," in *The Joseph Smith Translation: Restoring Plain and Precious Truths*, ed. Monte S. Nyman and Robert L. Millet (Provo, Utah: Religious Studies Center, Brigham Young University, 1985), p. 18.

5. See Kent P. Jackson, "The Appearance of Moroni to Joseph Smith," in *Studies in Scripture, Vol. 2: The Pearl of Great Price*, ed. Robert L. Millet and Kent P. Jackson (Salt Lake City: Randall Books, 1985), p. 341.

6. See Joseph Fielding Smith, *Doctrines of Salvation*, 3 vols., comp. Bruce R. McConkie (Salt Lake City: Bookcraft, 1954-56), 3:10-12; and Bruce R. McConkie, *Mormon Doctrine*, 2nd ed. (Salt Lake City: Bookcraft, 1966), p. 488.

7. Joseph Smith, October 5, 1840, recorded by Robert B. Thompson; Andrew F. Ehat and Lyndon W. Cook, comp. and ed., *The Words of Joseph Smith* (Provo, Utah: Religious Studies Center, 1980), pp. 42-44; see also pp. 50-51, note 1. All quotations from Joseph Smith in this chapter have been edited for spelling and punctuation.

8. See Joseph Fielding Smith, *Doctrines of Salvation* 3:93-94; Bruce R. McConkie, *Mormon Doctrine*, p. 666; *The Mortal Messiah* 1:128.

9. Joseph Smith, March 21, 1841, recorded by Martha Jane Coray; Ehat and Cook, *The Words of Joseph Smith*, p. 66.

10. See Kent P. Jackson, "The Signs of the Times: Be Not Troubled," in *Studies in Scripture, Vol. 1: The Doctrine and Covenants*, ed. Robert L. Millet and Kent P. Jackson (Salt Lake City: Randall Books, 1984), pp. 186-200.

11. The personification of the metaphor "sun" to the explicit "Son" need not be viewed as a scribal matter, regardless of what may have been either in Malachi's original text or on the gold plates of Mormon's abridgment. There is no reason not to assume that the Book of Mormon text here is deliberate and inspired.

12. In conjunction with this, see the interpretation of 3 Ne. 21:12-17 in chapter 17 of this volume.

13. Joseph Smith, August 27, 1843, recorded by Willard Richards; Ehat and Cook, *The Words of Joseph Smith*, p. 244, emphasis added.

14. See Charles R. Harrell, "Turning the Hearts of the Fathers and the Children," in *Studies in Scripture, Vol. 1*, pp. 57-63.

15. See Milton V. Backman, Jr., and Robert L. Millet, "Heavenly Manifestations in the Kirtland Temple," in *Studies in Scripture, Vol. 1*, pp. 426-29.

16. Joseph Smith, October 5, 1840, recorded by Robert B. Thompson; Ehat and Cook, *The Words of Joseph Smith*, p. 43.

17. Joseph Smith, January 21, 1844, recorded by Wilford Woodruff; Ehat and Cook, *The Words of Joseph Smith*, p. 318.

18. For example, see President Ezra Taft Benson, "The Book of Mormon: Keystone of Our Religion," in *Studies in Scripture, Vol. 7*, pp. 1-16.

19

BUILT UPON CHRIST'S GOSPEL
(3 Nephi 27–30)

KENT P. JACKSON AND DARRELL L. MATTHEWS

After the Savior appeared to the Nephites and established his church among them, the twelve disciples went through the land preaching the gospel and baptizing into the church those who repented. While traveling they became aware of disputes among the members of the church concerning the name by which it should be called. In order to obtain from the Lord an answer to the matter, they "united in mighty prayer and fasting." (3 Ne. 27:1.) In response to their prayers, Christ appeared to them and taught them. This visit of Jesus to his disciples is his last recorded visit to them.

The Name of the Church

While the disciples were praying to know by what name the church should be called, "Jesus came and stood in the midst of them, and said unto them: What will ye that I shall give unto you? And they said unto him: Lord, we will that thou wouldst tell us the name whereby we shall call this church; for there are disputations among the people concerning this matter." (3 Ne. 27:2-3; see Isa. 58:9, 11.) In response to this question, Jesus asked why the people should dispute over this issue: "Have they not read the scriptures?" (3 Ne. 27:5.)

The Savior then taught his disciples that those who wish to follow

---

Darrell L. Matthews is a doctoral student in ancient languages at Johns Hopkins University. Kent P. Jackson is associate professor of ancient scripture at Brigham Young University.

him must take upon themselves his name. He gave specific instructions concerning the name of the church: "Therefore ye shall call the church in my name; and ye shall call upon the Father in my name that he will bless the church for my sake. And how be it my church save it be called in my name? For if a church be called in Moses' name then it be Moses' church; or if it be called in the name of a man then it be the church of a man; but if it be called in my name then it is my church, if it so be that they are built upon my gospel." (3 Ne. 27:7-8.) In this explanation of the importance of the name of the church, two major points are emphasized. The first is that the true church must be named after Christ; the second is that it must be "built upon" his gospel. If only the first criterion were mentioned, any church using Christ's name could possibly be the true church. When the second requirement is added, it eliminates all churches that possess Christ's name while not containing his gospel in its fullness. It limits the true church to only one; The Church of Jesus Christ of Latter-day Saints meets both of these requirements. (D&C 115:4; 1:30.)

In addition to these requirements, Christ told the disciples: "If it so be that the church is built upon my gospel then will the Father show forth his own works in it." (3 Ne. 27:10.) From other scriptures we learn that some of the Father's works are spiritual gifts (1 Cor. 12:8-14; D&C 46:10-26), living prophets, service, and love—characteristics found in the Lord's church.

Christ continued by warning the disciples what would happen if the church were not built on his gospel: "But if it be not built upon my gospel, and is built upon the works of men, or upon the works of the devil, verily I say unto you they have joy in their works for a season, and by and by the end cometh, and they are hewn down and cast into the fire, from whence there is no return. For their works do follow them, for it is because of their works that they are hewn down; therefore remember the things that I have told you." (3 Ne. 27:11-12.) People who follow a false or incomplete gospel may have joy in their activities for a time during this life, but when the end comes they will not enjoy an inheritance in the celestial kingdom.

Thus the Lord has placed upon us the calling of missionary work, to make the blessings of the fullness of the gospel available for all people.

The Gospel

After Christ taught his disciples about the name and importance of his church, he taught them plainly what the true gospel consists of. In 3 Nephi 27:13-22 the Lord gave us the scriptures' fullest definition of his gospel. Christ taught his disciples: "This is the gospel which I have given unto you—that I came into the world to do the will of my Father, because my Father sent me." (3 Ne. 27:13.) He continued by teaching that his Father had sent him to be lifted up on the cross in order to draw the people of the world to him. "As I have been lifted up by men even so should men be lifted up by the Father, to stand before me, to be judged of their works, whether they be good or whether they be evil." (3 Ne. 27:14.) Jesus affirmed that those who repent and are baptized in his name will be blessed: "If he endureth to the end, behold, him will I hold guiltless before my Father at that day when I shall stand to judge the world. And he that endureth not unto the end, the same is he that is also hewn down and cast into the fire, from whence they can no more return, because of the justice of the Father." (3 Ne. 27:16-17.) This is the gospel of the Father, who "fulfilleth the words which he hath given, and he lieth not, but fulfilleth all his words." (3 Ne. 27:18.) Jesus taught that only those who repent of their sins and endure to the end will be worthy of God's kingdom.

The Savior continued: "Now this is the commandment: Repent, all ye ends of the earth, and come unto me and be baptized in my name, that ye may be sanctified by the reception of the Holy Ghost, that ye may stand spotless before me at the last day." (3 Ne. 27:20.) This statement is at the core of the gospel. Repentance allows Christ's atonement to become an active part in our lives, and those who live with and follow the promptings of the Holy Ghost will have the assurance that they have washed their garments in Christ's blood and will have a place at his right hand. Jesus then concluded: "This is my gospel; and ye know the things that ye must do in my church; for the works which ye have seen me do that shall ye also do; for that which ye have seen me do even that shall ye do; therefore, if ye do these things blessed are ye, for ye shall be lifted up at the last day." (3 Ne. 27:21-22.) These few verses contain the most concise and clear definition of the gospel, given by the Lord himself. It can be summarized as follows: (1) the atonement, (2) faith, (3) repentance, (4) baptism, (5) reception of the Holy Spirit, (6) enduring to the end, and (7) judgment. It is significant that in Christ's own definition the gospel consists essentially of two parts—the atonement of Christ, and the principles and ordinances required of us to make the atonement effective in our lives.

Jesus commanded his disciples to write the things they had been taught, "save it be those which are forbidden." (3 Ne. 27:23.) Because of the disciples' faithfulness in carrying out this command, we today have this beautiful section of scripture.

Results of Living the Gospel

After Jesus had commanded his disciples to write his teachings, he told them that their people would be judged out of their writings: "Write the works of this people, which shall be, even as hath been written, of that which hath been. For behold, out of the books which have been written, and which shall be written, shall this people be judged, for by them shall their works be known unto men." (3 Ne. 27:24-25.) He then taught his disciples that the Father keeps a record of all things and that all the world will be judged from those records. He also told them that they would be the judges of their people: "Ye shall be judges of this people, according to the judgment which I shall give unto you, which shall be just. Therefore, what manner of men ought ye to be? Verily I say unto you, even as I am." (3 Ne. 27:27.) This command is given to us all, to live our lives so we can be like Christ. In this instance, his disciples were specifically commanded to be like their Lord so they would be ready to be the judges of their people, following Jesus' example in judgment. To accomplish this assignment, they would need to become like their Savior, and by so doing their judgment would be just. (Cf. Moro. 7:18-19.)

The final verses of 3 Nephi 27 make clear to us some of the results of obeying or disobeying God's commandments. First Jesus spoke about prayer: "Whatsoever things ye shall ask the Father in my name shall be given unto you. Therefore, ask, and ye shall receive; knock, and it shall be opened unto you; for he that asketh, receiveth; and unto him that knocketh, it shall be opened." (3 Ne. 27:28-29.) Evidently these disciples had reached the point in their worthiness that they would not ask for anything unrighteously; Christ placed no conditions on this statement. Thus whatever they asked would be granted. (See also Nephi's example in Helaman 10:4-10.)

Christ told his listeners some of his joys and sorrows. We learn that he was pleased with those whom he was visiting: "My joy is great, even unto fulness, because of you, and also this generation; yea, and even the Father rejoiceth, and also all the holy angels, because of you and this generation; for none of them are lost." (3 Ne. 27:30.) Readers should pay special attention to the fact that our personal actions can cause Christ, the Father, and angels to rejoice or sorrow. Knowing God's feelings for us and his intense concern for each of us as individuals, we should conduct our lives so as to bring honor and joy to those heavenly beings who care so much for our welfare.

In 3 Nephi 27:30, we find an excellent example of what can be achieved in this mortal life. These people had achieved such righteousness that if they continued in it they would be saved in the Father's kingdom. After expressing his joy about those whom he visited, Christ told of his sorrow concerning the future generations of the Nephites: "It sorroweth me because of the fourth generation from this generation, for they are led away captive by [the devil] even as was the son of perdition; for they will sell me for silver and for gold, and for that which moth doth corrupt and which thieves can break through and steal. And in that day will I visit them, even in turning their works upon their own heads." (3 Ne. 27:32.) The Lord knew that the righteousness achieved by those he visited would not continue in all the later generations. He knew that it would decay as people became proud and materialistic, and he sorrowed for those who would be lost.

The Three Nephites

When Christ finished explaining his gospel to the Nephite disciples, he spoke individually to each of the Twelve: "What is it that ye desire of me, after that I am gone to the Father? And they all spake, save it were three, saying: We desire that after we have lived unto the age of man, that our ministry, wherein thou hast called us, may have an end, that we may speedily come unto thee in thy kingdom." (3 Ne. 28:1-2.) Jesus granted their request and told them that when they had reached the age of seventy-two they would join him in his kingdom.

The Savior then turned to the three who had not yet requested anything of him and asked them again what they desired of him. These three disciples still did not reply, because

> they sorrowed in their hearts, for they durst not speak unto him the thing which they desired. And he said unto them: Behold, I know your thoughts, and ye have desired the thing which John, my beloved, who was with me in my ministry, before that I was lifted up by the Jews, desired of me. [See John 21:21-23; D&C 7.] Therefore, more blessed are ye, for ye shall never taste of death; but ye shall live to behold all the doings of the Father unto the children of men, even until all things shall be fulfilled according to the will of the Father, when I shall come in my glory with the powers of heaven. (3 Ne. 28:5-7.)

The three would not "taste of death." While they continued in their earthly ministry, they would not experience pain of the flesh; the only pain they would feel would be sorrow for the sins of the world. "And all this will I do because of the thing which ye have desired of me, for ye have desired that ye might bring the souls of men unto me, while the world shall stand. And for this cause ye shall have fulness of joy; and ye shall sit down in the kingdom of my Father; yea, your joy shall be full." (3 Ne. 28:9-10.) In Doctrine and Covenants 7, we learn that the Lord told John that his desire was greater than that of the others because he had desired to continue to bring souls unto Christ while the others had wanted to finish their ministry and enter the kingdom of God. Both were righteous desires, but John and the Three Nephites desired a "greater work." (D&C 7:6.) Then "the heavens were opened, and they were caught up into heaven, and saw and heard unspeakable things." (3 Ne. 28:13.) The things which they saw and heard are not recorded because they were commanded not to reveal them to anyone. (3 Ne. 28:14.) This experience was so wonderful that the disciples were not even sure if "they were in the body or out of the body," because they were transfigured so "they could behold the things of God." (3 Ne. 28:15.)

Following this glorious experience, all of the disciples continued their ministries. The nine, when they had reached the age of seventy-two, were received into God's kingdom. The three who had chosen to continue their ministry until Christ's coming in glory remained. Mormon reported that these three "did go forth upon the face of the land, and did minister unto all the people, uniting as many to the church as would believe in their preaching; baptizing them, and as many as were baptized did receive the Holy Ghost." (3 Ne. 28:18.) In later generations, in spite of the works of righteousness that the Three Nephites performed, there were some who hated them. Because of this they were persecuted, but they were delivered by the hand of God. (3 Ne. 28:19-22; 4 Ne. 1:30-37; Morm. 1:13-16.)

Years later the Three Nephites ministered to Mormon. He wrote that they will also minister unto the Gentiles, the Jews, "the scattered tribes of Israel, and unto all nations, kindreds, tongues and people, and shall bring out of them unto Jesus many souls, that their desire may be fulfilled, and also because of the convincing power of God which is in them." (3 Ne. 28:26-29.) Their great righteousness makes it possible for them to show themselves to whomever they desire. Because of this, the work that they will perform before Christ's coming will be "great and marvelous."

At this point in the record, Mormon warned those who would reject the teachings of Jesus and those whom he sends to warn the world: "Wo be unto him that will not hearken unto the words of Jesus, and also to them whom he hath chosen and sent among them; for whoso receiveth not the words of Jesus and the words of those whom he hath sent receiveth not him; and therefore he will not receive them at the last day; and it would be better for them if they had not been born." (3 Ne. 28:34-35.)

Mormon's Counsel to the Gentiles

In the last two chapters of 3 Nephi, Mormon gave inspired counsel to his future readers, particularly the Gentiles. In the Book of Mormon, the term *Gentiles* generally refers to those who are neither Jews nor descendants of Lehi. Thus most Latter-day Saints today are Gentiles according to Book of Mormon terminology. Mormon's message has great relevance for us today; he saw our day and the pitfalls into which many of our time would fall. These last two chapters of 3 Nephi warn us of specific things against which we need to protect ourselves.

Mormon wrote that when the Book of Mormon would come forth, the restoration of scattered Israel would be starting: "When the Lord shall see fit, in his wisdom, that these sayings shall come unto the Gentiles according to his word, then ye may know that the covenant which the Father hath made with the children of Israel, concerning their restoration to the lands of their inheritance, is already beginning to be fulfilled." (3 Ne. 29:1.) The restoration of the house of Israel must of necessity follow the restoration of the gospel, the priesthood, the covenants, and true doctrine. The coming forth of the Book of Mormon played a vital role in this process.

Mormon followed with the assurance that although many would doubt that God could fulfill his promises to his covenant people, he would in reality do just that: "Ye need not imagine in your hearts that the words which have been spoken are vain, for behold, the Lord will remember his covenant which he hath made unto his people of the house of Israel." (3 Ne. 29:3.) Then he gave specific warnings of problems prevalent in our day. We are told that many would spurn the doings of God, "deny the revelations of the Lord, and . . . shall say the Lord no longer worketh by revelation, or by prophecy, or by gifts, or by tongues, or by healings, or by the power of the Holy Ghost." (3 Ne. 29:5-6.) Mormon continued:

> Yea, and wo unto him that shall say at that day, to get gain, that there can be no miracle wrought by Jesus Christ; for he that doeth this shall become like unto the son of perdition, for whom there was no mercy, according to the word of Christ! Yea, and ye need not any longer hiss, nor spurn, nor make game of the Jews, nor any of the remnant of the house of Israel; for behold, the Lord remembereth his covenant unto them, and he will do unto them according to that which he hath sworn. Therefore ye need not suppose that ye can turn

215

the right hand of the Lord unto the left, that he may not execute judgment unto the fulfilling of the covenant which he hath made unto the house of Israel. (3 Ne. 29:7-9.)

These words speak directly to our day. Mormon saw our time and warned us that many would deny revelation and the various gifts of the Holy Ghost; many would say that no miracles can be performed. Among the greatest of the miracles to which he referred would be the restoration of the house of Israel, which takes place in a miraculous fashion in the Church today, in accord with the ancient promises.

For centuries, many have believed that revelation and the gifts of the Spirit were lost from the world with the death of the early apostles and thus are no longer needed. Some believe that God has revealed all that will ever need to be revealed and is no longer active in the affairs of humanity: "He hath done his work." (2 Ne. 28:5-6.) Some who deny the existence of miracles and the gifts of the Spirit are also found within the Church and fail to see the hand of the Lord directing its affairs today. Some, still claiming to be Latter-day Saints, engage in personal or public opposition to doctrines and policies established by the Lord's prophets. This is one manifestation of the lack of faith foreseen by Mormon.

After Mormon had recorded the warnings to the Gentiles, he made a plea for repentance. He urged them to put away their wicked ways and accept the gospel:

> Hearken, O ye Gentiles, and hear the words of Jesus Christ, the Son of the living God, which he hath commanded me that I should speak concerning you, for, behold he commandeth me that I should write, saying: Turn, all ye Gentiles, from your wicked ways; and repent of your evil doings, of your lyings and deceivings, and of your whoredoms, and of your secret abominations, and your idolatries, and of your murders, and your priestcrafts, and your envyings, and your strifes, and from all your wickedness and abominations, and come unto me, and be baptized in my name, that ye may receive a remission of your sins, and be filled with the Holy Ghost, that ye may be numbered with my people who are of the house of Israel. (3 Ne. 30:2.)

In Mormon's plea for repentance he wrote to all the world. Since the problems of our generation, which Mormon saw, exist among some in the Church today, his call for repentance is also to us.

Conclusion

Before Jesus left the people of the American continent, he challenged them to accept his teachings and direct their lives accordingly. "Enter ye in at the strait gate; for strait is the gate, and narrow is the way that leads to life, and few there be that find it; but wide is the gate, and broad the way which leads to death, and many there be that travel therein, until the night cometh, wherein no man can work." (3 Ne. 27:33.) The events recorded in the Book of Mormon serve as a witness to us in the latter days that living by the principles of the gospel leads to temporal and eternal joy: "There was no contention in the land, because of the love of God which did dwell in the hearts of the people. And there were no envyings, nor strifes, nor tumults, nor whoredoms, nor lyings, nor murders, nor any manner of lasciviousness; and surely there could not be a happier people among all the people who had been created by the hand of God." (4 Ne. 1:15-16.) In 4 Nephi we have an example of a people who overcame their sins and obeyed the commandments of the Lord, which brought great joy into their lives. Because of this example we know that it is possible for us also to reach that high state of righteousness.

The Book of Mormon, which witnesses to the results of righteousness, is also a witness that rejection of gospel principles brings sadness and destruction. The final fate of the Nephites testifies to that truth. Since we decide by our actions if we will follow the Lord or not, let us choose to follow the righteous example of those among whom the Savior ministered in the Book of Mormon.

20

THE COURSE OF PEACE AND APOSTASY
(4 Nephi–Mormon 2)

ANDREW C. SKINNER

Nephi's prophecies concerning the condescension of God (1 Ne. 11:16; 2 Ne. 4:26) had been fulfilled to the fullest measure as Christ concluded his post-resurrection sojourn among his New World disciples. (3 Ne. 28:12.) A God had come to earth now on two continents. The pure gospel plan had been taught by its executor, old prophecies had come to pass and new ones been given, miracles had been performed, and people had been changed. The book of 4 Nephi is a testament of the profound effects of the Savior's visit on the lives of the American people.

Fourth Nephi is a record of great righteousness as well as tremendous wickedness. With the first two chapters of Mormon's personal account of his experience, it forms a cohesive unit that constitutes a classic study on the course and structure of apostasy, showing human beings at their best and worst. Perhaps this is the most significant contribution to our theological and spiritual education made by 4 Nephi, Mormon 1, and Mormon 2.

However, 4 Nephi is of singular importance in another distinct but related aspect. Nowhere is Mormon's inspired editorial ability and prophetic mantle better demonstrated or more apparent than in 4 Nephi. It cannot be doubted that Mormon was a *great* prophet. He received a personal visit from the Savior at age fifteen (Mormon 1:15) and, thus, retained from his youth the spirit of prophecy. For, as John

---

Andrew C. Skinner is instructor of history at Metropolitan State College, Denver, Colorado.

wrote, "The testimony of Jesus is the spirit of prophecy." (Rev. 19:10.) From Mormon's work of abridgment on the records that make up 4 Nephi, we might well conclude that one of the most important aspects of a true prophet's responsibility involves not just the prediction of the future, but also the presentation of the past in such a way as to reveal and teach the lessons of life needed to be learned for exaltation. Thus, Mormon desired to open up the past and the future to the understanding of generations who would follow. He wrote, for example: "It came to pass that two hundred years had passed away; and the second generation had all passed away save it were a few. And now I, Mormon, would that ye should know that the people had multiplied, insomuch that they were spread upon all the face of the land, and that they had become exceedingly rich, because of their prosperity in Christ." (4 Ne. 1:22-23.)

Here Mormon testified that though he was not an eyewitness, he knew that the source of prosperity in ancient times was Christ, with the implication that it is Christ who can also point the way to well-being in every age.

The actual eyewitnesses to the events recounted in 4 Nephi (those who kept the sacred records before Mormon became their custodian) include Nephi, son of Nephi the disciple of Christ and the person for whom the book was named; Nephi's son and grandson—both named Amos; and Ammaron. We do not know the size of the original records or the amount of information kept by these brethren. But we do know that it was Mormon's inspired and prophetic redaction of all the records that would bring to future generations the essential spiritual lessons of Nephite and Lamanite history in distilled form and, thus, by its very succinctness make those lessons more concentrated, compact, and poignant to us.

In forty-nine short verses we are shown the heights and depths of a civilization's spiritual and moral condition. In forty-nine short verses we are shown the practical workings of the law of the celestial kingdom, the true order of heaven on earth, and the ideal pattern of welfare service. Also, in forty-nine short verses the reader is shown the basest impulses of a telestial society. Also in these verses we are shown the circumstances and atmosphere that will exist during

Christ's millennial reign in stark contrast to Satan's avowed purposes, influence, and workings. And, finally, in these short verses we are taken through almost one-third (approximately 300) of all the years covered by the entire Book of Mormon (approximately 1,000). Truly the magnitude of Mormon's prophetic task and accomplishment is shown clearly here.

Some readers may lament the fact that one of the greatest periods of Nephite civilization—an era of ultimate earthly peace, prosperity, and spirituality—was given such relatively sparse historical treatment. Sidney Sperry observed that "it is unfortunate—at least vexing that the great Golden Era of Nephite history...should be so sparingly treated by Mormon, the abridger."[1]

However, it must be remembered, first, that sometimes things were commanded by the Lord not to be discussed in the records. (3 Ne. 26:11, 18.) A similar injunction may have applied to this portion of the abridgment. Second, Mormon's purpose was not the writing of history, nor was it historical embellishment or even enlargement. His abridgment was guided by inspiration and was first and foremost intended to teach the most important truths of the kingdom as they could be culled *from* history. Mormon said at one point:

> I do this for a wise purpose; for thus it whispereth me, according to the workings of the Spirit of the Lord which is in me. And now, I do not know all things; but the Lord knoweth all things which are to come; wherefore, he worketh in me to do according to his will. And my prayer to God is concerning my brethren, that they may once again come to the knowledge of God, yea, the redemption of Christ; that they may once again be a delightsome people. And now I, Mormon, proceed to finish out my record, which I take from the plates of Nephi; and I make it according to the knowledge and the understanding which God has given me. (Words of Mormon 1:7-9.)

It has been noted in commentaries that when originally published, 3 and 4 Nephi were both called "Nephi."[2] In 1879 Elder Orson Pratt added the separate titles, 3 and 4 Nephi, to help distinguish the works from one another. Each has a different emphasis and intent—one being an American Gospel recording the Savior's visit and physical presence, the other recounting the effect of that visit and the eventual decline of an entire culture.

Effect of the Savior's Visit

As 3 Nephi testifies, dramatic physical changes occurred on the American landscape immediately preceding the coming of the resurrected Christ to the New World. (3 Ne. 8.) They were some of the most impressive events ever to occur on the Western Hemisphere. And, yet, as significant as those changes were, even greater changes took place after the Savior finished his visit and departed. These greater changes occurred in the hearts, minds, and souls of the Nephites and Lamanites for one hundred and sixty-seven years after Jesus left.

As 4 Nephi reports, so powerful an effect did the Savior's presence and testimony have on the people that they were all converted to the Lord, joined the one true church that had been formed "in all the lands round about" (a phrase likely indicating the establishment of several branches or units of the Church in various geographic sectors), and began living the celestial law. There were no disputations among the people, justice everywhere prevailed, all earthly possessions were distributed equitably, and distinctions between rich and poor were eradicated. Such a condition recalls a similar circumstance found at the same time in the Old World when, after the Lord's ascension, members of the Church of Jesus Christ also enjoyed the blessings of the gospel, though perhaps to a lesser degree: "With great power gave the apostles witness of the resurrection of the Lord Jesus: and great grace was upon them all. Neither was there any among them that lacked: for as many as were possessors of lands or houses sold them, and brought the prices of the things that were sold, and laid them down at the apostles' feet: and distribution was made unto every man according as he had need." (Acts 4:33-35.)

Of course, the greatest difference between the New and Old World church is that the latter still had to contend with an outside culture in the throes of wickedness, while the former flourished in circumstances where all people were converted to the Lord. (4 Ne. 1:2.) Thus, the Book of Mormon peoples enjoyed their blessed state for a long time. As Mormon wrote: "How blessed were they! For the Lord did bless them in all their doings; yea, even they were blessed and prospered until an hundred and ten years had passed away; and the first generation from Christ had passed away, and there was no contention in all the land." (4 Ne. 1:18.)

Still, eventually the New World church succumbed to the same fate that befell the Old. Satan got hold upon the hearts of men and women (4 Ne. 1:28), and great apostasy ensued. We are left to lament and wonder whether or not the adversary is so powerful as to *always* triumph over good in the hearts of mortals if given enough time. After all, the people of Nephi had lived the Order of Zion for one hundred and sixty-seven years. Why not longer?

If we look at the example of the people of Enoch, we are taught that evil need not always conquer good, that mortals are capable of *continuing* to live in righteousness until they can no longer be withheld from God's abode. Witness the testimony of Moses: "The Lord called his people ZION, because they were of one heart and one mind, and dwelt in righteousness; and there was no poor among them. And Enoch *continued* his preaching in righteousness unto the people of God. . . . And it came to pass that the Lord showed unto Enoch all the inhabitants of the earth; and he beheld, and lo, Zion, *in process of time*, was taken up into heaven. And the Lord said unto Enoch: Behold mine abode forever." (Moses 7:18-19, 21; emphasis added.)

These examples show that in every age or dispensation when the Spirit of the Lord rests mightily upon God's children, and is heeded, the same unifying social and economic order predominates and produces a Zion society. This is confirmed by latter-day history and scripture. The order is called the law of the celestial kingdom. (D&C 105:4-5.) Fourth Nephi shows that it *is* a law of unity: "There were no robbers, nor murderers, neither were there Lamanites, nor any manner of -ites; but they were in *one*, the children of Christ, and heirs to the kingdom of God." (4 Ne. 1:17; emphasis added.)

In modern times the Lord has confirmed the importance of unity as an essential aspect of the law of the celestial kingdom. Said he: "Be one; and if ye are not one ye are not mine." (D&C 38:27.)

The most striking thing about the law of the celestial kingdom as it operated among the Nephites and Lamanites, and others as well, was the economic equality that prevailed. The scriptures use the phrase "all things common" to describe the condition. This was not a system of communal ownership such as has been advocated by nineteenth- and twentieth-century secular political theories. Nor did it mean that each person had exactly the same amount of personal goods. As the Lord explained in latter-day revelation concerning his divine law of economic equality: "You are to be equal, or in other words, you are to have equal claims on the properties, for the benefit of managing the concerns of your stewardships, every man according to his wants and his needs, inasmuch as his wants are just." (D&C 82:17.)

The following instruction may help to further clarify the matter:

> The scriptural phrase "they had all things common" (Acts 4:32; see also Acts 2:44; 3 Nephi 26:19; 4 Nephi 1:3) is used to characterize those who lived the law of consecration in ancient times. Some have speculated that the term *common* suggests a type of communalism or "Christian Communism." This interpretation is in error. The Prophet Joseph Smith taught clearly the true nature of having all things common: "I preached on the stand about one hour on the 2nd chapter of Acts, designing to show the folly of common stock (holding property in common). In Nauvoo every one is steward over his own (property)."[3]
>
> Each stewardship is considered private property, and the residues and surpluses consecrated for the storehouse became the "common property of the whole church" (D&C 82:18). It is referred to as the "common property" because every covenant member of the order had access to it, according to his just "wants" and "needs," including the need to improve his stewardship.[4]

Millennial Conditions Foreshadowed

Conformity to the law of the celestial kingdom (under which all were economically prosperous and without social distinctions) brought the combined Nephite and Lamanite people many blessings, not the least of which was peace in all the land. In fact, of all the varied things Mormon could have chosen to include in the highly abridged record, it is most significant that he chose to repeat the fact that peace pervaded the land. In the initial twenty-three verses of 4 Nephi, Mormon reported no fewer than five times that there were no contentions in the land and that peace abounded.

This peace resulted, directly, in great prosperity as well as the working of mighty miracles. These phenomena were centered in Christ. We learn that "the *Lord* did prosper [the people] exceedingly in the land" (4 Ne. 1:7) and that no miracles were done "save it were in the name of Jesus" (4 Ne. 1:5). Of course, Christ is the Prince of Peace, and when any of God's children at any time live the *gospel* of Christ then the *peace* of Christ is promised. In fact, the Lord said to the Nephites: "The mountains shall depart and the hills be removed, but my kindness shall not depart from thee, neither shall the *covenant of my peace* be removed, saith the Lord that hath mercy on thee." (3 Ne. 22:10; emphasis added.)

The conditions spoken of in 4 Nephi parallel and foreshadow those that will exist during the thousand-year period of Christ's millennial reign, the hallmarks of which are also righteousness, peace, and prosperity. During that future era, just as in bygone times described by Mormon, enmity shall cease (D&C 101:26), and nation will no longer lift up sword against nation (Isa. 2:4).

In other respects, too, the millennium and the celestial-like era described in 4 Nephi will be very much alike. Immediately after the Savior's departure from the American continent, his disciples formed the one true church of Christ in the lands round about, and many were baptized. Eventually all people were converted to the Lord (4 Ne. 1:1-2) and each received the Holy Ghost, which testified personally of the Savior. Regarding missionary activity during the millennium, Elder Bruce R. McConkie has written:

> With the destruction of the wicked and the fall of the great and abominable church (D&C 29:21; 88:94) — events destined to accompany the ushering in of the millennium — the conversion of men to the truths of the gospel will become easy. In due course every living soul on earth will come to

the knowledge of the truth. . . . This means that when "all things shall be made known unto the children of men" (2 Ne. 30:15-18), they all shall accept the gospel. . . . This will be the day when the great promise to Israel is fulfilled: "And they shall teach no more every man his neighbour, and every man his brother, saying Know the Lord: for *they shall all know me*, from the least of them unto the greatest of them." (Jer. 31:34.)[5]

Mormon wrote "that the people of Nephi did *wax strong*, and did *multiply* exceedingly fast." (4 Ne. 1:10; emphasis added.) We also gather from the record that all, except for a very small portion, of the second generation born after the coming of Christ to America grew up in the ways of the Lord (4 Ne. 1:18-22.) Concerning the millennium, we read about those same conditions that are to exist again: "They shall *multiply* and *wax strong*, and their children shall grow up without sin unto salvation." (D&C 45:48; emphasis added.) Thus, the people of the great Nephite golden age already had what the righteous of our day yearn to see—a millennial-like existence.

Zion Lost

It is one of the greatest tragedies of human history that what could have been a story with an ending very similar to that of the city of Enoch so quickly and thoroughly turned into one of complete iniquity. The Nephites and Lamanites from A.D. 36 to A.D. 200 possessed every good thing. As Mormon stated, "Surely there could not be a happier people among all the people who had been created by the hand of God." (4 Ne. 1:16.) However, after a time this great happiness was lost forever, and the decay of their civilization was absolute.

Just as spiritual rebirth is a process (see Alma 5), so too is spiritual death. The last half of 4 Nephi as well as Mormon 1 and 2 chronicle the course and structure of the final great Nephite apostasy, whose most striking features seem to be the loss of humility, the loss of unity, and the growth of greed and hardness of heart among the people. We may outline the progress of this spiritual death in a general way.

1. Tremendous prosperity brought unrighteous pride and haughtiness. The people forgot the source of their prosperity. (4 Ne. 1:23-24.)

2. Pride fostered the disintegration of unity among the people, both economically and socially. The law of the celestial kingdom was broken, and Zion was lost. (4 Ne. 1:25-26.)

3. Satan used class differentiation and social stratification as tools not only to foster enmity between groups of people (4 Ne. 1:29), but also to encourage greed (4 Ne. 1:26). People *en masse* began identifying themselves by many different names; there were all manner of "-ites." (4 Ne. 1:36.)

4. People's hearts were hardened; the true church was continually rejected, and sacred things such as the sacrament and other ordinances were trifled with. (4 Ne. 1:26, 34; see also D&C 6:11-12.)

5. Children were purposely taught to hate righteousness (4 Ne. 1:39), which goes against instructions to parents with children in Zion (D&C 68:25-28).

6. Secret oaths and combinations again began to be administered by the devil to combine against all righteousness. (4 Ne. 1:42; see also 3 Ne. 6:28-30.) Secret combinations spread to such an extent that "there were none that were righteous save it were the disciples of Jesus." (4 Ne. 1:46.)

7. Warfare spread over the face of the land. (Morm. 1:8.)

8. Finally, wickedness covered the whole face of the land, and the Lord removed his beloved disciples. Spiritual enlightenment, heavenly gifts, and miracles completely ceased, "the Holy Ghost did not come upon any" (Morm. 1:13-14), and the "day of grace" passed from the people (Morm. 2:15).

Mormon recorded that things eventually became so bad that all life and property were in jeopardy. (Morm. 2:10.) Such a condition produced sorrow and mourning. Yet, it was not sorrowing unto repentance, "but it was rather the sorrowing of the damned, because the Lord would not always suffer them to take happiness in sin." (Morm. 2:13.) Thus, the fate of a nation—indeed, a civilization—was sealed because they would not repent! (See Morm. 2:8.)

The More Sure Word

In the midst of recounting the course of Nephite apostasy and spiritual death, Mormon took time to tell us a little about himself. He recorded that he was a sober child, which we may take to mean one full of reason, self-control, and emotional balance, who was not extreme or frivolous but serious-minded and educated. (Morm. 1:2.) Like Nephi of old, he was large in stature while still a young man. But he was also like Nephi in one other important respect; he, too, was a living witness of the reality of Christ's divinity. As he testified: "I, being fifteen years of age and being somewhat of a sober mind, therefore I was visited of the Lord, and tasted and knew of the goodness of Jesus." (Morm. 1:15.)

In this regard, Mormon is reminiscent of others who had similar experiences. We have already mentioned Nephi, who, being very young, large in stature, and desirous to know the mysteries of God, cried unto the Lord and was visited by him. (1 Ne. 2:16.) The Old Testament prophet Samuel was another young man who was visited by the Lord. (1 Sam. 3:4-21.) In modern times, of course, we have the testimony of Joseph Smith, who, as a teenager, beheld the Father and the Son. (JS–H 1:17.) As these prophets and others of like experience teach us, young people can accomplish great and marvelous things, and the prophetic call does not depend on age, wealth, or circumstances.

Mormon suffered greatly because of the wickedness of his people. However, he was buoyed up and received some comfort in the sure knowledge that he would be lifted up at the last day just as the Savior had promised. (3 Ne. 27:14.) Said Mormon: "Wo is me because of their wickedness; for my heart has been filled with sorrow because of their wickedness, all my days; nevertheless, I know that I shall be lifted up at the last day." (Morm. 2:19.)

Mormon's knowledge was well founded. He had received the Second Comforter (D&C 88:3-4, 67-68) and possessed the more sure word of prophecy, as did other Nephite prophets including Alma (Mosiah 26:20), Enos (Enos 1:27), and the Twelve on the American continent (3 Ne. 28:3). Modern revelation teaches: "The more sure word of prophecy means a man's knowing that he is sealed up unto eternal life, by revelation and the spirit of prophecy, through the power of the Holy Priesthood." (D&C 131:5.) Such was the anchor to Mormon's soul in the face of the worst kind of calamity.

Knowing what he did and having the testimony he did, Mormon endeavored to preach to his people. However, the Lord forbade him from doing so. The people had "wilfully rebelled against their God" and sinned against the light. (Morm. 1:16.) Concerning the final outcome of these willful rebels, only the Lord can say definitively. However, the following statement is instructive and may apply in this situation: "Thus saith the Lord concerning all those who know my power, and have been made partakers thereof, and suffered themselves through the power of the devil to be overcome, and to deny the truth and defy my power—They are they who are the sons of perdition, of whom I say that it had been better for them never to have been born." (D&C 76:31-32.)

Whatever the eternal condition of the people of Nephi might be, we can say with certainty that their rebellion cost them dearly in this life and in the next.

Conclusion

Mormon's abridged record instructs us clearly on the nature and course of apostasy. Humility brought faith in Christ, which brought unity and peace, which then, in turn, brought pride as people forgot the real source of their achievements. Ultimately, hatred, destruction, and bloodshed filled the land while secret combinations raged against all righteousness. Peace was forever lost. Of these things Mormon's words are at once a report, an urging, and a warning. We can and ought to learn from the Nephites that living the law of the celestial kingdom transforms the world spiritually. But how can we live this law in our modern society? How can we even come close to conformity with the Lord's law when the rest of the world seems to be entrenched in sin, greed, avarice, and hatred?

While we may not be able to do everything, we can do something. Witness the words of President Marion G. Romney:

> Full implementation of the united order must, according to the revelation, await the redemption of Zion (See D&C

105:34.) In the meantime—while we are being more perfectly taught and are gaining experience—we should be strictly living the principles of the united order insofar as they are embodied in present Church requirements, such as tithing, fast offerings, welfare projects, storehouses, and other principles and practices. Through these programs we should, as individuals, implement in our own lives the basis of the united order.[6]

We also ought to learn from the Nephites that pride and envy lead to hatred, the breakdown of society, and the loss of peace. Modern prophets have given similar warnings. Elder Marvin J. Ashton said:

True Christians have no time for contention. Lasting peace cannot be built while we are reviling or hating others. Those who preach hate, ridicule, and untruths cannot be classified as peacemakers. Until they repent they will reap the harvest to which those engaged in the business of hatred are entitled. Feelings of enmity and malice can never be compatible with feelings of peace.

"The wicked are like the troubled sea, when it cannot rest, whose waters cast up mire and dirt. There is no peace, saith my God, to the wicked." (Isa. 57:20-21.)[7]

Mormon's record stands as a witness to his own prophetic calling and testifies of the greatness of the man. From personal experience, Mormon taught us that a witness of the Savior gives one strength and hope, even in the worst circumstances and surroundings. With the Spirit we are strong. Without the Spirit we are "left to ourselves," and we "become weak like unto our [unrighteous] brethren." (Morm. 2:26.) Let us resolve to learn the lessons that Mormon's record teaches.

NOTES

1. Sidney B. Sperry, *Book of Mormon Compendium* (Salt Lake City: Bookcraft, 1968), p. 434.
2. Ibid., for example.

3. Joseph Smith, *History of The Church of Jesus Christ of Latter-day Saints*, 2nd ed. rev., edited by B. H. Roberts (Salt Lake City: The Church of Jesus Christ of Latter-day Saints, 1932-51), 6:37-38.

4. *Doctrine and Covenants Student Manual: Religion 324–325* (Salt Lake City: Church Educational System, 1981), p. 425.

5. Bruce R. McConkie, *Mormon Doctrine*, 2nd ed. (Salt Lake City: Book-craft, 1966), p. 499.

6. *Ensign*, May 1977, p. 94.

7. *Ensign*, November 1985, p. 69.

21

MORMON AND THE DESTRUCTION OF NEPHITE CIVILIZATION
(Mormon 3–9)

THOMAS W. MACKAY

What Mormon must have felt, after nearly sixty years as general, historian, and prophet, as he helplessly witnessed his nation intent on spiritual suicide and utter annihilation! Although he found the behavior of his people reprehensible, still he had compassion for them. He offered his help, but he was unable to avert the imminent danger. And it was in this society that he had to rear his son and successor, Moroni. Mormon's humanity, his anguish, and his individuality all resound from the pages of the book, especially in that short segment entitled "The Book of Mormon."

Shaping the Historian's Mind

As we analyze Mormon's worldview, we realize from comments he made elsewhere in his abridgment of the historical record that certain people and events affected him deeply. For example, he wrote of king Benjamin in glowing terms, for ideals of industry, compassion, concern for the poor and needy, and a focus on the spiritual needs of people—these all leap out from Mormon's words. Mormon recounted how Alma's unwavering devotion to the gospel developed after he was moved by Abinadi's teachings and how it persisted in the face of adverse circumstances, despite the rebellion of people he

Thomas W. Mackay is professor of Greek and Latin at Brigham Young University.

loved, including one of his sons. Later, the conversion of the younger Alma—who resigned from political leadership to "preach the word of God" (Alma 4:19; cf. Alma 31:5)—and his experiences in teaching the people provided rich materials for the history. These individuals, with Moroni, Helaman, Nephi, and Samuel, also furnished patterns for Mormon's life.

But negative examples also abound in Mormon's account. What a contrast to these leaders Mormon made when he referred to Benjamin's contemporary, king Noah. But the wicked influence of individual apostates and leaders like Amlici, Nehor, Korihor, and Amalickiah pales in comparison to the social havoc wrought by the Gadianton robbers (contemporaneously, as though part of a worldwide phenomenon, robber bands and social deterioration were also a severe problem in the Roman Empire of the third century and again in the fifth century and later). So the prophet and historian noted at Mormon 1:18, 2:8, 28 the persistent presence of the Gadianton bands, answering his comment in Helaman 1-2, when the practice of a secret combination was introduced among the Nephites.[1] For at Helaman 2:12-14 Mormon observed, "More of this Gadianton shall be spoken hereafter.... And behold, in the end of this book ye shall see that this Gadianton did prove the overthrow, yea, almost the entire destruction of the people of Nephi. Behold I do not mean the end of the book of Helaman, but I mean the end of the book of Nephi, from which I have taken all the account which I have written." Thus we comprehend how Mormon had clearly seen from prophecy and from the social ills of his own lifetime the nature and origin of the destructive forces among the Nephites. This perspective was later echoed by his son Moroni, who lamented that "they [secret combinations] have caused the destruction of this people of whom I am now speaking [the Jaredite civilization], and also the destruction of the people of Nephi." (Ether 8:21.)

Other interests of Mormon included the military exploits of a man he deeply respected, the namesake of his own son: Moroni.[2] Of this great man Mormon said, "If all men had been and were, and ever would be, like unto Moroni, behold, the very powers of hell would have been shaken forever." (Alma 48:17; see 48:11-16.) This Moroni had delighted in preserving his people, not in shedding blood. Moroni's attitude, augmented by the example of the bravery and faith of Helaman's young warriors, became almost a preoccupation with Mormon.

The visit of the Savior and its effect on people nearly overwhelmed Mormon. And he had a special feeling for the three translated Nephite disciples; he had seen them himself. (3 Ne. 28:26; cf. Morm. 8:11.) In contrast to the three disciples, the response of his contemporary society must have struck Mormon forcibly, for despite his own preaching (Morm. 3:11-5:2), the Nephites refused to repent. Mormon learned how to evaluate society from experience, from abridging the Nephite records, and from heavenly visitants. So he based his historical judgment on the righteousness of the people, not on manifestations of military, political, financial, or cultural success. We discover this interpretation of history everywhere in Mormon's writings.

The first two chapters of Mormon continue the history recounted in 4 Nephi. The account begins with the injunction of the aged prophet Ammaron to the young Mormon, then but "about ten years of age" (Morm. 1:2), that he record the Nephite history of his lifetime. Nevertheless we must recall that this portion of Mormon's writings (Mormon 1-7) and the earlier bridge, "The Words of Mormon," between the small plates of Nephi (1 Nephi to Omni) and Mormon's abridgment of Mosiah from the large plates of Nephi were both made at the end of Mormon's life. Even the three chapters of Mormon's writings and teachings that Moroni inserted (Moroni 7-9) apparently antedate Mormon 7. Mormon's concluding message in Mormon 7 is poignant and direct. It thus reflects the maturity of his development as prophet-historian and offers his conclusion to the whole matter: the spiritual and cultural lessons future generations should learn from the disintegration of a once-flourishing civilization. These lessons are precisely the major motifs of the lengthy account of Nephite history that today bears his name.

An Age of Social Decay

As we pick up the story in Mormon 3, the prophet-historian had been divinely called to succeed the old prophet Ammaron. (Morm.

1:2-4.) Before this time, increasing tensions and conflicts split Nephite society into separate groups, and most people drifted from righteousness. (4 Ne. 1:27-38, 42-46; Morm. 1:7-11, 13-14.) Hence spiritual gifts and manifestations generally ceased (Morm. 1:14; cf. Morm. 9:20), though Mormon himself saw the Lord (Morm. 1:15). But in general the land was cursed; Gadianton robbers abounded; people hid up treasures, never to regain them; magic and witchcraft infected society, just as had been prophesied. (Hel. 13:30-38; 4 Ne. 1:45-46; Morm. 1:17-19; cf. Morm. 2:8, 10.) At fifteen, Mormon became military commander for the Nephites, but he had only limited success. (Morm. 2:1-11, 20-27.) Finally, in A.D. 350[3] a major mutual nonaggression pact was established among the Nephites, Lamanites, and Gadianton robbers. It did not last. Although ten years passed without battle, both Nephites and Lamanites made military preparations. (Morm. 3:1, 4.)

During the cessation of hostilities, the Nephites listened to Mormon only as their military and political leader, not as a prophet. (Morm. 3:1-3.) That was the same condition as twenty years previous, when the people lamented the wars and the degeneration of society, but only because those problems interfered with their own pleasures. Mormon pointedly commented that "their sorrowing was not unto repentance, because of the goodness of God; but it was rather the sorrowing of the damned, because the Lord would not always suffer them to take happiness in sin." (Morm. 2:13.)

In an epistle intended to intimidate his foe,[4] the Lamanite king announced his intention to resume war. In response, the Nephites fortified their cities and gathered "at the land Desolation, to a city which was in the borders, by the narrow pass which led into the land southward" (Morm. 3:5) — ironically, where the Jaredite armies had exterminated each other. In successive years (A.D. 361 and 362; Morm. 3:7-8) the Nephites repulsed the Lamanites, and those defensive victories altered Nephite desires: they wanted to go on the offensive against their enemies and utterly destroy *them*! Both sides were thoroughly infected with the same malady that afflicted the Jaredites and has been recorded of various nations: genocide of the opposition viewed as the only remedy.

In response, Mormon resigned, refusing to lead the offensive. He became "as an idle witness" (Morm. 3:16), as the Lord had commanded him. In the midst of this narrative, Mormon changed his authorial stance and directly addressed his audience, exhorting them to repentance and to an awareness of the impending final judgment. (Morm. 3:17-22.) So he indicated implicitly his disapproval of warfare, particularly for vengeance or for any purpose other than what had motivated Moroni.[5] Defense, not offense, and compassion, not annihilation, should be the motivating forces. He clearly stated this principle in his final words: "Know ye that ye must lay down your weapons of war, and delight no more in the shedding of blood, and take them not again, save it be that God shall command you." (Morm. 7:4.)

In an all-out offensive, the Lamanites assaulted and captured the key city Desolation, only to lose it again the following year. Lusting for each other's blood, both sides became depraved. Nearly a millennium before Mormon recorded the culmination of hostilities between Nephites and Lamanites, Nephi could boldly state that the invading house of Israel was more righteous than the prior inhabitants: "This people had rejected every word of God, and they were ripe in iniquity; and the fulness of the wrath of God was upon them; and the Lord did curse the land against them . . . unto their destruction, and he did bless it unto our fathers unto their obtaining power over it." (1 Ne. 17:35.) For Nephi, God "raiseth up a righteous nation, and destroyeth the nations of the wicked." (1 Ne. 17:37.) By contrast, to Mormon "the judgments of God will overtake the wicked; and it is by the wicked that the wicked are punished" (Morm. 4:5), for in his day he could discern no people who would qualify as righteous.

The belligerents fought ghastly battles, slaughtering women and children; but in their campaign of A.D. 367, the Nephites, furious because of the enemy's atrocities, drove out the invading and occupying forces of the Lamanites. (Morm. 4:10-16.) The next attack of the Lamanites, in A.D. 375, marked the point of no return for the genocidal war. (Morm. 4:18.) Overwhelming the pivotal stronghold of Desolation once more, the Lamanites quickly drove forward. Despite a repetition of wartime atrocities against their families, the

Nephites were so utterly terrorized that they fled, leaving all behind. (Morm. 4:19-22.) Under these circumstances, Mormon retrieved the records that Ammaron had deposited, but we may suppose that he had already abridged much of Nephite history from the various records while he was a nonparticipant in the battles from A.D. 362 (Morm. 3:11) to sometime after the Lamanites commenced their offensive in 375 (Morm. 5:1). He completed the abridgment and hid away his source records just before the final battle. (Morm. 6:6.)

Mormon was not deluded. He realized that the Nephites had not changed, yet his compassion led him to accept command once more. As Mormon and his armies swept by cities, they gathered Nephites into their retreating hosts. Many inhabitants would not believe that the Lamanites sought complete extermination of their enemies. However, the Nephite cities were soon obliterated. (Morm. 5:4-5.) Mormon's fuller account of these years on the plates of Nephi must have sickened him, and he summarizes only briefly for his modern audience. During these bleak days following the renewal of war in A.D. 375, the events described in Mormon's epistle to Moroni, recorded in Moroni 9, likely took place, for both there and in Mormon 5:16-18, Mormon lamented the moral, social, and spiritual degeneration of the Nephites. Their failure to repent left them as chaff blown on the wind, or as a storm-tossed ship without a rudder. (Mormon's similes are almost Homeric here [Morm. 5:18].) Then, as he did in Mormon 3, the prophet-historian again addressed his future audience, the Gentiles (Morm. 5:19-24), directing them to repent or to face destruction by "a remnant of the seed of Jacob" (Morm. 5:24).

The Final Battle and Its Aftermath

Mormon's account of the horrifying end of the war is brief—fifteen verses. His epistle to the Lamanite king set the battlefield: Cumorah. (Morm. 6:1-3.) The abundance of water in that region was striking enough to merit mention, perhaps indicating that the Nephites were often not in such terrain. The year was A.D. 384, the seventy-third year of Mormon's life. The entire populace, the full spectrum of age and physical strength, awaited the attack of the imposing Lamanite army (Morm. 6:7-8); as they did so, they experienced "that awful fear of death which fills the breasts of all the wicked" (Morm. 6:7).

In the fierce fighting that ensued, Mormon himself was wounded and left for dead amid his army. (Morm. 6:10.) The battle arrangements of the Nephites called for a general for every ten thousand combatants. Mormon named thirteen Nephite generals, including Mormon and Moroni, and noted "that there were ten more who did fall by the sword." (Morm. 6:15.) Every group of ten thousand was slaughtered, usually with their generals. Of the Nephite multitude, numbering roughly 230,000, that fought at Cumorah—and the Nephite host was dwarfed by "the greatness of their [the Lamanites'] numbers" (Morm. 6:8)—only twenty-four people survived, "and also a few who had escaped into the south countries and a few who had deserted over unto the Lamanites" (Morm. 6:15).[6] We learn from Moroni that those Nephites who escaped "were hunted by the Lamanites, until they were all destroyed." (Morm. 8:2, 7.) Among those slain was his father, Mormon, which left Moroni to a difficult and solitary life for another thirty-five years. (Morm. 8:3-5; Moro. 10:1.) If we may assume that Mormon 8:6 ("four hundred years have passed away since the coming of our Lord") marks the date of Moroni's first record on his father's plates, then Mormon, though aged and wounded, might have survived for a while. Perhaps the twenty-four survivors separated and agreed to rendezvous periodically, but within fifteen years of the battle, Moroni was without family or friend. Curiously, not all the demented fury and blood-lust was directed against the Nephites, for Moroni observed that "the Lamanites are at war one with another; and the whole face of this land is one continual round of murder and bloodshed; and no one knoweth the end of the war." (Morm. 8:8.) That is indeed poetic justice for the victorious nation.

Final Advice from a Dying Prophet, General, and Historian

After briefly recording the outcome of the battle (Morm. 6:1-15), Mormon lamented the insane destruction of his people. They simply refused to repent and to obey God's laws: "O ye fair ones, how could ye have departed from the ways of the Lord! O ye fair ones, how could ye have rejected that Jesus, who stood with open arms to receive you! Behold, if ye had not done this, ye would not have fallen. But behold, ye are fallen, and I mourn your loss." (Morm. 6:17-18.) As he proceeded, he referred to the last judgment, and this thought turned him to address his future audience directly. Whereas Mormon occasionally imbedded comments in his abridgment (as at 3 Ne. 30:1-2) and also composed an entire chapter on his approach to history (Hel. 12), we may view Mormon 7 as his final plea and loving advice to a civilization that would experience many of the same destructive forces that played out on the Americas anciently. This chapter warrants our careful and complete attention.

Speaking to the remnant of the house of Israel (that is, the descendants of the Lehi-Mulekite civilizations and others from among the Gentile nations who would read this record), Mormon proclaimed the following:

1. "Know ye that ye are of the house of Israel." (Morm. 7:2.) A correct sense of identity is essential to proper behavior. Pride in one's heritage and future, as prophesied in the scriptures, includes the blessings promised to Abraham, Isaac, and Jacob. Until you know who you are, you can never reach your potential. In positing this as his first instruction, Mormon combined the insight of the prophet with that of the historian. As long as people are oriented in time, with a historical perspective, they have a sense of identity; and Mormon, as other prophets in the Book of Mormon, always hearkened back to the religious origins of the house of Israel and its prophetic future.

2. "Know ye that ye must come unto repentance, or ye cannot be saved." (Morm. 7:3.) Through his account of Nephite history and through his own efforts with his contemporaries, Mormon always put matters into correct perspective: Put your life in order and be forgiven for sins through the atonement, or else all other accomplishments in life are transitory and vain.

3. "Know ye that ye must lay down your weapons of war, and delight no more in the shedding of blood, and take them not again, save it be that God shall command you." (Morm. 7:4.) This injunction

238

is stunning. First, it is specific and immediately follows the prophet-historian's call to repentance and his exhortation to understand our true identity. Second, it comes from one who was a military commander for fifty years. Nevertheless, he advocated a position not unlike that of the people of Anti-Nephi-Lehi; and certainly his hero Moroni also used restraint and took a defensive stance unless God directed otherwise. For a world with hundredfold overkill capability, what better message, what more apt charge could be written? This injunction is not the fanatical rambling of a demented, antisocial radical; rather it came from an active politician-general of many years. His historical and prophetic perspective also allowed him to deliver to our generation what we need desperately to know.

4. "Know ye that ye must come to the knowledge of your fathers, and repent of all your sins and iniquities, and believe in Jesus Christ, that he is the Son of God, and that . . . he hath risen again; . . . and he bringeth to pass the resurrection of the dead, whereby man must be raised to stand before his judgment-seat." (Morm. 7:5-6.) In a sense this repeats the first two points and joins to them Mormon's lament to the slain of his people. (Morm. 6:16-22.) We should live so that we will not be ashamed on judgment day; that is, we should repent and be forgiven for past misdeeds, then be inspired to do good in the future. By focusing on the final judgment, Mormon sought to motivate us to view life from an eternal perspective, the very thing the Nephites had lost.

5. "And he hath brought to pass the redemption of the world, whereby he that is found guiltless before him at the judgment day hath it given unto him to dwell in the presence of God in his kingdom . . . in a state of happiness which hath no end." (Morm. 7:7.) With his reaffirmation of the reality of the atonement and of the possibility of endless happiness following the brief period of trial in our mortal existence, Mormon tied back to the most important of the promises to Abraham, Isaac, and Jacob: that the Redeemer of the world would come from their posterity and perform the expiatory sacrifice for all, bringing about a universal resurrection, with individual rewards conditional upon faith, repentance, and obedience.

6. "Therefore repent, and be baptized in the name of Jesus, and

lay hold upon the gospel of Christ, which shall be set before you, not only in this record but also in the record which shall come unto the Gentiles from the Jews, which record shall come from the Gentiles unto you. For behold, this is written for the intent that ye may believe that; and if ye believe that ye will believe this also; and if ye believe this ye will know concerning your fathers, and also the marvelous works which were wrought by the power of God among them." (Morm. 7:8-9.) With the injunction to repent and be baptized, Mormon linked his message to his previous thought. Once acquired, an understanding of the principles of the gospel and of God's concern for his children is best reinforced by continual pondering of the scriptures. Mormon knew well that in our day, two major records, the Bible and the Book of Mormon, would corroborate each other and mutually support the restoration of the true gospel on the earth.

7. "And ye will also know that ye are a remnant of the seed of Jacob; therefore ye are numbered among the people of the first covenant; and if it so be that ye believe in Christ, and are baptized, first with water, then with fire and with the Holy Ghost, following the example of our Savior, according to that which he hath commanded us, it shall be well with you in the day of judgment." (Morm. 7:10.) Mormon now returned to his first injunction — to know and appreciate what it means to belong to the house of Israel. The historical anchor of personal and group identity not only has strong religious implications, but it is also a psychologically sound principle. By including the specific steps to take to abide by the gospel covenant, Mormon unified and summarized his statement: faith in Christ, baptism of water and of spirit, and constant obedience will lead to happiness when we are finally judged, as we will all surely be.

A Son Completes his Father's Work

As he sensed his life was coming to an end, Mormon gave his records to his son Moroni and directed him to complete the book. (Morm. 6:6; 8:1, 3; Moro. 9:24.) How was it not complete? The historical record after the visit of the Savior is extremely brief, by both choice and commandment. (Morm. 5:9; cf. 3 Ne. 26:6-12 [especially 11].) More significantly, when Mormon summarized the Jaredite record that Mosiah had translated, a record preserved for us in Moroni's abridgment under the name of Ether, he said, "This account shall be written hereafter; for behold, it is expedient that all people should know the things which are written in this account." (Mosiah 28:19.) This was one task he marked out for himself that he had not finished, and he perhaps spoke of this with Moroni. At least what Mormon mentioned in his epistle (Moro. 9:23) seems to be contemporary with the last year of the Nephite-Lamanite war, A.D. 384. (Or perhaps Moroni, while reading his father's record, came across the passage quoted above and, with filial devotion, did not want his father's promise to be unfulfilled.)

Moroni did continue his father's record. The trials and difficulties of his solitary existence are poignantly portrayed in Mormon 8:2-11, where even Moroni for some time seemed not to have been visited by the three Nephite disciples, who were translated and who had ministered among the Nephites and Lamanites until the wickedness of the people made it impossible to continue. Moroni dearly wanted his future readers to accept his record without being critical and negative, for he knew of his human weaknesses and failings. (Morm. 8:12-13, 17; cf. Ether 12:23-29, 35-36, 40.) Nevertheless, the record is true. It is divinely inspired. Perhaps he completed his first brief statement at Mormon 8:13 ("I make an end of speaking concerning this people. I am the son of Mormon, and my father was a descendant of Nephi"), for the next verse is almost another colophon that introduces the writer: "I am the same who hideth up this record unto the Lord" (Morm. 8:14). But our verse and chapter divisions are artificial and modern, not ancient, and so it seems that Mormon 8:13-14 is one continuous and unbroken statement. And Moroni's abridgment of Ether (that is, the twenty-four gold plates of the Jaredite record given by Limhi to the seer and king Mosiah, son of Benjamin) was probably accomplished at the same time as Mormon 8-9. However, to judge from Moroni 1:1, some time, perhaps as much as twenty years (Moro. 10:1), passed before Moroni composed the book that bears his name. As his father did, Moroni turned to his future audience and addressed them as though present, a voice crying from the dust. (Morm. 8:13-14.) His description of our days is precise and pointed, for he knew us through the spirit of prophecy. His concern was simple: as a civilization, we are following the same path as the Jaredites and Nephites, so he offered us a strong word of warning.

Just as his father prophesied how the Bible and the Book of Mormon would corroborate each other, Moroni made clear that no desire of personal fame or wealth and no intimidating threat will mar the appearance of the Nephite record in the last days. (Morm. 8:14-22.) But the book will be brought to a civilization where "miracles are done away" (Morm. 8:26) and where there are "secret combinations" (i.e., Gadianton-type groups; Morm. 8:27). Also, the social ills will pervade even the churches; corruption, rampant materialism, selfishness, and pride characterize the people. (Morm. 8:28-41.) Hence, because of social and spiritual problems left unattended, "the sword of vengeance hangeth over you." (Morm. 8:41.)

In the final chapter of Mormon, Moroni wrote with an apocalyptic view to the future. Though his audience was centuries removed, he addressed them directly. His message, echoing his father's warnings, emphasized the reality of the final judgment (Morm. 9:1-6), and Moroni linked together fall, atonement, resurrection, and judgment (Morm. 9:12-14). Disbelief in continuing revelation, miracles, and other religious matters is inconsistent with scriptural accounts of God's dealings with humanity. (Morm. 9:7-18.) For if God, who does not change, did miracles in the past, only a lack of faith can cause miracles to cease. Moroni then cited the Lord's injunction to his Nephite disciples or apostles (Morm. 9:22-25), a passage parallel to Mark 16:15-18.[7] Thus a cessation of miracles marks out the people as needing to change, to accept the gospel, and to look to the judgment. (Morm. 9:26-30.)

In an aside, Moroni referred to the language of the Nephites as "reformed Egyptian," and he also observed that the Nephites knew Hebrew—but in an altered form. (Morm. 9:32-34.) Since Nephite "reformed Egyptian" had been modified "according to our manner of speech," this was probably their primary written language. It was apparently also the primary language of the brass plates: "He [Lehi] having been taught in the language of the Egyptians therefore he could read these engravings." (Mosiah 1:4.) As we noted above, Moroni was a very self-conscious writer. He wanted people to read and to receive his message without worrying about minute details, for this book was to restore the gospel and its covenants to the house of Israel, particularly the latter-day remnant of Lehi's expedition. (Morm. 9:34-37.) He remained in harmony with his father's general scheme and purpose. Moroni dutifully completed what Mormon had undertaken.

NOTES

1. See also Alma 37:27-32 (about the secret combinations among the Jaredites), Helaman 6:17-32, and 4 Nephi 1:42, 46; also Hugh Nibley, *An Approach to the Book of Mormon* (Salt Lake City: Deseret Book, 1957), pp. 315-34 (now reprinted in a third edition [Salt Lake City: Deseret Book Company, and Provo, Utah: Foundation for Ancient Research and Mormon Studies, 1988], pp. 378-99).

2. Hugh Nibley, *Since Cumorah* (Salt Lake: Deseret Book Company, 1967), pp. 330-66.

3. The dating system *Anno Domini* or from the birth of Christ developed very early in Nephite records and accurately records the year as given. However, in the Greco-Roman world it was imposed on the historical narratives and records especially due to the influence of Dionysius Exiguus (sixth century) and the Venerable Bede (early eighth century). Unfortunately historical inaccuracies and lack of precise information apparently led to misplacing the birth of Christ about three to five years late, since Herod died in March, 4 B.C (F. F. Bruce, *New Testament History* [2nd ed.; London: Oliphants, 1977], p. 22), so if we wanted to put Book of Mormon dates in a timeline with traditional dating for the Roman world, we would need to adjust them accordingly. The year of the treaty would perhaps be circa 346/47. (For the date of Christ's birth, see Bruce R. McConkie, *The Mortal Messiah* [Salt Lake City: Deseret Book Company, 1979], 1:349-50, note 2; J. Reuben Clark, *Our Lord of the Gospels* [Salt Lake City: Deseret Book Company, 1954], p. vii; and Jack Finegan, *Handbook of Biblical Chronology* [Princeton: Princeton University Press, 1964], pp. 215-59; for the general problems and source materials for ancient chronology, see Alan E. Samuel,

Greek and Roman Chronology, Handbuch der Altertumswissenschaft, 1.7 [Munich: C.H. Beck'sche Verlagsbuchhandlung, 1972].)

4. Cf. Hugh Nibley, *Lehi in the Desert and the World of the Jaredites* (Salt Lake: Bookcraft, 1952), pp. 229-31.

5. Cf. Nibley, *Since Cumorah*, pp. 330-66 *passim*, but especially pp. 330, 340-41, 344, 348, 351-52.

6. Cf. Hugh Nibley, *Lehi in the Desert and the World of the Jaredites*, pp. 238-42.

7. There is no full parallel in the New Testament for Mormon 9:25 ("Whosoever shall believe in my name, doubting nothing, unto him will I confirm all my words, even unto the ends of the earth") except James 1:5-6. But Mormon 9:22-24 does give us cause to accept the longer ending of Mark as authentic early Christian scripture, despite textual questions based on manuscript tradition.

22

CHRIST AND THE JAREDITES
(Ether 1-4)

KENT P. JACKSON

As the ancient Jaredite civilization came to its dehumanizing end, the prophet Ether completed the record of his people, which he wrote on twenty-four plates of gold. He had been rejected by his people, as had other prophets, and now he saw their demise — living in a cave while he recorded the last days of a once-great society. (Ether 13:13-14.) Ether became a witness that the prophecies of annihilation had come true.[1] Once he had recorded that witness, he hid away the book, trusting it into the hands of God and knowing, we can be sure, that it would be made known to others in the due time of the Lord. (Ether 15:33.)[2]

Years later, a Nephite king named Limhi, son of Noah, sent an expedition of explorers to find the city of Zarahemla from which their ancestors had come. Limhi hoped to reunite his people with their fellow Nephites, from whom his colony had been separated for eighty years. Instead of finding Zarahemla, the explorers found the ruins of an ancient civilization and brought back artifacts to testify to their find. The most noteworthy of the artifacts was a record, written on "twenty-four plates which are filled with engravings, and they are of pure gold." (Mosiah 8:9; see also 8:7-14.) The due time of the Lord had arrived, and Ether's record had been discovered.

Limhi and his people could not read the plates but had an intense desire to know of their contents. Thus when Ammon and his party

---

Kent P. Jackson is associate professor of ancient scripture at Brigham Young University.

arrived from Zarahemla and told Limhi about King Mosiah—a seer who by means of some "interpreters" could make known the content of the record—Limhi "rejoiced exceedingly, and gave thanks to God, saying: Doubtless a great mystery is contained within these plates, and these interpreters were doubtless prepared for the purpose of unfolding all such mysteries to the children of men." (Mosiah 8:19; see also 8:12-14; 21:25-28.) Mosiah did translate the record, by means of "those two stones which were fastened into the two rims of a bow," which had been "prepared from the beginning, and were handed down from generation to generation, for the purpose of interpreting languages." (Mosiah 28:13-14; see also 28:11-18.)

The Nephites, anxious to learn about the nation whose history was on the record, mourned "exceedingly" and were "filled with sorrow" when they heard the tragic story of the Jaredites. Nonetheless, "it gave them much knowledge, in the which they did rejoice." (Mosiah 28:18.) In writing the book of Mosiah, Mormon noted that the Jaredite history would be included later in his record, for "all people should know the things which are written in this account." (Mosiah 28:19.) He died without including it in the Book of Mormon, but his son, Moroni, accomplished the task. "And now I, Moroni, proceed to give an account of those ancient inhabitants who were destroyed by the hand of the Lord upon the face of this north country. And I take mine account from the twenty and four plates which were found by the people of Limhi, which is called the Book of Ether." (Ether 1:1-2.) With these words, Moroni began his abridgment of the twenty-four gold plates of the Jaredite record.

Moroni found, as Mosiah had discovered earlier (Mosiah 28:17), that the Jaredite plates contained a history that extended from the creation of Adam to the time of Ether. He chose to begin his abridgment with the formation of the Jaredite colony at the time of the Tower of Babel, supposing that a record of the earlier period would already be available in the Bible at the time when the Book of Mormon would come forth. (Ether 1:3-4.)[3]

Jared and Mahonri Moriancumer

Moroni's abridgment of Ether's record devotes a third of its total space to the first generation of Jaredite history—the time of Jared and his brother and the successful establishment of their colony in the New World. The account begins at the time of the Tower of Babel, traditionally believed to be in Mesopotamia (modern-day Iraq).[4] Two great leaders are prominent at the beginning of the account—Jared and his brother, who is called in the narrative "the brother of Jared." There is no suggestion in Moroni's abridgment why he is known by this name. Perhaps his name was not recorded on Ether's twenty-four plates, or perhaps he was actually called "the brother of Jared."[5] In 1892, George Reynolds wrote that Joseph Smith had identified the brother of Jared's name as Mahonri Moriancumer.[6] Even though the reference comes from a late second-hand source, it has been accepted widely, and for the sake of convenience it will be used here. The narrative in the first chapter seems to suggest that the leader of the group was Jared. Yet he clearly recognized his brother's tremendous spiritual qualities and often took the initiative to ask him to inquire of the Lord for guidance in their collective mission. (See, for example, Ether 1:34, 36, 38.)

The Travels of the Jaredites

Knowing the intention of the Lord to confound the languages and scatter people over the earth, Jared asked his brother to pray that their language would not be confounded. Then he asked him to inquire about the relocation of their families and friends to another part of the world: "Who knoweth but the Lord will carry us forth into a land which is choice above all the earth? And if it so be, let us be faithful unto the Lord, that we may receive it for our inheritance." (Ether 1:38.) The Lord did, in fact, direct them to a promised land. With their families, their friends, and their friends' families, Jared and Mahonri Moriancumer trusted their future into the hands of God and followed his directions to a new home. With them they took flocks "of every kind," birds, fish, swarms of honeybees, and seeds of every kind. (Ether 2:1-3.) They traveled northward into a valley called "Nimrod," from which the Lord commanded them to travel "into the wilderness, yea into that quarter where there never had man been. And it came to pass that the Lord did go before them, and did talk with them as he stood in a cloud, and gave directions whither they should travel." Their journey included crossing "many waters, being directed continually by the hand of the Lord." (Ether 2:5-6.) It continued until they arrived at the "great sea which divideth the lands," at which point they stopped their journey for four years. It was from this location, which they named Moriancumer (Ether 2:13), that they later sailed across the ocean to their land of promise. The record does not give much specific information about the route of the group's travels from the valley of Nimrod to Moriancumer. Elder George Reynolds suggested: "It is evident that they first traveled northward, but whether they turned east or west is not so apparent. The general idea is that they turned eastward and crossed Central Asia."[7]

A Promised Land

In his discussion of the journeys of the Jaredites, Moroni took the opportunity to interject some profound information about the land of promise to which Jared and his people were traveling. Certainly he was in a unique position to write about the covenants and curses associated with a promised land. He knew the history of his own people and had himself witnessed their destruction. He also knew the final end of the Jaredite civilization, which makes his comments on their beginning most meaningful. He made his point clearly:

> Whoso should possess this land of promise, from that time henceforth and forever, should serve him, the true and only God, or they should be swept off when the fulness of his wrath should come upon them.
>
> And now, we can behold the decrees of God concerning this land, that it is a land of promise; and whatsoever nation shall possess it shall serve God, or they shall be swept off when the fulness of his wrath shall come upon them. And the fulness of his wrath cometh upon them when they are ripened in iniquity. (Ether 2:8-9.)

Those who desire to live in a land of promise must serve the true and only God. Those who fail to do so will be "swept off" when they reach the point of being "ripened in iniquity," that is, when their wickedness reaches the point at which punishment is inevitable.

Moroni was speaking of the Americas, which was the promised

land to the peoples of the Book of Mormon—the Jaredites, the Mulekites, and the Lehites. As he mentioned in verse 10, it was "choice above all other lands." Because the land was so vast, fertile, and rich, both the Nephites and the Jaredites were able to become extremely prosperous within a short time after their arrivals. (1 Ne. 18:24-25; Ether 6:28.) But when Moroni wrote his record, both of those civilizations had already gone to ruin for failing to serve God. He was not writing to them but to us in the latter days, the modern readers of his book.

Since the European discovery of the New World, when people from many lands began colonizing the Americas, they found a land in which God had provided an incredible richness of natural resources. Using those resources, they built, in a relatively short time, a civilization of unprecedented prosperity. Yet Moroni, who saw the world in the last days, gave somber warnings to the people of our time, explaining why the records of these fallen peoples were preserved for our benefit: "This cometh unto you, O ye Gentiles, that ye may know the decrees of God—that ye may repent, and not continue in your iniquities until the fulness come, that ye may not bring down the fulness of the wrath of God upon you as the inhabitants of the land have hitherto done." (Ether 2:11.)

Perhaps Moroni had in mind specifically those modern readers who would live in the land once promised to his own people—America—whose inhabitants now are already, collectively speaking, "ripening in their iniquity." But his warnings are appropriate for all people everywhere, for all nations are ripening in iniquity. He wrote these words so people in all lands could repent and avoid the calamities to which the Jaredites and his own people had subjected themselves.

Not all covenant people share the same promised lands. Palestine was the promised land and gathering place for the Israelites in ancient times; the Americas were the promised land and gathering place for the ancient Jaredites and the children of Lehi. Today each land is the land of promise and the place of gathering for those who live in it,[8] and the warnings and promises that Moroni gave in Ether 2:8-12 apply to all Latter-day Saints in their own nations. We can enjoy the blessings and the promises only if we and our fellow citizens, wherever we may live, "serve the God of the land, who is Jesus Christ." (Ether 2:12.)

Obtaining Light

Having been instructed by the Lord to build boats to convey his people across the waters, the brother of Jared successfully fulfilled the Lord's wishes. Yet God's instructions did not include showing him how light would be provided in the boats. For this he needed to exert his own initiative and make the best use of his God-given intellectual and spiritual resources. The Lord gave the brother of Jared an opportunity to grow. By making it necessary for him to find a way to light the barges, the Lord was challenging him to exercise his *agency*, his *intelligence*, and his *faith*.

The Lord motivated the brother of Jared to exercise his agency by placing on *him* the responsibility to find light for the barges. He had to make a decision himself rather than expecting God to do all that was needed. Mahonri exercised his intelligence by devising a solution that was functionally possible. His solution was, in fact, a good one; but it still required divine approval (which it received). And it still needed a miracle to make it work; only the Lord himself could create the light. Concerning the experience of the brother of Jared, Elder Harold B. Lee wrote: "It was as though the Lord were saying to him, 'Look, I gave you a mind to think with, and I gave you agency to use it. Now you do all you can do to help yourself with this problem; and then, after you've done all you can, I'll step in to help you.' "[9] Mahonri's enormous faith was demonstrated when he asked the Lord to touch the stones and provide light. He knew that the Lord would hear his plea, once he had exerted himself as the Lord required: "I know, O Lord, that thou hast all power, and can do whatsoever thou wilt for the benefit of man. . . . O Lord, thou canst do this. We know that thou art able to show forth great power." (Ether 3:4-5.) And the Lord did.

An Encounter with Christ

What followed is one of the greatest events in scriptural history: "The veil was taken from off the eyes of the brother of Jared, and he saw the finger of the Lord; and it was as the finger of a man, like unto flesh and blood." (Ether 3:6.) Seeing the Lord's finger was a startling revelation to him: "I saw the finger of the Lord. . . . I knew not that the Lord had flesh and blood." (Ether 3:8.) In response to Mahonri's faith, Jehovah decided to reveal more to him about the nature of God: "Because of thy faith thou hast seen that I shall take upon me flesh and blood. . . . Sawest thou more than this? And he answered: Nay; Lord, show thyself unto me." (Ether 3:9-10.) The Lord showed himself to the brother of Jared with these words: "Seest thou that ye are created after mine own image? Yea, even all men were created in the beginning after mine own image. Behold, this body, which ye now behold, is the body of my spirit; and man have I created after the body of my spirit; and even as I appear unto thee to be in the spirit will I appear unto my people in the flesh." (Ether 3:15-16.)

Mahonri was speaking with Jehovah, who later was born on earth, received a physical body, and was called Jesus Christ. Like other ancient prophets, he beheld the Lord's spirit body, in the image of which all men were created. (Gen. 1:26; Moses 1:6; Ether 3:15-16.) We cannot tell from the account exactly what the brother of Jared knew about the nature of God prior to this vision. But it appears in verse 8 that he was startled to see what he thought was a body of "flesh and blood." The Lord's comments in verse 16 make it clear that it was a body of spirit that the prophet saw. His misunderstanding shows that a spirit body resembles the flesh-and-blood body with which we are familiar. (D&C 77:2.)

Moroni provided a valuable summary: "Jesus showed himself unto this man in the spirit, even after the manner and in the likeness of the same body even as he showed himself unto the Nephites." (Ether 3:17.)

A most remarkable aspect of this experience is the powerful demonstration of faith on the part of Mahonri Moriancumer. Because he so completely *knew* that God would provide the light, the Lord could not keep him inside the veil that separates the earthly realm from the divine. "Never has man come before me with such exceeding faith as thou hast," said Jehovah. (Ether 3:9.) The prophet showed even greater faith when he requested, "Lord, show thyself unto me."

(Ether 3:10.) He testified that he believed the Lord's words before hearing them, knowing that God cannot lie. (Ether 3:12.) As Moroni reported, "Having this perfect knowledge of God, he could not be kept from within the veil." Indeed, "the Lord could not withhold *anything* from him, for he knew that the Lord could show him *all* things." (Ether 3:20, 26, emphasis added; see also Ether 12:20-21.) As a result of this faith, his exaltation was assured. His ultimate return to the presence of God had been given divine confirmation, and he then was permitted to see God and abide in his presence. (Ether 3:12-13.)[10]

Then came a statement from the Lord that sets the brother of Jared apart from every other person who had ever lived on earth up to that time: "*Never* have I showed myself unto man whom I have created, for *never* has man believed in me as thou hast." (Ether 3:15, emphasis added; see also verse 9.) The uniqueness of Mahonri Moriancumer's faith justified the uniqueness of Jehovah's revelation to him. No one else—including such prophets as Adam, Seth, Enoch, and Noah—had ever experienced in mortality such a manifestation of God, because no one else had ever exercised such faith.

Although the first part of verse 15 is difficult to understand, it is clear that there was something extraordinary about the appearance of the Lord to the brother of Jared, whose faith exceeded that of every other person since the beginning of time. We know from the scriptures that others had seen God, yet the Lord stated to the brother of Jared: "Never have I showed myself unto man."[11] Perhaps the following discussion will explain the Lord's statement.

The brother of Jared was speaking with Jehovah, "the Lord Omnipotent who reigneth, who was, and is from all eternity to all eternity, . . . the Father of heaven and earth, the Creator of all things from the beginning." (Mosiah 3:5, 8; see also Alma 11:39.) Under the direction of God the Father, whom we call Elohim, Jehovah is God of the universe, presiding over all things. Having been endowed by Elohim with infinite power, glory, and authority, Jehovah *is* the Father. He is God who spoke and still speaks to the prophets, who designed and reveals laws for the blessing of his people, and who directs the affairs of mortals on earth.

We know also that Jehovah is the same being who later came into the world as Jesus Christ. He became a being of dual nature: *Father* and *Son, God* and *Man.* (See Mosiah 15.) Prior to his mortal birth, he was the Lord Jehovah (Father, God); while he walked the earth he was the mortal Jesus Christ (Son, Man). Now he sits again on a throne of glory in the heavens. (See Philip. 2:5-11; Col. 1:12-20.)[12]

Concerning Jehovah's work, Elder Joseph Fielding Smith wrote:

> All revelation since the fall has come through Jesus Christ, who is the Jehovah of the Old Testament. In all of the scriptures, where God is mentioned and where he has appeared, it was Jehovah who talked with Abraham, with Noah, Enoch, Moses and all the prophets. He is the God of Israel, the Holy One of Israel; the one who led that nation out of Egyptian bondage, and who gave and fulfilled the Law of Moses. (1 Ne. 19:10; 3 Ne 11:10, 14; 15:2-9.) The Father [that is, Elohim] has never dealt with man directly and personally since the fall, and he has never appeared except to introduce and bear record of the Son.[13]

President Smith also taught: "The Father has honored Christ by placing his name upon him, so that he can minister in and through that name *as though he were the Father;* and thus, so far as power and authority are concerned, *his words and acts become and are those of the Father.*"[14]

Since Jehovah is empowered with the fulness of Elohim and is commissioned to speak in his behalf, he stands in the place of the Father and speaks the Father's words. Thus when he appeared in ancient times he was the Father, filling in every way the role of God. When giving revelation to prophets, he spoke of the mortal mission of Jesus Christ in the third person—that is, with the words of and from the perspective of God the Father, as though Jesus Christ were someone else. This explains Jehovah's discussion of Christ in Moses 1 and in many other scriptures.[15]

It seems from the scriptures that with one exception, in all the recorded manifestations of Jehovah prior to his birth in the flesh, he appeared in his role as God the Father, speaking the words of the Father. The exception is this appearance to the brother of Jared in

Ether 3. He said: "Behold, I am Jesus Christ. I am the Father and the Son. In me shall all mankind have life, and that eternally, even they who shall believe on my name; and they shall become my sons and my daughters. And never have I showed myself unto man whom I have created, for never has man believed in me as thou hast." (Ether 3:14-15.)

It appears that the uniqueness of this situation, brought about because of Mahonri Moriancumer's unparalleled faith, was the fact that Jehovah appeared to him in his role as Jesus—whereas to others he had shown himself as the Father. Never before, as far as we can tell from the scriptures, had Jesus Christ shown himself unto man. And, in fact, nowhere else in the scriptures do we have an example of Jehovah appearing in his role as Jesus until his coming in the flesh. As Moroni reported, "Having this perfect knowledge of God, *he could not be kept from within the veil; therefore he saw Jesus;* and he did minister unto him." (Ether 3:20, emphasis added.) To the brother of Jared the Lord revealed his complete nature: God who would become Man. Perhaps that is a reason why he commanded that the account of the appearance not be known in the world until after his mortal ministry. (Ether 3:21.)

Exercising Faith in the Lord

Mahonri's vision was not over with the appearance of Christ. The Lord "showed unto the brother of Jared *all* the inhabitants of the earth which had been, and also *all* that would be; and he withheld them not from his sight, even unto the ends of the earth." (Ether 4:25, emphasis added; cf. Moses 1:27-28.)[16] The Lord had told him that if he believed he could be shown all things, it would be so. Because he did, God "*could not* withhold *anything* from him, for he knew that the Lord could show him all things." (Ether 3:26, emphasis added.) This was no ordinary man; few people who have ever lived have been greater. Faith is the process of reaching out beyond our knowledge. The more knowledge we possess, the farther we can reach. The faith of Mahonri Moriancumer was so great that *nothing* could be withheld from him. Nowhere in the scriptures do we have an example of more perfect faith.

The sacredness of the event required that the record of it be kept sacred as well. The brother of Jared was commanded to write down what he had experienced and to seal it up, along with two stones that the Lord provided for interpreting such sacred records. (Ether 3:22-23, 27-28; 4:2.) Moroni, the inspired historian of the account, knew that the record was a treasure of inestimable worth, to be preserved to come forth among a righteous generation. Until humanity is worthy of such an endowment of knowledge, the record will remain sealed. (Ether 4:6-7.) To see what Mahonri Moriancumer saw will require the same kind of faith that he had. Likely that level of faith will not be had in the Church sufficiently until the Millennium. (See D&C 101:32-34.)[17]

Lack of faith and lack of faithfulness are the sicknesses that create spiritual blindness. No one knew that better than Moroni, who had witnessed it to the fullest extent — in his own lifetime and vicariously through the records entrusted into his care. Using the faith of the brother of Jared as a standard, he recorded the Lord's words that challenge us to enlarge the boundaries of our own faith: "I will show unto you the greater things, the knowledge which is hid up because of unbelief. . . . When ye shall rend that veil of unbelief which doth cause you to remain in your awful state of wickedness, and hardness of heart, and blindness of mind, then shall the great and marvelous things which have been hid up from the foundation of the world" be made known. (Ether 4:13, 15.)

Those with such faith will not be kept within the veil that separates the holy from the earthly. They shall see what the prophets have seen and know what the prophets have known.

NOTES

1. The book of Omni contains a brief reference to a Jaredite matter, written by Amaleki before Ether's history was discovered. Sometime between the arrival of the Mulekites in the New World and their joining with king Mosiah and the Nephites (Omni 1:12-15), the Mulekites came upon a

large inscribed stone. It was written by a man named Coriantumr, who was alive at the time of the discovery and lived for nine months among the Mulekites. (Omni 1:20-22.) This was undoubtedly the same Coriantumr who was a contemporary of Ether and who played a major role in the final events in the history of the Jaredite nation. (See Ether 12-15; especially 15:29-34.)

2. We are not informed of Ether's sources for the compilation of his record, which covered over two thousand years. But knowing how other sacred histories were written, including that of Mormon and Moroni, it is certainly possible that Ether had earlier Jaredite writings from which he compiled his account.

3. I suppose that it would not be inappropriate to wish that Moroni had included the account of history from Adam's time to that of Jared. Since we know from the Joseph Smith Translation and the Book of Mormon that the Old Testament did not arrive in the latter days without suffering major omissions, it is likely that the Jaredite equivalent of Genesis 1-11 would reveal fascinating information to us that is not available elsewhere.

4. Without question, the book of Ether clearly substantiates the historicity of the Tower of Babel and the account of the confounding of the languages that took place because of it. Whatever the exact circumstances may have been, at least we know because of Ether's account — untainted by textual manipulation and uninspired tradition — that there was such a tower and that the Lord did indeed confound the languages of his children in order to scatter them throughout the earth. (Ether 1:33-37.)

5. Arab men frequently have secondary names constructed from "Abu" ("father of"), often followed by the name of the first-born son (i.e., Abu-Ibrahim, "father of Ibrahim," etc.).

6. The account was published in a footnote in the *Juvenile Instructor*, May 1, 1892, p. 282. It reads as follows: "While residing in Kirtland Elder Reynolds Cahoon had a son born to him. One day when President Joseph Smith was passing his door he called the Prophet in and asked him to bless and name the baby. Joseph did so and gave the boy the name of Mahonri Moriancumer. When he had finished the blessing he laid the child on the bed, and turning to Elder Cahoon he said, the name I have given your son is the name of the brother of Jared; the Lord has just shown [or revealed] it to me. Elder William F. Cahoon, who was standing near heard the Prophet make this statement to his father; and this was the first time the name of the brother of Jared was known in the Church in this dispensation."

7. *Juvenile Instructor*, May 1, 1892, p. 284, note. Elder Reynolds also wrote: "We have no direct information in regard to the locality of Morian-

cumer, but those who believe that the Jaredites traveled eastward through Central Asia, are of the opinion that it was near the mouth of one of the great rivers that flow through the Chinese empire into the Pacific Ocean." (*Juvenile Instructor*, May 1, 1892, note.)

8. Spencer W. Kimball, *The Teachings of Spencer W. Kimball*, ed. Edward L. Kimball (Salt Lake City: Bookcraft, 1984), pp. 439-40; see also Harold B. Lee, citing Bruce R. McConkie, in *Conference Report*, April 1973, pp. 6-7.

9. "How to Receive a Blessing from God," *Improvement Era*, October 1966, p. 862.

10. See Joseph Smith, *Teachings of the Prophet Joseph Smith*, selected by Joseph Fielding Smith (Salt Lake City: Deseret Book Company, 1938), p. 150.

11. Several explanations have been given for this passage. See Joseph Fielding Smith, *Answers to Gospel Questions*, 5 vols. (Salt Lake City: Deseret Book Company, 1957-66), 2:124-25; Bruce R. McConkie, *The Promised Messiah* (Salt Lake City: Deseret Book Company, 1978), pp. 47, 599-600; Sidney B. Sperry, *Answers to Book of Mormon Questions* (Salt Lake City: Bookcraft, 1967), pp. 47-51; Daniel H. Ludlow, *A Companion to Your Study of the Book of Mormon* (Salt Lake City: Deseret Book Company, 1976), p. 318.

12. See Kent P. Jackson, "Jesus and the Gospels," *Studies in Scripture, Vol. 5: The Gospels*, ed. Kent P. Jackson and Robert L. Millet (Salt Lake City: Deseret Book Company, 1986), pp. 2-5.

13. Joseph Fielding Smith, *Doctrines of Salvation*, 3 vols., comp. Bruce R. McConkie (Salt Lake City: Bookcraft, 1954-56), 1:27.

14. Ibid., p. 30, emphasis added.

15. It also helps clarify the identities in Isaiah 53 (see especially verse 10). For a detailed discussion of the role of Christ as Father, see Robert L. Millet, "The Ministry of the Father and the Son," in *The Book of Mormon: The Keystone Scripture*, ed. Paul R. Cheesman (Provo, Utah: Religious Studies Center, Brigham Young University, 1988), pp. 44-72.

16. Rodney Turner wrote concerning Moses' similar vision in Moses 1:27-28: "Nor did he simply view them en masse as one might look at a vast concourse of people without discerning any one individual. By the incomprehensible power of the Holy Ghost he perceived each man, woman, and child comprising the human race *at one and the same time!* In doing so, he experienced something of the omnipresent nature of the Spirit of the Lord." ("The Visions of Moses," *Studies in Scripture, Vol. 2: The Pearl of*

Great Price, ed. Robert L. Millet and Kent P. Jackson [Salt Lake City: Randall Book Company, 1985], p. 55.)

17. See Bruce R. McConkie, "The Doctrinal Restoration," in *The Joseph Smith Translation: The Restoration of Plain and Precious Things*, ed. Monte S. Nyman and Robert L. Millet (Provo, Utah: Religious Studies Center, Brigham Young University, 1985), pp. 15, 20-21.

23
PROMISES FULFILLED
(Ether 5–8)

ANDREW C. SKINNER

Long before the ancient patriarch Abraham, father of the Hebrews, went out from Ur and journeyed to his land of promise as part of the great covenant, others had already left the Near East and traveled thousands of miles in search of yet another promised land. Moroni's abridged account of the voyage and arrival of the Jaredites, found in Ether 5-8, is inspiring as well as instructive theologically, prophetically, historically, culturally, and politically. It provides us with many instances of prophecies and promises fulfilled by the Lord.

Perhaps God sends people to covenant lands so that they might establish a special relationship with him as they struggle in the midst of ungodliness. Five such examples immediately come to mind: the Jaredites, Abraham and his people, the Israelites under Moses, the Nephites, and the nineteenth-century Latter-day Saint pioneers.

That Deity takes seriously the giving of certain lands or territories, viewing them as *special* gifts and important symbols of favored status, seems certain. (See 2 Ne. 3:2; and 9:1-2, for example.) All the lands of the earth are God's, just as the psalmist wrote: "The earth is the Lord's, and the fulness thereof." (Ps. 24:1.) God may give *whatever* land he chooses to *whomever* he chooses. But those who receive come under strict requirements of righteous living, as the Jaredite record demonstrates: "But he would that they should come forth even unto the land of promise, which was choice above all other

---

Andrew C. Skinner is instructor of history at Metropolitan State College, Denver, Colorado.

lands, which the Lord God had preserved for a righteous people. And he had sworn in his wrath unto the brother of Jared, that whoso should possess this land of promise, from that time henceforth and forever, should serve him, the true and only God, or they should be swept off when the fulness of his wrath should come upon them." (Ether 2:7-8.)

Thus, God may also sweep off from the face of his property whomever he chooses; and this he has done in the past. (See Gen. 6:7; Deut. 7:1-2; 1 Sam. 15:3, 8; Ether 15.)

Moroni interrupted the story of Jaredite travel and settlement in the land of promise by inserting some direct and personal instructions to the future translator of the record he had produced. Moroni warned him not to touch the portion of the record that was sealed up unless God so commanded him. (Ether 5:1.) According to Moroni, the sealed portion contained "the very things which the brother of Jared saw" (Ether 4:4) on Mount Shelem; in particular "all the inhabitants of the earth which had been, and also all that would be; and he withheld them not from his sight, even unto the ends of the earth" (Ether 3:25). These are some of the things other great prophet-patriarchs have also viewed, as attested to by Enoch (Moses 6:36), Abraham (Abr. 3:22), Moses (Moses 1:8, 28), and even our first father, Adam (D&C 107:56).

Having been instructed by the Lord that this "revelation from God, from the beginning of the world to the ending thereof" (2 Ne. 27:7) would not be given to other people until they became sanctified like Jared's brother (Ether 4:7), Moroni told the future prophet (Joseph Smith) that it was not to be translated. However, Moroni was able to promise him that the plates containing the record would be shown to three witnesses who would help him translate the appointed portion. Their testimony was to stand as evidence to the rest of the world of the record's reality and truth.

The Law of Witnesses

So it was in June 1829, some 1,400 years after Moroni's prophetic instructions to a future prophet, that three men asked Joseph Smith if they could be the special witnesses spoken of by Moroni in Ether 5:2-4. Joseph Smith's own words recount the episode:

> In the course of the work of translation, we ascertained that three special witnesses were to be provided by the Lord, to whom He would grant that they should see the plates from which this work (the Book of Mormon) should be translated; and that these witnesses should bear record of the same, as will be found recorded [2 Ne. 11:3; Ether 5:2-4]. Almost immediately after we had made this discovery, it occurred to Oliver Cowdery, David Whitmer and the aforementioned Martin Harris (who had come to inquire after our progress in the work) that they would have me inquire of the Lord to know if they might not obtain of him the privilege to be these three special witnesses; and finally they became so very solicitous, and urged me so much to inquire that at length I complied.[1]

The revelation that followed promised the fulfillment of Moroni's earlier prophecy; it is set forth in modern scripture as section 17 of the Doctrine and Covenants. It begins with these words: "Behold, I say unto you, that you must rely upon my word, which if you do with full purpose of heart, you shall have a view of the plates, and also of the breastplate, the sword of Laban, the Urim and Thummim, which were given to the brother of Jared upon the mount, when he talked with the Lord face to face." (D&C 17:1.)

According to the Prophet Joseph Smith, not many days after the revelation was received, the four men (Joseph Smith, Martin Harris, David Whitmer, and Oliver Cowdery) went into some woods near David Whitmer's house to try to obtain the actual fulfillment of the promises made in the revelations from God. (Ether 5; D&C 5; 17.) Each man, beginning with Joseph Smith, took a turn at praying vocally for an answer or divine manifestation. The same procedure was repeated after the first attempt failed to produce the desired result. After a second failure, Martin Harris withdrew himself, believing that he was the cause of the difficulty. The men, without Martin Harris, again prayed and in a matter of minutes received a glorious manifestation of the plates held by an angel. They also heard a voice from heaven that confirmed the very words Moroni had uttered many centuries earlier when he prophesied precisely that the plates would be "shown by the power of God." (Compare the wording in Ether 5:3 and *History of the Church* 1:55.)

Joseph Smith left the two in order to check on Martin Harris. Joseph and Martin joined in prayer with the following result, as reported by the Prophet himself: "Before we had yet finished, the same vision was opened to our view, at least it was again opened to me, and I once more beheld and heard the same things; whilst at the same moment, Martin Harris cried out, apparently in an ecstasy of joy, ' 'Tis enough; 'tis enough; mine eyes have beheld; mine eyes have beheld;' and jumping up, he shouted, 'Hosanna,' blessing God, and otherwise rejoiced exceedingly."[2]

These episodes constitute the final link in an ancient chain going all the way back to the Jaredites. For it is, in part, the things that happened to Jared, his brother, and their families, that the three witnesses attested to. Oliver Cowdery, David Whitmer, and Martin Harris were the physical, literal fulfillment of Moroni's promise. They became living witnesses not only of the things the Prophet Joseph Smith was doing but also of the importance of the law of witnesses itself. Because of this law of witnesses, Joseph Smith did not have to stand alone as he fielded the abuses and injuries inflicted by an apostate world. Thus, we may more fully appreciate his remarks made soon after his experience with the three witnesses: "Father, mother, you do not know how happy I am; the Lord has now caused the plates to be shown to three more besides myself. They have seen an angel, who has testified to them, and they will have to bear witness to the truth of what I have said, for now they know for themselves that I do not go about to deceive the people, and I feel as if I was relieved of a burden which was almost too heavy for me to bear, and it rejoices my soul that I am not any longer to be entirely alone in the world."[3]

At the time Moroni prepared his abridgment of the account of the people of Jared, circa A.D. 400, the law of witnesses was already a very ancient one. It was an integral part of the cultural, legal, and moral heritage carried by Moroni's ancestors from Jerusalem in 600 B.C. Though nothing is said in the Bible about qualification, it is likely that a witness in biblical times was considered to be any free man who had firsthand knowledge of a fact or an event.[4] During early Christian times, those who had firsthand knowledge of Jesus were called witnesses. Eventually the Greek word for witness, *martus*, came to denote those who had given up their lives or met violent deaths in pursuit of the Christian cause, martyrs.

Moroni's understanding of the law of witnesses parallels that of the Apostle Paul; that is, "In the mouth of two or three witnesses shall every word be established." (2 Cor. 13:1.) The knowledge of both Paul and Moroni regarding the law was undoubtedly based, in part, on several Mosaic prescriptions that required the testimony of at least two witnesses to establish with certainty any claim. (Num. 35:30; Deut. 17:6; 19:15.) It was the intention of the law in ancient Israel to establish as securely as possible any information being attested to. For this reason, three witnesses were preferable to two. Multiple witnesses decreased the possibility of shoddy, perverted, or "plotting witnesses" (*edim zummim*).[5] It is significant that where the plates and sacred records are concerned, the Lord provided, first, three witnesses and, later, many more for these latter days. Concerning the law of witnesses, Elder Bruce R. McConkie wrote:

> Whenever the Lord has established a dispensation by revealing his gospel and by conferring priesthood and keys upon men, he has acted in accordance with the *law of witnesses* which he himself ordained. This law is: "In the mouth of two or three witnesses shall every word be established." (2. Cor. 13:1; Deut. 17:6; 19:15; Matt. 18:15-16; John 8:12-29.) Never does a prophet stand alone in establishing a new dispensation of revealed truth, or in carrying the burden of such a message and warning to the world. In every dispensation, from Adam's to the present, two or more witnesses have joined their testimonies, thus leaving their hearers without excuse in the day of judgment should the testimony be rejected.[6]

A Miraculous Journey

After Moroni made an end of his prophecies and promises, he gave an account of the great voyage of the people of Jared. With the many necessary preparations finally completed, the people entered their barges and set forth into the sea, putting their trust in the Lord. We are told that they were in the water an incredible 344 days — almost a full year.

Moroni's abridgment gives us some small idea of the truly miraculous and spectacular nature of the Jaredite adventure, wherein the eight barges were propelled toward their destination by a furious wind, created by the Lord, which "did never cease to blow towards the promised land." (Ether 6:8.) While some may question the veracity of such a story, it should be remembered that God is Lord over all the elements of the earth. As he himself told Moroni, "At my command the heavens are opened and are shut; and at my word the earth shall shake." (Ether 4:9.)

Even those modern-day skeptics who most disbelieve maritime theories concerning the ancient peopling of the Americas admit that some early transoceanic voyages are probable due to oceanic currents and prevailing winds. From the work of one writer we read:

> The winds and current of the North Pacific trend eastward. Any craft caught helpless in their embrace can easily be carried across the ocean; in fact, there are records to show that, for example, between 1775 and 1875 about twenty Japanese junks were blown, against their will, to the west coast of America and deposited at various points between Alaska and Mexico. If Japanese vessels in the last century, why not Chinese or Indian or Malaysian during all the long centuries that preceded the arrival of Columbus? There must have been a certain number that ended a storm-tossed journey on this side of the Pacific. Perhaps a few of the hardier spirits among their crews risked the long sail back home, but most must have chosen to live on where they landed. Eventually they either died out or became wholly absorbed, leaving behind only tantalizing indirect reminiscences of their presence such as art motifs, pottery shapes, and the like.[7]

Other less skeptical scholars have long recognized the reality of transoceanic crossings but have opted to support Atlantic-route theories also based, in part, on the existence of "gentle climatic conditions and extremely favorable ocean currents and prevailing winds."[8]

In fact, journeys like that of the Jaredites are in harmony with ancient Near Eastern cultural and literary motifs as well as historical circumstances of the late fourth and early third millennium B.C., which is the time-frame posited by recent scholarship for the rise of Jaredite civilization in the New World.[9] Very early Near Eastern records abound with references to ships and voyages. "No motif is more common in the miniature art of the Mesopotamian cylinder seals than the reed boats used by the legendary heroes in the period of settlement."[10] Mesopotamia was known for its seagoing excursions, and it is also generally accepted as the land of the tower where the Jaredites originated. The earliest Mesopotamian people, known as the Sumerians, incorporated into their literature the episode of the great flood. Regarding the period of settlement after the flood, Sumerian writings indicate that the survivors landed in a big ship at a place called Dilmun and from there went to Mesopotamia, also by sea.[11] Thus, seagoing ventures were, early on, a significant part of the Mesopotamian cultural milieu. Some scholars have suggested that the oldest sign for *ship* in ancient Sumer was the same as the one used for the *marine* in the hieroglyphic script of Egypt.[12] These writing systems both date to before 3000 B.C..

The ancient Jaredite record gives us some idea concerning the construction of the barges, which were "tight like unto a dish." The record compares them to the ark of Noah. (Ether 6:7.)

Because the Jaredite barges were watertight, they could be "buried in the deep" without harm to their passengers. It was this construction that made necessary the special system of lighting (sixteen transparent stones) designed by the brother of Jared and put into operation by the finger of the Lord. The King James Version of the Old Testament reports that Noah's ark was to have a "window" for a light: "A window shalt thou make to the ark." (Gen. 6:16.) However, some modern Jewish translators of the Hebrew text render this passage: "A *light* shalt thou make to the ark." The word in question, *tsohar*, in the dual form means "noon" or "midday." Ancient Jewish legend relates that it was not just a light in the ark but was actually "a precious stone which illuminated the whole interior of the Ark."[13]

In another interesting parallel to the Jaredite barges found in ancient Near Eastern literature, one of the heroes of the Gilgamesh Epic is commanded to build a ship in the face of an impending flood. This hero (Utnapishtim) is told by one of the gods to build it according to proper specifications and to caulk or seal it. The boat will take him down into "the (watery) Deep . . . to dwell."[14]

Suffice it to say that nonscriptural sources provide an important historical and cultural context for the events recounted by Moroni. In Joseph Smith's day, such things as these were almost totally unknown. Nowadays we know that the Jaredite record fits the pattern of the ancient world. And yet our conviction of its truth is a matter of faith.

Jaredite Kingship

Perhaps we cannot appreciate from Moroni's brief account the great joy felt by the people of Jared when they finally landed in the promised land. They stood upon a land that was both promised and promising. It represented, in tangible form, the very fulfillment of the Lord's words: "I will go before thee into a land which is choice above all the lands of the earth." (Ether 1:42.) It represented, in tangible form, a covenant kept. We may only guess at the kind of powerful revelations the people received as they were "taught from on high" in their new home. (Ether 6:17.)

After not too long a time, as the record seems to indicate, the people of Jared voiced their desire to have a king rule over them. History confirms that monarchy has existed since the earliest periods of human culture. Some peoples have believed that kingship was instituted by, and serves as the agent of, divine will. The situation of the Jaredites at this juncture in their history immediately brings to mind the people of Israel, who also clamored for a king. They were told by Samuel the prophet the same thing the brother of Jared told his people centuries earlier: "Surely this thing leadeth into captivity." (Ether 6:23.)

Perhaps because they knew the risks associated with kingship, several of the Jaredites refused the office. Finally, one of the sons of Jared — Orihah — was anointed. He was a righteous and successful king because he "did walk humbly before the Lord, and did remember how great things the Lord had done for his father, and also taught his people how great things the Lord had done for their fathers." (Ether 6:30.)

Orihah is a perfect example of the Lord's teachings on righteous kingship as presented by Mosiah. If just rulers could always be chosen, then kingship would be an expedient form of government. However, not all leaders are just, and it is therefore usually not expedient to have kings rule. As Mosiah taught, "How much iniquity doth one wicked king cause to be committed, yea, and what great destruction!" (Mosiah 29:17.)

Clearly the brother of Jared well understood the Lord's teachings regarding kingship, for it was not long after the reign of Orihah that his prophetic words were fulfilled when Orihah's successor was brought into captivity. (Ether 7:5.) What followed was one of the bright spots in the history of the Jaredite people—a history filled with rebellion, treachery, warfare, and extreme wickedness. That bright spot was the reign of Shule, who "remembered the great things that the Lord had done for his fathers in bringing them across the great deep into the promised land; wherefore he did execute judgment in righteousness all his days." (Ether 7:27.)

Secret Combinations: Freedom Assaulted

Several things made Orihah and Shule successful and blessed rulers, bringing peace and prosperity to the Jaredites. These things include those important institutions to which all of us most owe our loyalties and allegiance: God, family, and fellow beings. After a time, when these things were rebelled against and forgotten, the Jaredite culture began to collapse. The steady slide of the Jaredite people toward destruction began in earnest with the rebellion of one Jared (son of Omer and grandson of Shule), who took his own father into captivity and sought, without moral restraint, "the kingdom and . . . the glory of the world." (Ether 8:7.)

It is significant that Jared's own daughter, following the wicked example he himself had set, provided the impetus to introduce into their society the most insidious and cunning of all Satan's wicked schemes, secret combinations. (Ether 8:9.) She reminded her father that part of the record brought by their ancestors to the promised land contained "an account concerning them of old, that they by their secret plans did obtain kingdoms and great glory." Eventually, one Akish was persuaded to become involved in these secret plans. "And it was the daughter of Jared who put it into his heart to search up these things of old; and Jared put it into the heart of Akish; wherefore, Akish administered it unto his kindred and friends, leading them away by fair promises to do whatsoever thing he desired." (Ether 8:17.)

As to what was contained in that part of the ancient record referred to by Jared's daughter, we have been given an outline from various sources. According to Ether, the secret plans consisted of "oaths which were given by them of old who also sought power, which had been handed down even from Cain, who was a murderer from the beginning." (Ether 8:15.) Nephi reported that these oaths were "administered by the devil, to combine against all righteousness." (3 Ne. 6:28.) The record of Moses confirms the veracity of the previous two statements in a graphic and frightening manner: "Satan said unto Cain: Swear unto me by thy throat, and if thou tell it thou shalt die; and swear thy brethren by their heads, and by the living God, that they tell it not; for if they tell it, they shall surely die; and this that thy father may not know it; and this day I will deliver thy brother Abel into thine hands." (Moses 5:29.)

Moroni testified that secret combinations lead to destruction — the destruction of life, property, and freedom. (Ether 8:25.) The overthrow of freedom or free agency was Satan's plan from the beginning. (Moses 4:1-4.) Thus, secret combinations can be found in many elements of society among all people. (Ether 8:20.) Perhaps this may frighten us in the latter days. But it may also make us more conscious of Moroni's warning for our times — which warning he was commanded to write (Ether 8:26): "Whatsoever nation shall uphold such secret combinations, to get power and gain, until they shall spread over the nation, behold they shall be destroyed. . . . Wherefore, O ye Gentiles, it is wisdom in God that these things should be shown unto you, that thereby ye may repent of your sins, and suffer not that these murderous combinations shall get above you, which are built up to get power and gain—and the work, yea, even the work of destruction come upon you, yea, even the sword of the justice of the Eternal God shall fall upon you, to your overthrow and destruction if ye shall suffer these things to be." (Ether 8:22-23.)

If there is one lesson we learn from reading Ether 5-8, it is that when the Lord makes a prophecy or promise it must surely come to pass. Latter-day Saints must resolve to fight against Satan through personal righteousness and by avoiding the very appearance of evil. Does something degrade rather than edify? Is it done solely to get gain? Or does it attempt to stay hidden from Deity? If so, we must leave it alone.

Conclusion

The book of Ether is a record of great importance. It teaches of righteous leaders who were surely among the noble and great souls seen by Abraham. (Abr. 3:22-23.) It discloses glimpses of unspeakably glorious matters reserved for a future time of great righteousness. (Ether 4:7.) It bears testimony of the prophet Joseph Smith and three other latter-day witnesses called by God. (Ether 5.) It describes the customs and culture of an ancient people. (Ether 6.) It is full of verifying traditions.

The book of Ether (especially chapters 5-8) is important as well as interesting because it contains a number of parallels to be found in other scriptures. These include a great ocean voyage, barges like Noah's ark, prayers and praises sung unceasingly (compare Enos and others), a great family gathering before the death of the patriarchs (compare Ether 6:19-20 and D&C 107:53), the request for kingship, and secret combinations.

However, the great value of Ether, in particular chapters 5-8, lies in the spiritual lessons it provides: The promises of God are sure and must be fulfilled, and if we are righteous we shall prosper in the land. Just as Moroni wrote these things in his record so that "evil may be done away," let us read and apply them for the same reason.

NOTES

1. Joseph Smith, *History of the Church of Jesus Christ of Latter-day Saints*, 2nd ed. rev. (Salt Lake City: The Church of Jesus Christ of Latter-day Saints, 1932-51), 1:52-53.

2. Ibid., p. 55.

3. Ibid., p. 56, footnote.

4. Josephus reported that women and slaves were disqualified as witnesses. Josephus, *Antiquities* 4:8, 15.

5. J. H. Hertz, ed., *The Pentateuch and Haftorahs*, 2nd ed. (London: Soncino Press, 1967), p. 830.

6. Bruce R. McConkie, *Mormon Doctrine*, 2nd ed. (Salt Lake City: Bookcraft, 1966), p. 436.

7. Jamake Highwater, *Native Land, Sagas of the Indian Americas* (Boston: Little, Brown and Company, 1986), p. 16.

8. Ross T. Christensen, ed., *Transoceanic Crossings to Ancient America* (Provo: Brigham Young University, 1970), p. 25.

9. John L. Sorenson, *An Ancient American Setting for the Book of Mormon* (Salt Lake City: Deseret Book Company, and Provo, Utah: Foundation for Ancient Research and Mormon Studies, 1985), pp. 116-18.

10. Thor Heyerdahl, *The Tigris Expedition* (Garden City, N.Y.: Doubleday and Company, 1981), p. 8.

11. Ibid., p. 23.

12. Ibid., p. 8.

13. Hertz, *Pentateuch and Haftorahs*, pp. 26-27.

14. James B. Pritchard, ed., *The Ancient Near East Volume 1, An Anthology of Texts and Pictures*, 2 vols. (Princeton: Princeton University Press, 1973), p. 66.

24

A MORE EXCELLENT WAY
(Ether 9–15)

CATHERINE THOMAS

The Book of Mormon belongs to that group of ancient religious records known as Two-Way documents. A number of other ancient records may be described as Two-Way documents: the Qumran Manual of Discipline, the early Christian Didache, the Epistle of Barnabas, and so on.[1] Two-Way literature presents a philosophy that describes life as consisting of only two ways, each antithetical to the other; it identifies only two inclinations in man, also antithetical. For example, 2 Nephi 10:23-24 describes two ways: "Therefore, cheer up your hearts, and remember that ye are free to act for yourselves — to choose the way of everlasting death or the way of eternal life. Wherefore . . . reconcile yourselves to the will of God, and not to the will of the devil and the flesh." At the end of Ether 8, Moroni anticipated the reader's question as to why he occupied so much space with the grim, nearly unrelieved saga of the fall of the Jaredite nation. He answered with a two-way statement: "I . . . am commanded to write these things that evil may be done away, and that the time may come that Satan may have no power upon the hearts of the children of men, but that they may be persuaded to do good continually, that they may come unto the fountain of all righteousness and be saved." (Ether 8:26.)

We could illustrate the Two Ways on a line, with *Evil/Satan's Will* on one end and *Righteousness/God's Will* on the other. The

Catherine Thomas is a doctoral student in ancient history at Brigham Young University.

Book of Mormon describes no in-between states. Moroni observed later in his own book that an evil person cannot do good, and a follower of Christ cannot do evil. (Moro. 7:6-11.) One's life is characterized either by directing his energies to the right side where he or she experiences abundant life, or toward the left where he or she suffers a diminution of life and, if undeterred, self-annihilation. A nation's life is characterized by the same polarity. Moroni presented this two-way energy principle in the rise and fall of the Jaredites.

War and Peace

Moroni compressed several hundred years in chapters 9-11 of Ether. We read 9:15-25 carefully because it describes an atypical period of over 225 years of peace, perhaps somewhat similar to that in 4 Nephi. Moroni supplied little description of these years except that the people enjoyed harmony and plenty, with even an appearance of the Son of Righteousness to Emer.

But we do not need Moroni to give us details. All righteous societies have energy flows in common. They direct their energies toward discerning the word of the Lord and supporting and nurturing one another. Their growth in the Lord is unhindered by ego-conflicts and contention. Peaceful societies never happen by accident. They result from steady devotion to selflessness: they take thought on what causes human beings to thrive; they speak to nurture one another; they act to develop each other. They have laid down their natural self-wills and have taken on the image of Christ. They experience loving, sustained closeness.

It is sobering how readily people trade inner peace for something less. These gospel societies would never cease if it were not that people begin to choose something other than peace. Akish, for example, chose power (Ether 9:11); Riplakish chose wives, concubines, and gold (Ether 10:5-8); Shiblom chose secret combinations (Ether 11:7). Before obvious signs of deterioration appear, people begin to think in terms, not of unity and mutual support, but of separateness.

Separation begins in such subtle ways. We unwittingly begin to look for trouble, picking at this, complaining at that. We take offense over a real or imagined slight; we get angry because people around us do not do what we want; we grow cold or irritable, or we retaliate to get what we want; we insist on being right at the expense of precious relationships; we reject others who seem to lack love, failing to perfect love in ourselves. We disturb ourselves with self-seeking. Thus keeping the water rippling around us, we are not still and at rest in the principles of tolerance and love, of overlooking, of letting go, of forgiving, of ceasing to expect anything—except tolerance and kindness in ourselves. In candid moments we may wonder if we would singlehandedly dismantle a Zion society.

In achieving separateness, people are left with emptiness and alienation. They try to fill the void with external things, or power, or self-gratification, when the cause of their emptiness is their spiritual death; what they are hungry for is the love of Christ and relationships built on loving commitment. Their misery drives them to create more misery, and finally to destroy life.

This pattern of the pursuit of misery recurs in Ether. By Ether 9:26 the murderous secret oaths had taken root again. From this point the Jaredites traced a familiar curve: up and down from obedient to depraved king, from peace to desperation. Each dip in the curve brought a more severe response from the Lord as the spiritual law of the harvest operated on each generation. The ancient oaths found willing hearts. They gained so great a grasp on the people that the Lord threatened a destruction "as never had been upon the face of the earth, and their bones should become as heaps of earth upon the face of the land except they should repent of their wickedness." (Ether 11:6.) Finally the Lord swore to execute judgment of utter destruction and to bring forth another people to possess the land. (Ether 11:20-21.) This prophecy was fulfilled with the final destruction of the Jaredites and the nearly simultaneous arrival of the Nephites and Mulekites.

As this once so-promising Jaredite world approached genocide, Ether found refuge in visions of a better world; the reader senses that Moroni too was brooding over his own Nephite brethren who faced the same fate. Moroni also gazed soberly forward into the world of latter-day Israel. He provoked his modern reader with this question: How shall *we* escape the Jaredite and Nephite fate?

How do any people halt their precipitous decline? Ether declared: "By faith all things are fulfilled—wherefore, whoso believeth in God might with surety hope for a better world." (Ether 12:3-4.) Deliverance hangs on a total reversal of mental, physical, and spiritual energy flows. But Ether's people would not believe because (1) they had chosen something other than peace and unity; they did not any longer want a better world, and (2) they could not *see* the evidence of Ether's promise. (Ether 12:5.)

Faith and Sight

"By faith all things are fulfilled." (Ether 12:3.) Moroni used Ether's thought as the springboard for his own discussion of faith. He illustrated with several examples that the fulfillment of heavenly promises comes only after people have demonstrated their faith. In every apostasy that ever developed on the earth, people declined to that state in which, like Korihor, they declared: "Ye cannot know of things which ye do not see; therefore ye cannot know that there shall be a Christ." (Alma 30:15.) They preferred their own power to God's power, since God's power required of them more than they wanted to give.

"Dispute not because ye see not, for ye receive no witness until after the trial of your faith." (Ether 12:6.) In the scriptures, *faith* assumes *faith in Jesus Christ*. (See Ether 12:18.) Why is it so important to have a trial—a period of proving—of one's faith in Jesus Christ? Why is one more blessed for believing in Jesus without having seen him? Here we come to an essential spiritual fact: one key purpose of earth life is to develop faith, to learn to "walk by faith, not by sight." (2 Cor. 5:7.) Moroni observed that people first had to have faith in Christ before he could show himself to them. But how can people have faith in that which they have not seen? Why should people believe in Christ more than in Buddha? Why should they believe in any God at all?

God can hold people responsible for faith in Christ for three reasons: (1) Jesus Christ *is* the Savior of all. (2) God created people such that they could discern truth from error. Their existence and progression involve the divine substances of light, spirit, truth, intelligence, and glory. (D&C 93.) This divinity underlies the nature of God and man. People may enlarge their portion of divinity until like Christ they obtain the fullness, at which point they too become gods. Another term for the divine element in mortals is "Spirit of Christ." (Moro. 7:16; John 1:4.) (3) God can hold people responsible for truth because faith implies a desire, a *choosing* to know. Many people have sensed spiritual truths but have not wanted to exert the effort leading to personal sanctification. Amulek said, "I knew . . . , yet I would not know." (Alma 10:6.)

Here is the distinction between testimony-seeking and sign-seeking: the sign-seeker wants to keep his disobedient life and still have spiritual power. He wants to reap where he has not sown. The testimony-seeker wants to submit to God, repent, and live by the light that the Lord gives through the Holy Ghost.

When a messenger of God teaches the gospel by the Holy Spirit, that spirit bears witness to the truth. The listener is now responsible; shall he or she accept or reject the witness? We recall that God held Korihor responsible for his deception. Korihor confessed that he chose Satan's lie because it was pleasing to his carnal mind. (Alma 30:53.) When gospel truth has been revealed, deception is a choice; spiritual blindness is self-induced. (Alma 13:4.)

If we have come to earth to develop this inner truth-discernment, then we understand why Jesus told his disciples that he must for their sakes go away. That is, if they were to develop this inner spiritual capacity independent of what they could see, spiritual realities had to be removed behind a veil. Moroni calls this spiritual organ of truth discernment the "eye of faith." (Ether 12:19.) We understand that after one's faith has developed through the power of the Holy Ghost, one may receive the Second Comforter or the tangible and visible presence of the Godhead. Thus one who has developed this inner capacity is more blessed spiritually than one who depends only on the senses for knowledge. Such a one *knows* more. Elder Bruce R. McConkie bore powerful personal witness to this spiritual knowing:

> As pertaining to Jesus Christ, I testify that he is the Son
> of the living God and was crucified for the sins of the world.
> He is our Lord, our God, and our King. This I know of myself

independent of any other person. I am one of his witnesses, and in a coming day I shall feel the nail marks in his hands and in his feet and shall wet his feet with my tears. But I shall not know any better then than I know now that he is God's Almighty Son, that he is our Savior and Redeemer, and that salvation comes in and through his atoning blood and in no other way.[2]

"[Christ] prepared a way that thereby others might be partakers of the heavenly gift, that they might hope for those things which they have not seen. Wherefore, ye may also have hope, and be partakers of the gift, if ye will but have faith. . . . In the gift of his Son hath God prepared a more excellent way; and it is by faith that it hath been fulfilled. For if there be no faith among the children of men God can do no miracle among them." (Ether 12:8-12.) Moroni presented another two-way concept: two kinds of life are available to mortals: natural life and spiritual life. (Cf. Mosiah 3:19.) He referred to this higher life as "the heavenly gift." He meant the quality of life given first through the Holy Ghost as the First Comforter and then through Christ himself.

Men of old, in the beginning having the same standing as their brethren, chose to live so righteously because of their strong confidence in Christ that they entered into the holy order of God, and into the *rest of God*. (Alma 13:12.) This state of rest does not always refer to some distant state for which we must wait until exaltation; rather, we obtain that state of rest here through our faith in Christ and take it with us into the kingdom. (See Moroni 7:3, where Mormon commended the members for having entered into the rest of the Lord; cf. Alma 33:23.)

Faith progresses from one's having confidence in God to God's having confidence in that person and permitting him or her to witness and even to administer divine power, as did Moses, Alma, Amulek, Nephi and Lehi, Ammon, the three Nephite disciples, and those — like the brother of Jared, whom Moroni described in Ether 12:19-21, whose inner spiritual capacity was so well-developed from obedience — who had obtained Christ's word (or mind of Christ, 1 Cor. 2:16) to such a degree that they could, with their immanent oneness in Christ, compel his presence. We will learn before the end of chapter 12 that Moroni himself was such a man.

Students of the scriptures ask how one closes the gap between where he or she is and where such people as Moroni and the brother of Jared were. Joseph Smith said: "Here, then, is eternal life — to know the only wise and true God; and you have got to learn how to be Gods yourselves, and to be kings and priests to God, the same as all Gods have done before you, namely, by going from one small degree to another, and from a small capacity to a great one; from grace to grace, from exaltation to exaltation, until you attain to the resurrection of the dead, and are able to dwell in everlasting burnings, and to sit in glory, as do those who sit enthroned in everlasting power."[3] Even Jesus "received not of the fulness at first, but continued from grace to grace, until he received a fulness." (D&C 93:13.)

One does not usually leap ahead from one capacity level to a level much farther away; we usually develop patiently by making small adjustments, gradually increasing our capacity, building a solid foundation on the most simple principles of the gospel: "Ye are not able to abide the presence of God now, neither the ministering of angels; wherefore, continue in patience until ye are perfected." (D&C 67:13.)

We make spiritual progress through two means: our own agency and God's timetable. He does not always reveal his timetable. To possess some capacities, we wait on the Lord. We make a mistake if we think that by going into some kind of spiritual overdrive, we can suddenly assume great spiritual capacity or compel spiritual experience.

Strength in Weakness

The truth is that we were born into an imperfect state in a fallen world. We chafe against our imperfection, but we cannot completely eradicate our humanity in this life. Here power is an attribute of God, not of man. We were created weak so that we would turn to the only source that could develop real spiritual stamina in us. Moroni recorded his conversation with the Lord on this subject in Ether 12:23-37. He feared that the Gentiles would not accept the precious records because of the weaknesses in their writing. (Ether 12:25.) The Lord comforted him with this wonderful principle: "My grace is sufficient for the meek, that they shall take no advantage of your weakness; and if men come unto me I will show unto them their weakness. I give unto men weakness that they may be humble; and my grace is sufficient for all men that humble themselves before me; for if they . . . have faith in me, then will I make weak things become strong unto them." (Ether 12:26-27.) When the Lord told the Apostle Paul, "My grace is sufficient for thee: for my strength is made perfect in weakness," Paul declared, "Most gladly therefore will I rather glory in my infirmities, that the power of Christ may rest upon me." (2 Cor. 12:9.)

The idea of heavenly community continued to direct Moroni's thoughts. He remembered that Christ had said that he had prepared a house for man among the mansions of his Father for which a man must hope [a gift of the Holy Ghost] or he could not inherit that excellent place. (Ether 12:32.) He recalled that Christ secured this excellence by laying down his life. (Ether 12:33.) Moroni was moved by this charity that made the heavenly place possible. Charity is another spiritual gift given to mortals in increments called *grace*. The Greek word behind *grace* in the New Testament means "divine gift." It refers to divine gifts of power unlocked by the Atonement. Grace, like all divine gifts, is administered to mortals through the Holy Ghost. It helps them do what they could not do by themselves.[4]

Moroni prayed that God would endow the Gentiles with grace. Here the Lord taught Moroni another principle: "If they have not charity it mattereth not unto thee, thou hast been faithful; wherefore, thy garments shall be made clean. And because thou hast seen thy weakness thou shalt be made strong, even unto the sitting down in the place which I have prepared in the mansions of my Father." (Ether 12:37.)

The Lord confirmed Moroni's calling and election here as he reassured him that because Moroni in his weakness drew on God's strength, he would sit down in the mansion that Christ had prepared for him. (Ether 12:37.) Moroni sealed his prophecies with his witness that they were true because Christ had told him face to face, in plain humility, in his own language. He bade us to seek Jesus, that his grace, his heavenly gifts, would abide in us forever.

New Jerusalem and the End of the Jaredites

The thread of the heavenly community continues to weave through Ether's tale of dissolution. Moroni resumed his narrative (chapter 13) with Ether's description of a new heaven and earth, a world with two centers of heavenly power: the New Jerusalem, that holy sanctuary of the Lord that would descend to the new world, joining with the earthly New Jerusalem, and contain the seed of Joseph. The rebuilt, sanctified city of Jerusalem in the ancient world would be headquarters for other tribes of scattered Israel, gathered from the the whole earth. These heavenly-city dwellers are partakers of the fulfilling of the Abrahamic covenant, or the covenant of exaltation. These cities will stand during the Savior's millennial reign until the celestialization of the earth. (Ether 13:8; D&C 101:16-38; Moses 7:60-64.) Those offered the gospel first, the Jews, have been reserved for redemption last because they were so tardy in accepting their Savior; the Gentiles, last to be taught the gospel in ancient times, will have been saved first. (Ether 13:12.)

Ether witnessed these harmonious scenes with the eye of faith as the Jaredites clamored on in mutual extinction. By day he lived in a cave and at night went out to witness the days' destruction, gathering material to finish his record. War rose in terrible crescendo through the next four years. Besides the prophet Ether, only Coriantumr would survive his people. He would not fall by the sword but would be buried by the very people who would supplant the Jaredite nation in the Lord's favor. (Ether 13:21; 14:24.) The chosen people are only those who choose the Lord.

"The Spirit of the Lord had ceased striving with them, and Satan had full power over the hearts of the people; for they were given up unto the hardness of their hearts, and the blindness of their minds that they might be destroyed." (Ether 15:19.) Ether recorded, "All the people upon the face of the land were shedding blood, and there was none to restrain them." (Ether 13:31.) Civil order had collapsed. In reflection of the slipperiness and the utter perishability of their lives and works, they held on to nothing but their swords; no security offered itself. The relentless law of the harvest rolled upon them, and they lived out their remaining days like specters in a terrifying nightmare of anger—sickness, howling, stench, and blood. The lives they had chosen had filled them, not with desire for peace and abundant, thriving life, but with hatred and self-destruction. The ultimate end of evil is death.

Coriantumr and Shiz shared the last scene together. Ether, looking on secretly from his hiding place, saw Coriantumr behead Shiz in a memorably gory scene, after which Coriantumr fell to the earth "as if he had no life." (Ether 15:32.) But he was not dead, as the Lord foresaw. Coriantumr appeared again among the Mulekites as one who pathetically straddled that transition from a fallen group to a new chosen people. (Omni 1:21.)

Conclusion

One of the greatest lessons of the Book of Mormon is that whatever the Lord prophesies is fulfilled every whit, in every specific detail, nothing omitted. One day not far hence we will read those pages that precede the annihilation of the Jaredites, or the destruction of the Nephites before the Lord's first appearance, or the extinction of the Nephites in Moroni's day, and understand that the Book of Mormon was given to us in our day as a manual by which we could read the signs of the times and escape the irrevocable judgments of God.

Between the lines, however, we learn about the qualities of a Zion people. Undoubtedly Zion will be built up with some grand gestures, with some dramatic acts, but by and large it will be built up and sustained by those who have learned how to overcome in the most simple issues of life: to live in sweet, tolerant, humble peace—not just absence of war—but real, deep peace and real love with those around them. Only those who practice inner peace will survive in Zion.

Earlier we observed that the Book of Mormon describes no states between God's will and man's self-will, even though we may think we ourselves occupy intermediate positions. The question does not concern position but direction. As simplistic as this two-way philosophy seems at first, we must finally conclude that there really are only two ways. Anyone who operates from the ego impulses of self-will must admit that he or she spends his or her energies in the one way. Only that energy spent to grasp and respond to Christ's voice allows us to claim the other way. When we feel inner disturbance, it is a blessing to be able to check our own energy flow and correct its course. Only Christ makes us alive; every other way of life results in death.

NOTES

1. For a discussion of Two-Way literature, see A.R.C. Leaney, *The Rule of Qumran and Its Meaning* (Philadelphia: Westminster Press, 1966) pp. 46f.

2. *Ensign*, May 1985, p. 11.

3. Joseph Smith, *Teachings of the Prophet Joseph Smith*, selected by Joseph Fielding Smith (Salt Lake City: Deseret Book Company, 1938), pp. 346-47.

4. See "Grace" in "Bible Dictionary," Holy Bible (Salt Lake City: The Church of Jesus Christ of Latter-day Saints, 1979).

25

THE PRACTICES OF THE CHURCH
(Moroni 1–6)

ROBERT E. PARSONS

This final book in the Book of Mormon was written by Moroni after his father's death and some fifteen to thirty-five years after the battle at Cumorah. Moroni's dangerous and lonely situation is expressed in the opening verses: "Now I, Moroni, after having made an end of abridging the account of the people of Jared, I had supposed not to have written more, but I have not as yet perished; and I make not myself known to the Lamanites lest they should destroy me. For behold, their wars are exceedingly fierce among themselves; and because of their hatred they put to death every Nephite that will not deny the Christ. And I, Moroni, will not deny the Christ; wherefore, I wander whithersoever I can for the safety of mine own life." (Moro. 1:1-3.)

The first six chapters of Moroni deal with procedures and practices of the Church in Moroni's day. What is written is somewhat "ordinary" for active Latter-day Saints because the procedures are so similar to Church practices today. Thus, there often is a tendency to skim these chapters quickly and move on to more exciting material. However, a different view is needed if we acknowledge that Moroni was writing to our generation and had seen our day and time:

> Behold, the Lord hath shown unto me great and marvelous
> things concerning that which must shortly come, at that day
> when these things shall come forth among you. Behold, I speak

---

Robert E. Parsons is associate professor of ancient scripture at Brigham Young University.

unto you as if ye were present, and yet ye are not. But behold, Jesus Christ hath shown you unto me, and I know your doing. And I know that ye do walk in the pride of your hearts; and there are none save a few only who do not lift themselves up in the pride of their hearts, unto the wearing of very fine apparel, unto envying, and strifes, and malice, and persecutions, and all manner of iniquities; and your churches, yea, even every one, have become polluted because of the pride of your hearts. (Morm. 8:34-36.)

In connection with seeing our day, I like to think that Moroni also saw the practices of modern-day Christianity. This makes it easier to understand his concern and interest in telling us the correct procedures for such basic practices as conferring the Holy Ghost, ordaining to offices in the priesthood, administering the sacrament, and conducting church meetings. If one were to visit Catholics, Baptists, Lutherans, Pentecostals, and Unitarians on successive Sundays, what would he or she observe regarding the sacrament, ordinations, and church meetings? In that framework, it is easy to understand Moroni's concern with basic procedure and why he wrote what he did to this generation.

Power to Minister for Christ

Moroni's straightforward explanation in chapters 2 and 3 clarifies the statement of Jesus in John: "Ye have not chosen me, but I have chosen you, and ordained you, that ye should go and bring forth fruit." (John 15:16.) What does it mean that Christ ordained the apostles? The Christian world lays on unauthorized hands, confers divinity degrees to bestow authority, or assumes power by simple desire. In clear, unmistakable words, Moroni stated:

The words of Christ, which he spake unto his disciples, the twelve whom he had chosen, as he laid his hands upon them—And he called them by name, saying: Ye shall call on the Father in my name, in mighty prayer; and after ye have done this ye shall have power that to him upon whom ye shall lay your hands, ye shall give the Holy Ghost; and in my name shall ye give it, for thus do mine apostles. (Moro. 2:1-2.)

> The manner which the disciples, who were called the elders of the church, ordained priests and teachers — After they had prayed unto the Father in the name of Christ, they laid their hands upon them, and said: In the name of Jesus Christ I ordain you to be a priest, (or, if he be a teacher) I ordain you to be a teacher, to preach repentance and remission of sins through Jesus Christ, by the endurance of faith on his name to the end. Amen.
>
> And after this manner did they ordain priests and teachers, according to the gifts and callings of God unto men; and they ordained them by the power of the Holy Ghost, which was in them. (Moro. 3:1-4.)

As we read these words, there can be no question as to how one is ordained with power to minister for Christ and how that power is used to bestow the Holy Ghost. Another plain and precious teaching has been restored in the Book of Mormon, and we can now read biblical statements on receiving the priesthood and bestowing the Holy Ghost without misunderstanding.

Verse 2 of Moroni chapter 2 ends, "for thus do mine apostles." Obviously the Nephites were familiar with this term as well as the sacred office, notwithstanding the constant use of the terms "twelve" or "disciple." Concerning the presence of apostles among the Nephites and the office in their church administration, Joseph Smith stated:

> This book also tells us that our Saviour made His appearance upon this continent after His resurrection; that He planted the Gospel here in all its fullness, and richness, and power, and blessing; that they had Apostles, Prophets, Pastors, Teachers, and Evangelists; the same order, the same priesthood, the same ordinances, gifts, powers, and blessings, as were enjoyed on the eastern continent, that the people were cut off in consequence of their transgressions, that the last of their prophets who existed among them was commanded to write an abridgment of their prophecies, history, &c, and to hide it up in the earth and that it should come forth and be united with the Bible for the accomplishment of the purposes of God in the last days.[1]

Elder Joseph Fielding Smith added: "While in every instance the Nephite twelve are spoken of as disciples, the fact remains that they had been endowed with divine authority to be special witnesses for Christ among their own people. Therefore, they were virtually apostles to the Nephite race, although their jurisdiction was, as revealed to Nephi, eventually to be subject to the authority and jurisdiction of Peter and the twelve chosen in Palestine."[2]

Sacramental Prayers

As Moroni saw our day and observed a typical Christian Sabbath, he must have been amazed at the multitude of apostate practices surrounding the holy yet simple ordinance of the sacrament in the various Christian churches. Visiting the Catholics, Presbyterians, Congregationalists, or Pentecostals, one would see a variety of practices. No wonder Moroni wrote the prayers and manner of administering and said, "We know the manner to be true." (Moro. 4:1.)

Both of the sacramental prayers contain the phrase "always remember him." We learn something of the importance of this phrase in the account recorded in 3 Nephi 1-2. A plan had been made to slay the righteous, and a day had been set apart to do this if the sign spoken of by Samuel the Lamanite should not come to pass. As Nephi pleaded with God in mighty prayer, the Lord spoke, saying: "Lift up your head and be of good cheer; for behold, the time is at hand, and on this night shall the sign be given, and on the morrow come I into the world, to show unto the world that I will fulfil all that which I have caused to be spoken by the mouth of my holy prophets." (3 Ne. 1:13.)

The sign was given, and the effect of this sign on those in the promised land is recorded as follows: "From this time forth there began to be lyings sent forth among the people, by Satan, to harden their hearts, to the intent that they might not believe in those signs and wonders which they had seen; but notwithstanding these lyings and deceivings the more part of the people did believe, and were converted unto the Lord." (3 Ne. 1:22.)

Although it is common to say "signs do not convert," it is clear that this sign was so tremendous that "the more part of the people did believe, and were converted to the Lord."

A great lesson is now taught in the Book of Mormon, for we learn that after conversion one must continue in works of faith to retain this conversion. Only three or four years after the people were converted, we read: "Thus passed away the ninety and fifth year also, and the people began to forget those signs and wonders which they had heard, and began to be less and less astonished at a sign or a wonder from heaven, insomuch that they began to be hard in their hearts, and blind in their minds, and began to disbelieve all which they had heard and seen." (3 Ne. 2:1.)

How do people "begin to forget"? Could they actually forget they had seen a day, a night, and a day as one day? Certainly not, but they could forget the spiritual significance of that experience. They could forget their spiritual feelings and thus could lose their spiritual conversion. Unfortunately, we see the same thing in the lives of a few Church members today. For example, a returned missionary will never forget where he served his mission, but he may forget his spiritual feelings and conversion. How does this happen? By neglecting the sacred ordinance given that "we might always remember." If we always remember, we certainly cannot forget. If we neglect the sacred ordinance of the sacrament, or do not partake of the emblems worthily and with the proper attitude, it is not long until we do not "always remember him" and "always have his spirit to be with us." If we lose his spirit, we are no longer numbered with the faithful. Although the Nephites in 3 Nephi 2 did not have the ordinance of the sacrament (it had not yet been instituted among them), they obviously had sacrificial ordinances designed to point them to Christ and to help them always remember him. They lost the spirit that converted them and could keep them faithful. The necessity of faithful sacrament observance in remembering the Lord was discussed by President Spencer W. Kimball: "When you look in the dictionary for the most important word, do you know what it is? It could be remember. Because all of you have made covenants—you know what to do and you know how to do it—our greatest need is to remember. That is why everyone goes to sacrament meeting every Sabbath day, to take the sacrament and listen to the priests pray that they 'may always remember him and keep his commandments which he has given them.' Nobody should ever forget to go to sacrament meeting. Remember is the word. Remember is the program."[3]

Sacred Ordinances

Elder Boyd K. Packer said, "Good conduct without the ordinances of the gospel will neither redeem nor exalt mankind; covenants and the ordinances are essential."[4]

Elder Packer was speaking of the ordinances of salvation—beginning with baptism and progressing on to the sealing ordinances of the temple. Why should ordinances be so important? Certainly most Protestant churches place little saving value on them. The following four points may help solidify our understanding of their purpose and importance.

First, God has commanded them. This in and of itself should be sufficient: "Wherefore he that prayeth, whose spirit is contrite, the same is accepted of me if he obey mine ordinances. He that speaketh, whose spirit is contrite, whose language is meek and edifieth, the same is of God if he obey mine ordinances." (D&C 52:15-16.)

Second, ordinances are the legal means for the orderly accomplishment of stated purposes. Priesthood is used in God's kingdom so that the work performed is legal. So it continues with ordinances. God could remit sins through any means he decreed. If he said that one must read the Bible eight times to be forgiven of sins, that decree would stand. However, for good reasons he instituted the principle that sins are to be forgiven through faith in the Lord Jesus Christ, repentance of sins, and participation in the ordinance of baptism. Thus, this becomes the legal or authorized means for remitting sins. Performed under the direction of his priesthood, it is and remains an orderly procedure, without confusion, carefully and harmoniously regulated.

Third, ordinances are effective teaching symbols that clearly portray what is happening. The ordinance of baptism is a perfect example. How gracious of God to institute a procedure that portrays forgiveness. Water itself is a cleansing agent. The burial in the water symbolizes the burying of the man of sin in a watery grave. The rising of the person from immersion in water is analogous to the dead rising from an earthly grave. The rising or resurrection is to a new life — a spiritual life. As we wash away our sins in a watery grave and bury the man of sin in a watery tomb, so we also come forth to a new, spiritual life, cleansed and forgiven through the sacred ordinance of baptism.

Fourth, ordinances serve as witnesses to spiritual agreements between God and man. As one puts his signature to a document to bind himself to the written terms, so we bind ourselves to the terms of ordinances by participating in them. Such a seal of intent and participation is noted in heaven itself and is also recorded on earthly records kept by the Church. When the day of judgment arrives and the books are opened, records of our participation in and binding ourselves to the terms of ordinances will be brought forth. Both our making of these ordinances and our keeping of the terms entered into will play a major role in the judgment rendered upon us.

Nourishing New Members

Moroni 6 is most interesting and enlightening concerning Nephite church practices. We read: "After they had been received unto baptism, and were wrought upon and cleansed by the power of the Holy Ghost, they were numbered among the people of the church of Christ; and their names were taken, *that they might be remembered and nourished by the good word of God*, to keep them in the right way, to keep them continually watchful unto prayer, relying alone upon the merits of Christ, who was the author and the finisher of their faith." (Moro. 6:4; emphasis added.)

To illustrate the importance of nourishing new members, I would like to include excerpts from a lesson taught to a Book of Mormon class at Brigham Young University during the fall of 1987. I asked the class to indicate where they had family members serving on missions and then to estimate how many hours a day the missionary was working and how much the mission was costing per month.

Teacher: We have suggested time and cost of missionary work. Let us examine another question. Why do some converts not remain active in the Church? My own experience has been that if we were to pick the one central thing that causes more people to go inactive than anything else, the answer would have to be lack of fellowshipping. But that has ramifications. You can say, well they weren't really converted, but what that means is that as long as someone fellowshipped them they were converted enough to keep coming and to grow. But if you stop the fellowshipping, they weren't able to keep on by themselves. If we had fellowshipped them another one or two years, maybe they would have been strong enough to stand by themselves.

The reason we've discussed this is that I did a little calculating. Although these figures may not be exactly up to date, they are not too far off. These figures were worked out in the early 1980s. I took the number of converts we get in the Church per year, and the number of missionaries we have, and an estimated number of hours they work, and the estimated average cost. What I came up with was that it was taking about 468 hours of missionary work per convert, and it was costing about $540 per convert. If you go on a mission and know that it is going to take that many hours to make a convert and cost that much money, do you want to go or stay home? Do you find members objecting to spending that much money and that much time to convert somebody to the Church? We don't object to that. We say we would like to be more economical because we want more people to hear the gospel. But, if that is what it takes, we'll spend the time and the money. Now, isn't it a shame to spend all that time and all that money to bring somebody into the Church, and then lose him? And the main reason we lose him is what? Lack of fellowshipping. We should keep many more converts in the Church. We should be much more successful.

Have you ever gone to sacrament meeting, stood at the back of the hall for ten or fifteen minutes before the meeting began, watched people come in and sit down, and noticed who looked like he might be all alone? Have you ever watched for somebody sitting all by himself? Did you ever have enough compassion and spirit of fellowshipping to go sit down by that person and say, "I'm so-and-so and you're who?" Did you get acquainted and make that person feel at home and go through the meetings with him? No, we don't do that. That's as much a part of missionary work for this time and circumstances as to accept a full-time mission when the call comes.

Now, in the light of all I've said, let's read a passage from Moroni chapter 6. We want to pick it up in verse 4. We are talking about converts who come into the Church. "After they had been received unto baptism, and were wrought upon and cleansed by the power of the Holy Ghost, they were numbered among the people of the church of Christ; and their names were taken, that they might be remembered and nourished by the good word of God, to keep them in the right way."

We have a system for keeping track of people. Isn't that what Moroni was saying they did? They were numbered, and their names were taken. Now, they didn't have computers like we do today, but they kept track of people so they could be nourished and kept in the right way. They fellowshipped them to strengthen them in the kingdom.

We do a very good job in missionary work and are willing to spend money and time to convert people to the Church. We don't do a very good job currently in fellowshipping. There are some exceptions to that; once in a while you go to a ward where they really take care of strangers.

Student: Sometimes we, as missionaries, hated to take someone to a ward knowing how cold that ward was going to be. We had something so precious that we wanted to share with them, but we were afraid of what the members would do.

Teacher: That's not too flattering to us, is it? As we reflect on our efforts to strengthen converts and keep track of members in the Church today, it is edifying to read Moroni's statement of similar concern in his day and of the practices of the Church among the Nephites.

Is it not faith-promoting to know that the Church in earlier dispensations not only practiced faith, repentance, and baptism, but also recorded the names of members and watched over and nourished them that they might be kept in the faith? Today we call such practices fellowshipping, home teaching, or visiting teaching, but the purpose in each dispensation has been the same—first to convert and then to perfect members of Christ's Church. President Gordon B. Hinckley commented on the tragedy of losing souls after once having brought them into the kingdom: "The greatest tragedy in the Church . . . is the loss of those who join the Church and then fall away. With very few exceptions it need not happen. I am convinced that almost universally those who are baptized by the missionaries have been taught sufficiently to have received knowledge and testimony sufficiently to warrant their baptism. But it is not an easy thing to make the transition incident to joining this Church. It means cutting old ties. It means leaving friends. It may mean setting aside cherished beliefs. It may require a change of habits and a suppression of appetites. In so many cases it means loneliness and even fear of the unknown. There must be nurturing and strengthening during this difficult season of a convert's life. A tremendous price has been paid for his presence in the Church. The long efforts of the missionaries and the cost of their service, the separation from old relationship and the trauma associated with this makes it imperative that these precious souls be welcomed, reassured, helped in their times of weakness, praised for what they do, given responsibility under which they may grow strong, and encouraged and thanked for all they do."[5]

Conducting Meetings

Moroni 6 concludes: "The church did meet together oft, to fast and to pray, and to speak one with another concerning the welfare of their souls. . . . And their meetings were conducted by the church after the manner of the workings of the Spirit, and by the power of the Holy Ghost; for as the power of the Holy Ghost led them whether to preach, or to exhort, or to pray, or to supplicate, or to sing, even so it was done." (Moro. 6:5, 9.)

Those who preside over meetings today are concerned that what is done is under the influence of the Holy Ghost. Meetings should be planned under the inspiration of the Holy Spirit, and meetings should be conducted under that same spirit. This will necessitate, at times, that on-the-spot changes be made in the songs sung and those called upon to speak and the subjects spoken upon—all this that God may be glorified and that Church members may be watched over and strengthened as was done in the ancient church among the Nephites.

NOTES

1. Joseph Smith, *History of the Church of Jesus Christ of Latter-day Saints*, ed. B.H. Roberts, 7 vols. (Salt Lake City: The Church of Jesus Christ of Latter-day Saints, 1932-51), 4:538, March 1842.

2. Joseph Fielding Smith, *Answers to Gospel Questions* (Salt Lake City: Deseret Book Company, 1957), 1:122.

3. "Circles of Exaltation," *Charge to Religious Educators*, 2nd ed. [Salt Lake City], 28 June 1968.

4. *Conference Report*, Oct. 1984, p. 105.

5. President Gordon B. Hinckley, Regional Representatives' Seminar, April 3, 1987.

26

HOPE, FAITH, AND CHARITY
(Moroni 7–8)

Monte S. Nyman

Many members of the Church can quote some of the verses from Moroni 7, such as "All things which are good cometh of God" (v. 12); "The Spirit of Christ is given to every man" (v. 16); and "Charity is the pure love of Christ" (v. 47). However, few have ever seen the great overall message and the unity of the whole chapter. It is my opinion that Mormon's sermon ranks as one of the greatest, surpassed only by those of the Savior.

Mormon identified his audience as those "of the church, that are the peaceable followers of Christ, and that have obtained a sufficient hope by which [they] can enter into the rest of the Lord, from this time henceforth until [they] shall rest with him in heaven." (Moro. 7:3.) While we do not know exactly when Mormon delivered his sermon, we do know that it was in a period when great trials and afflictions were upon the Church. In A.D. 345, Mormon, who was then about thirty-four years old, lamented that "a continual scene of wickedness and abominations has been before mine eyes ever since I have been sufficient to behold the ways of man." (Morm. 2:18.)[1] As these conditions only worsened over the next forty years of his life, those whom Mormon addressed as the faithful members of the Church would have endured the sufferings and persecutions of their corrupt society.

When Mormon presented the sermon recorded in Moroni 7, he

Monte S. Nyman is professor of ancient scripture at Brigham Young University.

was a disciple of Jesus Christ (3 Ne. 5:12-13), a special witness, grounded in the knowledge of the gospel. His office not only gave him the authority but also the responsibility to declare the gospel "according to the power of the Holy Ghost." (D&C 18:32.) His message to the Nephites is as applicable to us today as it was to those who heard it in his own time. As will be shown, it represents a three-step plan of salvation: hope, faith, and charity. While these terms have become common in our modern Christian world, we may also have become complacent in really understanding them. That they are of universal importance is demonstrated by Paul's use of them in writing to the Corinthians. (1 Cor. 13.)[2]

Hope Produces Good Works

Those faithful members of the Church to whom Mormon spoke had been brought to their present spiritual status through the principle of hope—the hope of eternal life (Titus 1:2; 3:7) obtained through Jesus Christ (Jacob 2:19). This hope gives people the courage to follow the commandments, thereby producing good works in their lives. Both ancient and modern scriptures tell us all people will be judged of their works, whether they be good or evil. (2 Cor. 5:10; Morm. 3:20.) This is enlarged upon by Mormon.

Mormon commenced the body of his sermon by saying: "The word of God . . . [says] by their works ye shall know them . . . a man being evil cannot do that which is good." (Moro. 7:5-6.)[3] This statement serves as a warning or refutation of the idea of earning or buying salvation through a specified number of good deeds. As Mormon continued, "if [a man] offereth a gift, or prayeth unto God, except he shall do it with real intent it profiteth him nothing." (Moro. 7:6.) In other words, we must do the right thing for the right reason. After expounding upon the idea that it is impossible for an evil person to do good things, Mormon declared that this is because "all things which are good cometh of God; and that which is evil cometh of the devil." (Moro. 7:12.) Doing something for the right reason is doing it not only because it is what God would want us to do, but also because it is what we want to do. Consequently, work will demonstrate a love of God and be a service to humanity. It will further

God's work of bringing "to pass the immortality and eternal life of man." (Moses 1:39.) It will be inspired of God. (Moro. 7:13.)

Mormon added a further warning about how we perceive works. He cautioned us against judging what is good to be from the devil and what is evil from God. (Moro. 7:14.) As an answer to this dilemma of how we can know which is which, he reminded his congregation and us that "the Spirit of Christ is given to every man, that he may know good from evil." He then noted that the way to judge whether a thing is good or not is to determine whether it "inviteth to do good, and to persuade to believe in Christ." (Moro. 7:15-16.) If it does, it is good. After giving a similar but contrasting description of how the devil's operations entice us to do evil, Mormon cautioned that the way we judge will determine the way we will also be judged. (Moro. 7:17-18.)

Through a hope in Christ, we produce good works in this life and gain the right to receive the Spirit in our lives. This is one criterion for the judgment for every individual. By following the directions of the Spirit of Christ, given to everyone who is born into this world, we can make the proper selection of which good works to accomplish.

Faith Produces Ordinances

Mormon told his listeners that they could lay hold upon every good thing through their faith, for a good thing comes through Christ; and God, who knows all things, sent angels to minister to mortals and make known Christ's coming. (Moro. 7:19-22.) Mormon added that God also declared to prophets that Christ would come and that there were various ways that good things were manifest: "Wherefore . . . men began to exercise faith in Christ; and thus by faith, they did lay hold upon every good thing; and thus it was until the coming of Christ." (Moro. 7:23-25.)

Mormon further attested that people were saved by faith in Christ, thus becoming the sons and daughters of God. (Moro. 7:26.) We become his sons and daughters through being born again. (Mosiah 5:7; Ether 3:14; Gal. 4:1-7.) As the Prophet Joseph Smith taught: "Being born again, comes by the Spirit of God through ordinances."[4] Thus faith produces ordinances necessary for salvation. Mormon equated these saving ordinances with miracles, which he said had not ceased since the coming of Christ in the flesh, neither had angels ceased to minister to God's children. (Moro. 7:27-29.) He noted that there are two prerequisites for angels to minister to mortals: first, angels must be commanded to come by Jesus; and second, the recipient must be "of strong faith and a firm mind." (Moro. 7:30.)

There are two basic purposes for which angels come: (1) to call people to repentance, and (2) to fulfill and to do the work of the covenants of the Father. (Moro. 7:31.) The calling of people to repentance is illustrated in various places in the Book of Mormon. (See, for example, 1 Ne. 3:29; Mosiah 27:11.) The appearance of angels to fulfill and to do the work of the covenants of the Father is the work of providing ordinances for salvation. For ordinances to be efficacious, they must be done by the authority of the priesthood. The keys of the priesthood are the directing power of the priesthood.[5] When apostasy has occurred and the keys of the priesthood have been lost, making it necessary to restore these keys again, God has used angels to restore them. In our own dispensation, John the Baptist restored the keys of the Aaronic Priesthood (D&C 13); Peter, James, and John restored the keys of the Melchizedek Priesthood (D&C 27:12-13); Moses brought back the keys of the gathering of Israel, Elias the keys of the Abrahamic covenant, Elijah the keys of sealing power (D&C 110:11-16); other angels from Adam to the present all declared their dispensation, their keys, and so on (D&C 128:21). Thus the way is once more prepared for individuals to attain salvation through the exercise of faith to receive the ordinances of the priesthood. The chosen vessels of the Lord (priesthood leaders) bear testimony of Christ, and the ordinances necessary for salvation through him (baptism, etc.), and the covenants of the Lord are fulfilled. (Moro. 7:31-32.) By faith, miracles are performed and angels minister to God's children. Without faith, these ordinances are not performed, angels do not minister, and individuals are not fit to be numbered among the people of the Church. (Moro. 7:37-39.)

Mormon proclaimed that such faith would not be obtainable without hope. This hope, which motivates us to do things, is a necessary companion of faith. We hope for eternal life, and because of our hope we have faith in Christ. Because of our faith in Christ, we do the works of the Father. We could not exercise faith to receive the ordinances if we did not hope for eternal life through the atonement. (Moro. 7:40-42.)

Charity Brings Grace

Through the humility required to obtain hope and faith, one is also able to obtain the essential quality for salvation, charity. This enables him or her to confess "by the power of the Holy Ghost that Jesus is the Christ." Without this celestial quality, Mormon says, mortals are considered as nothing. (Moro. 7:44.) Similar testimony of this concept was previously borne in the Book of Mormon by Nephi (2 Ne. 26:30) and Amulek (Alma 34:28-29). Mormon gave or quoted a lengthy definition of charity. The definition concludes with the familiar statement: "Charity is the pure love of Christ." (Moro. 7:45-47.)

Mormon bore witness that it will be well at the time of judgment for those who possess charity. (Moro. 7:47.) He then gave the formula for obtaining this gift of God: "Pray unto the Father with all the energy of heart," and the gift will be "bestowed upon all who are true followers of his Son, Jesus Christ; that [they] may become the sons [and daughters] of God." (Moro. 7:48.) The obtaining and maintenance of this pure love is possible through "diligence unto prayer, until the end shall come." (Moro. 8:26; see also 2 Ne. 33:6-9.) Therefore, charity is the pure love of God and is a gift from God based on prayer and true discipleship. Gaining it is required for salvation in the celestial kingdom, and it is bestowed through God's grace. As one shares the love, he or she receives more of God's grace—he or she receives "grace for grace." (D&C 93:12; John 1:16.)

Three Steps to Salvation

Basically, three things are required for salvation: works, faith, and grace. Some religions emphasize that salvation comes only through faith and the grace of God. Others emphasize that salvation comes from ordinances. Still others preach the necessity of works. The scriptures show that all three are required for salvation. Because hope for eternal life produces works, individuals will be judged according to their works. Through faith we gain the ordinances prerequisite for salvation. However, after we receive all of the ordinances and do all of the works, it is the grace of God that prepares and purifies us for salvation. This is what Nephi meant when he said, "It is by grace that we are saved, after all we can do." (2 Ne. 25:23.)

The Doctrine of Christ Concerning Children

The sermon we have just considered was placed in the record by Moroni as he concluded his engravings on the plates. He also included a letter he had received from his father concerning the baptism of little children, a pernicious doctrine that had been introduced into the Nephite church and seemed always to creep into the church as apostasy began to set in. (Moro. 8:4-6.)[6] The placement of Mormon's letter following his sermon does not seem to be accidental. Mormon testified to his son that those who suppose that little children need baptism are "in the gall of bitterness and in the bonds of iniquity; for he hath neither faith, hope, nor charity." (Moro. 8:14.)

Before considering Mormon's explanation of the relationship of Christ and little children, we should affirm the source of his reasoning. He had received the word of the Lord by the power of the Holy Ghost and had received the authority and responsibility from God to boldly declare his words. Therefore, we will not be considering merely the opinion of Mormon but the very "words of Christ" that came to him. (Moro. 8:7-8, 16.)

The Lord revealed three reasons to Mormon as to why children do not need to be baptized. The first is that little children are not capable of committing sin. The second is that the atonement of Christ has paid for the transgressions of little children. The third is that little children cannot repent. These three reasons will each be considered separately.

Mormon was told that little children were not capable of committing sin. After being reminded of Jesus' teaching that he came into the world not to call the righteous but sinners to repentance (cf. Mark 2:17), Mormon was told that the curse of Adam (the fall into an environment of sin) was taken from children and had no power over them. In other words, Satan has no power to tempt little children. (D&C 29:47.) Furthermore, Mormon was informed that the law of circumcision was done away or revoked by Christ (Moro. 8:8) because this law had served its purpose. Prior to the Savior's advent, circumcision at eight days typified the principle that children are not accountable until they are eight years old. (JST Gen. 17:11-12.) When the atonement was accomplished, circumcision, like Mosaic sacrifice, was done away. Thus Mormon concluded that it was solemn mockery to baptize little children when the atonement of Christ had taken care of whatever transgressions they may have committed.

Mormon next explained to Moroni that "little children are alive in Christ, even from the foundation of the world." The plan of salvation was based upon the foreknowledge of God. God, knowing that many little children would not live to the age of accountability, provided for their salvation through the atonement, without the necessity of baptism. (Moro. 8:11-12.) As revealed to Joseph Smith, "All little children who die before they arrive at the years of accountability are saved in the celestial kingdom of heaven." (D&C 137:10.) Not to have provided for these little children would have rendered God "a partial God," for "many little children have died without receiving baptism." (Moro. 8:12.) Based on his foreknowledge, God sent those spirits who were of a celestial character to the bodies of those who would die in their infancy. In the words of Joseph Smith:

> We have again the warning voice sounded in our midst, which shows the uncertainty of human life; and in my leisure moments I have meditated upon the subject, and asked the question, why it is that infants, innocent children, are taken away from us, especially those that seem to be the most intelligent and interesting. The strongest reasons that present themselves to my mind are these: This world is a very wicked world; and it is a proverb that the "world grows weaker and wiser"; if that is the case, the world grows more wicked and corrupt. In the earlier ages of the world a righteous man, and a man of God and of intelligence, had a better chance to do good, to be believed and received than at the present day; but in these days such a man is much opposed and persecuted

by most of the inhabitants of the earth, and he has much sorrow to pass through here. The Lord takes many away even in infancy, that they may escape the envy of man, and the sorrows and evils of this present world; they were too pure, too lovely, to live on earth; therefore, if rightly considered, instead of mourning we have reason to rejoice as they are delivered from evil, and we shall soon have them again.[7]

These children needed to receive a body, that they might go on in their eternal progression.[8] Of course other great and noble spirits were needed to administer the plan of salvation upon the earth and were also chosen in the premortal councils to be leaders on the earth at various times in mortality. (Abr. 3:22-23.) In the wisdom and foreknowledge of God, the assignments were made based upon the faith and good works of the spirits in the first estate, meaning the premortal life. (Alma 13:1-5.) Without an acceptance of the omniscience of God, the doctrine of salvation for little children is incompatible with God being unchangeable and no respecter of persons.

Mormon's final point that little children are unable to repent (Moro. 8:19) is also based upon the law of accountability. Repentance includes the recognition of sin, a remorse for mistakes, and a restitution for the damage or hurt that has been done. Until the child matures enough to be able to do this, he is not accountable; until the child is able to understand right and wrong and the effects of his actions, the Lord does not hold him accountable. To believe in the need for baptism of infants, in Mormon's words, "denieth the mercies of Christ, and setteth at naught the atonement of him and the power of his redemption." (Moro. 8:20.) Mormon invited the readers to give heed, for his words will stand for or against them at the judgment seat of Christ. (Moro. 8:21.)

Mormon added another dimension to his treatise on little children; he said that those who are without the law are also alive in Christ. This would include all people who are born into a situation where they are never taught,[9] as well as those who through some imparity are also incapable of understanding the law. (Moro. 8:22; see also D&C 29:50.)

Become Like Little Children

Mormon admonished his missionary son to teach "repentance and baptism unto those who are accountable and capable of committing sin; yea, teach parents that they must repent and be baptized, and humble themselves as their little children, and they shall all be saved with their little children." (Moro. 8:10.) Jesus taught similar things during his mortal ministry. (Matt. 18:2-6.) Paul taught the saints to be children in the sense that they were devoid of malice, but to be adults in regard to understanding. (1 Cor. 14:20.) Mormon further taught that the first fruit of repentance was baptism, "and baptism cometh by faith unto the fulfilling the commandments; and the fulfilling the commandments bringeth remission of sins; and the remission of sins bringeth meekness, and lowliness of heart; and because of meekness and lowliness of heart cometh the visitation of the Holy Ghost, which Comforter filleth with hope and perfect love, which love endureth by diligence unto prayer, until the end shall come, when all the saints shall dwell with God." (Moro. 8:25-26.) The plan of redemption is to fill all of us, like Christ, full of charity. Those who have hope and bring forth works unto repentance will receive a remission of their sins through their faith in accepting the ordinances. Through the ordinances they will receive the Holy Ghost, who will fill them with hope to do more and more good works in and through the love of Christ, which is charity. This charity will then enable them to endure to the end.

Mormon followed this plan and attained the desired goal. He was filled with everlasting charity for all people, and he especially loved little children. He urged his son Moroni to pray for the Lamanites, his enemies who were seeking his life. (Moro. 8:27-29.) With the exception of the Savior himself, we may have no better example of a charitable person than Mormon. Moroni took his father's advice and seems to have attained that same quality of love. As he later abridged the record of the Jaredites, he prayed for the Gentiles unto whom his record would come. (Ether 12:33-41.) As he added a few more chapters to the records of his father, he also did so for the benefit of the Lamanites. (Moro. 10:1-4.) With such examples and admonitions to follow, we should be encouraged to strive to attain the same quality of love in our lives, "for charity never faileth" and "all [other] things must fail." (Moro. 7:46.)

NOTES

1. Mormon was about ten years of age in A.D. 321, making him about thirty-four in the year A.D. 345. (4 Ne. 1:48-49; Morm. 1:2.)

2. Charges of plagiarizing have been leveled against the Prophet Joseph Smith because of the similarities between 1 Corinthians 13 and Moroni 7. There are several possibilities for these similarities: (1) The Holy Ghost inspired both men; (2) Jesus taught these things to both the Jews and the Nephites and they were not recorded (John 21:25; Acts 1:3; 3 Ne. 26:8-12); (3) Paul and Mormon both were quoting from an earlier source that was lost from the original text of the Bible with other plain and precious things (1 Ne. 13:24-29). Some support of the latter is given by references to charity in Old Testament times by Nephi. (2 Ne. 26:30.) The last two possibilities are supported by modern biblical critics who question Paul as the originator of the message of 1 Corinthians 13. For their theories and evidences, see Richard L. Anderson, *Understanding Paul* (Salt Lake City: Deseret Book Company, 1983), pp. 118-19 and notes.

3. Mormon's quotation is very similar to 3 Nephi 14:16-20 or Matthew 7:14-20. Because these sources use "fruits" instead of "works" and "a tree" rather than "a man," it is possible that Mormon was paraphrasing these teachings. Another possibility is that he was quoting from an Old Testament source that is no longer in the Bible because of the loss of plain and precious parts. (1 Ne. 13:24-29.) Further support for the latter possibility is that much of the so-called Sermon on the Mount was known to the Nephites before it was given as a collective sermon to the Nephites. (See Matt. 7:7 and 2 Ne. 32:4.)

4. *Teachings of the Prophet Joseph Smith*, comp. Joseph Fielding Smith (Salt Lake City: Deseret Book Company, 1976), p. 162.

5. Joseph F. Smith, *Gospel Doctrine*, 11th ed. (Salt Lake City: Deseret Book Company, 1959), p. 136.

6. The washing of little children was a false doctrine instituted in the days of Abraham and refuted by the Lord in a revelation. (JST Gen. 17:3-6.) The Lord on this same occasion made the covenant with Abraham that every male child should be circumcised when eight days old. (Gen. 17:9-

12.) The circumcision being performed at eight days was symbolic of the child becoming accountable at eight years. (JST Gen. 17:11-12; see also D&C 68:25-27.)

7. *Teachings*, pp. 196-97.

8. The Prophet Joseph Smith taught: "We came to this earth that we might have a body and present it pure before God in the celestial kingdom. The great principle of happiness consists in having a body. The devil has no body, and herein is his punishment. He is pleased when he can obtain the tabernacle of man, and when cast out by the Savior he asked to go into the herd of swine, showing that he would prefer a swine's body to having none." (*Teachings*, p. 181.) These little children, being pure, did not need to be tested further. Their gaining of earthly experience, another purpose for coming to mortality, will be provided for them in the millennium. (See *Gospel Doctrine*, pp. 453-54.) See also Joseph Fielding Smith, *Doctrines of Salvation*, 3 vols., comp. Bruce R. McConkie (Salt Lake City: Bookcraft, 1954-56), 2:56-57; Bruce R. McConkie, "The Salvation of Little Children," *Ensign*, April 1977, p. 6.

9. Paul taught that "where no law is, there is no transgression." (Rom. 4:15; see also 2 Ne. 9:25-26.) However, while those who have no law are not taught, it must also be remembered that without the law there is no progression. Those who die without the law are only terrestrial beings unless they accept the gospel in the spirit world. (D&C 76:72; see also Joseph Fielding Smith, *Answers to Gospel Questions*, 5 vols., compiled by Joseph Fielding Smith, Jr. [Salt Lake City: Deseret Book Company, 1957-66], 4:10.)

27

COME UNTO CHRIST
(Moroni 9–10)

S. BRENT FARLEY

"My beloved son, I write unto you again that ye may know that I am yet alive; but I write somewhat of that which is grievous." (Moro. 9:1.) Thus began the final known letter of Mormon to his son Moroni. The ravages of war threatened to annihilate an entire nation; yet the prophet-father reached his prophet-son with the news that he was yet alive. His only joy was the knowledge of their faithfulness. (See Moro. 9:6, 22, 25-26.)

Mormon's report on the condition of their people was appalling. They had, by choice, gone beyond the point of repentance. Inspired warnings were met with anger; they refused to repent. Their feelings for the dignity of the human race had dwindled from smoking embers to cold ash. They thirsted for blood and craved immorality. They had become so hardened that they delighted in torture and murder; they even ate the flesh of their victims as a token of bravery. They were without civilization, without principle, and beyond feeling.

The bleakness of the letter was broken by the hope of reunion and the transferral of sacred records. (Moro. 9:24.) The closing reflected the sacred trust that though a nation might perish, a faithful saint would be raised up to the glory of eternal life. (Moro. 9:25.) With a final "amen," Mormon disappeared from known history.

S. Brent Farley is an instructor at the LDS Institute of Religion at Utah State University.

Moroni's Promise

In the ensuing years, Moroni concluded his sacred commission with the golden plates. His final message to the world began with a promise that will help change the world as its inhabitants come unto Christ (a millennial destiny). It is called "the promise of the Book of Mormon."

"Behold, I would exhort you that when ye shall read these things..." (Moro. 10:3.) Moroni was referring specifically to the sacred records, a portion of which would be revealed in the restoration of the gospel to Joseph Smith. The portion would be translated and published for all the world to read. *"If it be wisdom in God that ye should read them."* The book could be read and laid aside as any other piece of literature. But if the reader sought wisdom about God and his kingdom, he would be taking a step upward in his relationship with the divine. It would be the wisdom of God ingested to one's spirit from the printed page. To further qualify for this great promise, the reader is encouraged, *"Remember how merciful the Lord hath been unto the children of men, from the creation of Adam even down until the time that ye shall receive these things."* This provides a perspective that spans time and races, and causes one to realize that God is a personal and loving individual who has been dealing with humanity for their salvation since time began on this planet. It implies a reference to the Bible, for it is the most commonly possessed scripture that provides knowledge of God's dealings with his children since the creation. Having an understanding of biblical accounts provides a foundation for an understanding and an acceptance of the Book of Mormon as another testament for Christ. *"And ponder it in your hearts."* Pondering is thinking seriously, thoughtfully considering something, or reflecting upon a topic. To ponder in the heart adds the dimension of the feelings of the soul, wherein heart and mind are combined in an effort to understand.

Such an attitude of consideration begins with the "reading" and leads to the "receiving." (Moro. 10:4.) As Alma explained, truth (applied in this case to the Book of Mormon—the experiment being tested) has an effect upon the soul, for truth "will begin to swell within your breasts; and when you feel these swelling motions, ye will begin to say within yourselves—It must needs be that this is a good seed, or that the word is good, for it beginneth to enlarge my soul; yea, it beginneth to enlighten my understanding, yea, it beginneth to be delicious to me." (Alma 32:28.) This is a gradual but very noticeable process. As one reads and receives, the admonition of the promise continues: *"I would exhort you that ye would ask God, the Eternal Father, in the name of Christ, if these things are not true; and if ye shall ask with a sincere heart, with real intent, having faith in Christ, he will manifest the truth of it unto you, by the power of the Holy Ghost."* (Moro. 10:4.) Nephi, an earlier Book of Mormon prophet, testified that "if ye shall believe in Christ ye will believe in these words, for they are the words of Christ." (2 Ne. 33:10.) A simpler deduction would be hard to obtain; the promise of the Book of Mormon is a guarantee that this logical point will be proven. The proof, however, is not an empirical test open to the view of all. It is open only to the view of all who perform the test in the specified way; it is a test that affects the soul and the mind. The heart must be "sincere"; the intent must be "real." The sincerity and intent must be of such a nature and force as to produce change in the heart of the reader upon verification of the truth. And it requires faith, a quality difficult to measure for mortals, but which is definitely measurable to God. When such conditions are adequately met, the grand promise is: *"He will manifest the truth of it unto you, by the power of the Holy Ghost."* (Moro. 10:4.) A direct communication from God through the Holy Ghost will occur.

The promise originates with God. Thousands upon thousands have tested the promise and obtained the blessing of positive and undeniable proof. Many are the witnesses who verify the validity of fulfillment. Such evidence is referred to as a testimony. Through varying degrees and in differing manners, one may, as Moroni testified, "know the truth of all things" by the power of the Holy Ghost. (Moro. 10:5.)

Gifts of the Spirit

Moroni prophetically declared: "Nothing that is good denieth the Christ, but acknowledgeth that he is. And ye may know that he is, by the power of the Holy Ghost." (Moro. 10:6-7.) He then rehearsed some of the gifts of God that come by the Spirit (much as Paul did in 1 Corinthians 12).

"To one is given by the Spirit of God, that he may teach the word of wisdom." (Moro. 10:9.) Wisdom is the ability to understand and use principles and ideas that are correct and true; it is the ability to incorporate those principles into life for the betterment of humanity. The greatest source of wisdom is God. James declared, "If any of you lack wisdom, let him ask of God, that giveth to all men liberally, and upbraideth not; and it shall be given him." (James 1:5.) It was this scripture that led Joseph Smith into the sacred grove and the presence of God. Wisdom embraces the use of principles both spiritual and temporal, great and small; but all wisdom results in the benefit of mankind and their ultimate progression toward God. The ability to teach the word of wisdom is the ability to emulate and propagate that which benefits and improves mankind.

"And to another, that he may teach the word of knowledge by the same Spirit." (Moro. 10:10.) Knowledge is attained when one grasps truth. "Truth is knowledge of things as they are, and as they were, and as they are to come." (D&C 93:24.) Knowledge is not a distorted grasp of the facts; it is a clear attainment and understanding of that which is. It is not the varying interpretations of mortals that produce knowledge most readily; it is the guidance of the Spirit of the Lord that brings things into view "as they really are, and . . . as they really will be." (Jacob 4:13.) The greatest knowledge is that which opens the way to exaltation. As with wisdom, there are varying degrees of knowledge, temporal and spiritual, greater and smaller. The ultimate and sublime purpose of knowledge is "for the salvation of our souls." (Jacob 4:13.)

Firsthand knowledge comes with the aid of the Spirit. To read the scriptures gives one knowledge of what others have said. That is secondhand knowledge. When the Spirit bears witness to the truth of what the prophets have written, it becomes the personal and firsthand knowledge of the reader. The knowledge thus obtained is a gift of God, and the ability to teach knowledge is the capacity to aid others in their grasp of truth.

"And to another, exceedingly great faith." (Moro. 10:11.) "Faith is the assurance of things hoped for, the evidence of things not seen." (JST Heb. 11:1.) Faith comes in varying degrees for a variety of situations, both temporal and spiritual, from the farmer who plants the seeds to the prophet who sees within the veil the things of God. Its exercise develops power and undying trust. Abel, Enoch, Noah, Abraham, and Sarah are cited for their faith. (Heb. 11:4-13; see also Ether 12:19.) Faith was the power that saved Israel when they were led through the waters of the Red Sea. (Heb. 11:29.) Faith in its perfection is embodied in God, who framed the worlds through this power. (Heb. 11:3.)

Faith is the ability to trust explicitly in someone or something. In its truest sense, it binds one to God and the principles of his kingdom. Great faith is a peak in spiritual development. The brother of Jared illustrated this when he saw the Savior. (Ether 3:4-13.)

"And to another, the gifts of healing by the same Spirit." (Moro. 10:11.) Healing is the process by which the sick are restored to health. The priesthood ordinance of administering to the sick by use of pure olive oil and the authority of God is designed for this purpose. Many could testify to the miracle of healing through priesthood ordinances. The scriptures are replete with examples of healing, the prime focus centering in Christ himself, who went about "healing all manner of sickness and all manner of disease among the people which believed on his name." (JST Matt. 4:22.) The gift of healing by the Spirit is a special and notable ability to perceive the situations in which the miracle of restoration of health may be called forth by faith and priesthood power.

The gift to heal is not limited solely to physical maladies; it also extends to the ability to restore health to the spirit. The sicknesses of sin and depression affect spirituality. Some have the ability to teach or speak in such a manner that hope and enlightenment are brought to those who are down in spirit; they are thereby able to grasp that healing balm provided in the word of another and work their way back to full spiritual health.

"And again, to another, that he may work mighty miracles." (Moro. 10:12.) A miracle is something perceived by others as "supernatural," or beyond the normal power of mortals to produce. It is a manifestation of divine power, usually in response to faith.[1] Miracles have affected the earth, the elements of nature, and the inhabitants of the world. Some miracles appear greater than others. The greatest miracle of all was the atoning sacrifice and resurrection of the Savior.

"To another, that he may prophesy concerning all things." (Moro. 10:13.) The ability to prophesy is the spiritual power to foresee and foretell events in the future. The greatest prophecies were the predictions of the prophets of the mission of Jesus Christ before it actually occurred.

To prophesy is greater than to predict; people predict weather and events based upon logic and consistency of occurrences. Often they are wrong. Prophecy is a gift of the Spirit, sure and validated by the workings of God. "The testimony of Jesus is the spirit of prophecy." (Rev. 19:10.) As judged appropriate by God, certain individuals have the gift to know of things in the future.

"To another, the beholding of angels and ministering spirits." (Moro. 10:14.) This gift enables one to see people who are normally beyond the veil limiting mortal sight. It is to behold heavenly beings. "Ordinarily the word *angel* means those ministering persons who have a body of flesh and bone, being either resurrected from the dead (re-embodied), or else translated, as were Enoch, Elijah, etc. (D&C 129). . . . Spirits are those beings who either have not yet obtained a body of flesh and bone (unembodied), or who have once had a mortal body and have died, and are awaiting the resurrection (disembodied)."[2]

"And again, to another, all kinds of tongues; and again, to another, the interpretation of languages and of divers kinds of tongues." (Moro. 10:15-16.) The gift of tongues applies to the understanding of various languages. It may come suddenly in the ability to speak in one language and be understood in another, as on the Day of Pentecost. (Acts 2:1-11.) More commonly, it is the ability given to missionaries to quickly acquire the skill to speak in and understand a foreign tongue spoken in the mission area to which they are called.

"And all these gifts come by the Spirit of Christ; and they come unto every man severally, according as he will." (Moro. 10:17.) The

Spirit of Christ is the "true light, which lighteth every man who cometh into the world" (JST John 1:9); it is the power that enlightens eyes and "quickeneth your understandings" (D&C 88:11). It is referred to by many as the "conscience." Through that medium, the gift of the Holy Ghost brings about the greater spiritual gifts to those who are obedient to God's commandments. Every person has a spiritual gift or gifts; they are determined and given by an all-wise God for the benefit of the individual and those with whom he or she relates. All gifts are designed to bring people to Christ.

Moroni testified to "all the ends of the earth—that if the day cometh that the power and gifts of God shall be done away among you, it shall be because of unbelief." (Moro. 10:24.) He had lived in such a society.

"And again I would exhort you that ye would come unto Christ, and lay hold upon every good gift, and touch not the evil gift, nor the unclean thing." (Moro. 10:30.) As the good gifts came from God and led to eternal happiness, so the evil gifts would refer to powers and abilities of wickedness derived from obedience to Satan, which would lead to eternal misery. Implied in the exhortation to "lay hold upon every good gift" is that all gifts from God may be enjoyed at some point in time—their fullness undoubtedly reserved for the next life for those who are exalted. To "lay hold" would imply not only the use of individual gifts, but also the enjoyment available from the emanation of gifts exercised by others.

Becoming Perfected in Christ

A concise and concluding formula for coming unto Christ is given by Moroni. (Moro. 10:32-33.) "Come unto Christ, and be perfected in him." In the records Moroni was about to seal was the recorded commandment of the Savior: "I would that ye should be perfect even as I, or your Father who is in heaven is perfect." (3 Ne. 12:48.) Being close to Christ carries this requirement: "Deny yourselves of all ungodliness." To become godlike is the supreme goal in gospel progression. Satan would thwart that goal by cloaking evil enticements in attractive garbs. To resist them requires denial. It requires saying no to the attractive show of Satan's wares. Success also requires the exertion to "love God with all your might, mind and strength." In turning away from Satan, one must turn to God. A complete commitment and devotion fosters a love that takes on a divine characteristic, for it transcends all other relationships. It moves more and more toward charity, which is "the pure love of Christ." (Moro. 7:47.) It becomes more and more a privilege than a command as one grows in love of God. As that occurs, "then is his grace sufficient for you, that by his grace ye may be perfect in Christ." That which is beyond the capability of an individual to achieve on his or her own is granted by divine providence. The power of increased spiritual strength brings one closer to the attributes of godliness, and thus closer to the eternal goal of perfection. Perfection in mortality is possible in a limited way; that is, one does the best in gospel progression of which he or she is capable within the confines of mortality. It is to gain the triumph over sin. Thus it was recorded that "Noah found grace in the eyes of the Lord; for Noah was a just man, and perfect in his generation." (Moses 8:27.) Ultimately, perfection is attained in the eternal sense when one becomes like God: "He that receiveth my Father receiveth my Father's kingdom; therefore all that my Father hath shall be given unto him." (D&C 84:38.) These, Christ said, will "sit with me in my throne, even as I also overcame, and am set down with my Father in his throne." (Rev. 3:21.)

The perfection in mortality involves qualifying to be "sanctified in Christ by the grace of God, through the shedding of the blood of Christ, which is in the covenant of the Father unto the remission of your sins, that ye become holy, without spot." (Moro. 10:33.) To be sanctified is to be cleansed by the spirit of the Holy Ghost because of the efficacy of the atonement of Jesus Christ, made possible by baptism into the Lord's church. It leaves one pure and clean. In mortality, it is an ongoing and renewable process, for throughout mortality one keeps overcoming mistakes and progressing. Sins are repented of quickly and regularly, and the seriousness is less and less when compared with the mistakes of earlier development. The cleansing is a type of that which becomes permanent when one enters the kingdom of God in eternity. Then that which was known in part is achieved in a fullness, that the one so sanctified may remain in that state forever.

Moroni knew by the spirit of prophecy that such would be his case after death. "I soon go to rest in the paradise of God, until my spirit and body shall again reunite, and I am brought forth triumphant through the air, to meet you before the pleasing bar of the great Jehovah, the Eternal Judge of both quick and dead. Amen." (Moro. 10:34.)

NOTES

1. See "Bible Dictionary," Holy Bible (Salt Lake City: The Church of Jesus Christ of Latter-day Saints, 1979), p. 732.
2. Bible Dictionary, p. 608.

Scripture Index

THE OLD TESTAMENT

THE NEW TESTAMENT

THE BOOK OF MORMON

3:21	254	12:3	274	7:6-11	272
3:22-23	255	12:3-4	274	7:12	293, 294
3:25	260	12:5	274	7:13	295
3:26	252, 254	12:6	274	7:14	295
3:27-28	255	12:8	24	7:15-16	295
4:2	255	12:8-12	276	7:16	275, 293
4:4	260	12:18	274	7:17-18	295
4:6-7	255	12:19	275, 308	7:18-19	211
4:7	260, 269	12:19-21	276	7:19-22	295
4:9	264	12:20-21	252	7:23-25	295
4:13	255	12:21	22	7:26	295
4:15	255	12:23-29	241	7:27-29	296
4:17	191	12:23-37	277	7:30	296
4:25	254	12:25	278	7:31	296
5	269	12:26-27	278	7:31-32	296
5:1	260	12:32	278	7:37-39	296
5:2-4	261	12:33	278	7:38-48	34
5:3	262	12:37	278	7:40-42	297
6	269	13:8	279	7:41-42	24
6:7	265	13:12	279	7:44	27, 297
6:8	264	13:13-14	245	7:45-47	297
6:17	266	13:21	279	7:46	302
6:19-20	269	13:31	279	7:47	293, 297,
6:23	266	14:24	279		311
6:28	249	15:19	279	7:48	297
6:30	267	15:29-34	256	8:4-6	298
7:5	267	15:32	280	8:7-8	298
7:27	267	15:33	245	8:8	299
8:7	267	23:35-36	241	8:10	301
8:9	267	23:40	241	8:11-12	299
8:15	94, 268	13:10-12	190	8:12	299
8:17	268			8:14	298
8:20	268	**MORONI**		8:16	298
8:21	232	1:1	241	8:19	300
8:22-23	269	1:1-3	282	8:20	300
8:25	268	2:1-2	283	8:21	300
8:26	268, 271	2:1-3	161	8:22	300
10:5-8	272	3:1-4	284	8:25-26	301
9:11	272	4:1	285	8:26	297
11:6	273	6:4	288, 290	8:27-29	301
11:7	272	6:5	291	9:1	304
11:20-21	273	6:9	291	9:6	304
9:15-25	272	7:3	276, 293	9:22	46, 304
12–15	256	7:5-6	294	9:23	241
		7:6	294		

THE DOCTRINE AND COVENANTS

THE PEARL OF GREAT PRICE

Subject Index

Abinadi, 59

Abraham: lawful heirs of, 169; covenant of, 188-19, 193

Accountability, 300

Actions, thoughts precede, 156

Adultery, 155-56

Agency: as part of plan of salvation, 31-32; involves accepting consequences, 107; role of, in receiving blessings, 182-83 n. 9; Satan desires to overthrow, 268

Alma: Korihor is brought before, 1; testifies of God to Korihor, 5; undertakes Zoramite mission, 19; gives discourse on faith, 22-25; departs out of land forever, 37, 125-26; counsels his sons, 41-42; conversion and testimony of, 43-44; entrusts Helaman with records, 45-46; calls Corianton to resume mission, 54; discussion by, of resurrection, 59-60; is compared with Nephi, son of Helaman, 136 n. 1

Alms, 156

Amalickiah, 75-76, 81

Americas as promised land, 249

Aminadab, 102

Ammaron, 233

Ammon, people of: outcast Zoramites join, 36; withdraw from Jershon to Melek, 36; nearly break oath of peace, 84-85; two thousand sons of, go to war, 85-87

Ammoron, 81, 83-84, 90, 129-30

Amlulek, teachings of, to Zoramites, 29-34

Angels: sent to Alma, 44; ministering of, 296; definition of, 309

Anger, sin of, 155

Annalistic writing, 92, 104 n. 1

Anti-Christ, Korihor as, 1, 10-11, 18, 26 n. 2

Antipus, 86

Apostasy: of Nephites, 103, 108, 117-18, 127; resulting from pride, 141; first mistakes of, involve nature of God, 173-74; classic study of, 218; steps into, after Golden Era, 226

Apostles, 284-85

Ark of Noah, 265

Ashton, Marvin J., 229

Assassins, 94, 104 n. 3

Atonement: Korihor denied need for, 9-10; Amulek explains necessity of, 30; as part of plan of salvation, 32, 37; required infinite sacrifice, 32; infinite effects of, 39 n. 10, 53; repentance depends on, 53; makes mercy possible, 64, 120

Augustine, 30-31

Authority: Jesus bestows, on Nephite Twelve, 151-52, 178; Jesus proclaims his, 162; Moroni reemphasizes, 283-84

Ballard, Melvin J., 40 n. 21, 180-81

Holy Ghost: truth confirmed by, 12-13, 37; sin against, 30, 49-50, 55 n. 1; role of, in prayer, 176-77, 180; power to bestow, 178-79, 284; developing faith through, 275; conducting meetings under influence of, 291-92; gifts of, 307-10

Hope, 24, 294-95

Humanity: naturalistic view of, 7-8; fallen mortal nature of, 30-31, 110-11, 277; divine element in, 275

Humility, 19-20, 48, 152, 278

Inequality, 140, 146

Irenaeus, 172

Isaiah, 167-68, 196-97

Israel: God's covenants with, 42; Mormon prophesies concerning, 135-36, 215-16; lost tribes of, Jesus to preach to, 164-66; restoration of, in latter days, 167-68, 184; by blood or by belief, 169; scattering of, 191-92; to return with rich treasures, 194-95 n. 2; Mormon addresses descendants of, 238, 240

Jacob, wicked king, 142

Jared, 247

Jared, brother of, 22, 247, 250-52, 254-55

Jared, wicked son of Omer, 267-68

Jaredites: record of, 240-41, 245-46; travels of, 247-48, 263-64; barges of, 250, 265-66; kings of, 266-67; destruction of, 279-80

Jehovah. See Jesus Christ

Jerusalem, New, 186-88, 279

Jesus Christ: Korihor denied, 9-10; twofold role of, 10; denial of, four cases of, 16-19; Amulek testifies of, 29; role of, as Mediator, 62-64; as sure foundation, 104, 159; Samuel the Lamanite prophesies of, 119-20; birth of, signs accompanying, 126-27; death of, signs accompanying, 143-44, 147; voice of, comes to Nephites through darkness, 144-45; visits temple in Bountiful, 149-51,

161; bestows authority on Nephite twelve, 151-52, 161, 283-84; proclaims his authority, 162; resurrection of, in flesh, 174; prays for and blesses Nephites, 175; all prophets testify of, 188; taught fullness of gospel to Nephites, 196; messengers preparing way for, 198; as Sun or Son of Righteousness, 201; church of, to be named after, 208-9; as source of prosperity, 219; effects of visit of, 221; shows body to brother of Jared, 251-52, 254; speaks in Father's behalf, 253; exercising faith in, 274-75

John the Baptist, 198

John the Beloved, 213

Joseph of Egypt: seed of, to deliver Israel from bondage, 170-71; covenant land of, 186-87

Judgment: righteous, exercising, 158-59; according to works, 294

Justice: is essence of law, 33; balance of, with mercy, 62-64; as attribute of God, 65

Kimball, Spencer W., 20, 121, 286-87

King-men, 31

Kings: Jaredites desire, 266; just, vs. wicked, 267

Kishkumen, 94, 96-97

Knowledge: methods of gaining, 3-5, 12; gained through Holy Ghost, 12-13, 307; secular, does not imply spirituality, 20-21; in excess of wisdom, 22; cycle of faith and, 23; reveals choices and consequences, 107; of mysteries, 181, 255; increasing in, through faithfulness, 204-5; desire for, 275

Korihor, 1, 18, 275; naturalistic viewpoint of, 4-5, 8; denies possibility of sin, 8-9; demands sign and is struck dumb, 10-11

Lachoneus, 128, 130, 139

Lamanites: Teancum decoys, out of stronghold, 81; capture Zarahemla

ing, might have saved Nephites, 147; signaling beginning of Restoration, 191; seeking, contrasted with seeking testimony, 275; are quickly forgotten, 285-86

Sin: Korihor denied possibility of, 8-9; atonement redeems us from effects of, 10; sexual, seriousness of, 49, 50-51; unpardonable, 49-50, 55 n. 1; forsaking, 51-52; new definitions of, on higher plane, 155-56; little children are incapable of, 298-99

Smile of God, 180-81

Smith, Joseph: Book of Mormon bears testimony of, vii; on revelation, 13 n. 5, 22; on Savior, 32; on hell, 58; on resurrection, 59, 60, 67 n. 11; on God's justice, 65; on fundamental elements of body, 67 n. 12; on correctness of Book of Mormon, 107; received keys to gather Israel, 166; on comprehending God, 172-73; on mysteries of God, 181; Christ prophesies of, 190-91; as messenger to prepare way for Christ, 198; on sons of Levi and priesthood restoration, 199-200; on mission of Elijah, 202-3; on three witnesses, 261-62; on Church organization in New World, 284; on salvation of little children, 299-300; on importance of gaining body, 303 n. 8

Smith, Joseph F., 52, 59

Smith, Joseph Fielding, 68 n. 14, 253, 285

Spirit world, 34-35, 56-58, 67 n. 10-11

Stripling warriors, two thousand, 85-87

Teancum, 81, 90

Temptation, praying to avoid, 157-58

Ten tribes, Jesus to preach to, 164-66

Teomner, 87

Testimony: gaining, 44-45; seeking, contrasted with seeking signs, 275; promise of, in Book of Mormon, 306

Theism, shift from, to naturalism, 6-7

Three Nephites, 213-14, 233

Three Witnesses to Book of Mormon, 260-62

Thoughts, actions preceded by, 156

Tithing, 200

Title of Liberty, 75

Tongues, gift of, 309

Tower of Babel, 247, 256 n. 4

Tribal organizations among Nephites, 141-42

Truth, responsibility to accept, 274-75

Twelve Nephite disciples, 151-52, 178-79; Christ's final visit to, 208; speak individually to Savior, 212-13; ordain priests and teachers, 284; as apostles, 284-85

Two-Way literature, 271

United order, 223, 228-29

Unity: celestial law of, 221-23; as characteristic of righteous societies, 272; dissolving of, 272-73

Universe: view of, as self-acting, 5-7; inanimate, 7-8

Unpardonable sin, 49-50, 55 n. 1

Vengeance, 74, 234-35

War: varying motivations for, 70-72; defensive, can be justifiable, 72-74; righteous individuals in, 77-78; earth will never be free from, 78; can harden or soften hearts, 80; final, between Nephites and Lamanites, 234-37; continues among Lamanites, 237; Mormon's injunction against, 238-39

Warnings, prophetic, 118-19, 147

Weaknesses, 277-78

Wealth: setting hearts upon, 103; love of, crowds out love of God, 117, 158; of Nephites, "slipperiness" of, 118-19; pride accompanying, 140-41, 226

Whitmer, David, 261-62

Whitney, Orson F., 53-54

Wickedness: death does not erase, 60-61; is personal choice, 98, 107; led